David Pierini

Natalie Y. Moore is the South Side bureau reporter for WBEZ, Chicago's NPR–member station. Before joining WBEZ, she covered Detroit's City Council for *Detroit News*. She worked as an education reporter for the St. Paul *Pioneer Press* and as a reporter for the Associated Press in Jerusalem. Her work has been published in *Essence, Black Enterprise,* the *Chicago Reporter, In These Times,* the *Chicago Sun-Times*, and the *Chicago Tribune*. She lives in Chicago.

Additional Praise for *The South Side*

"A reminder that, even though great gains have been made in the development of integrated neighborhoods and suburbs, Chicago is still shackled by the chains of segregation, chains that limit the potential of hundreds of thousands of African Americans and impoverish the lives of all residents of the region . . . A clarion call for us to break the chains that bind us and allow our imaginations to be free to take on—and change—the systemic reality of segregation and its impact on all of us."

—*Chicago Tribune*

"What's important about Natalie Y. Moore's new book is less that it's about Chicago's South Side and more that it's *of* the South Side, deeply and lovingly, in a way journalism about the area rarely is. . . . A powerful political document."

—*Chicago Reader*

"*The South Side* is a comprehensive iconoclastic investigation of segregated black Chicago, past and present. . . . An essential book for anyone interested in the history and current state of race in the urban United States."

—*Shelf Awareness*

"Moore strikes an admirable balance between palpable love for Chicago's diversities and clear-eyed anger at the powerful forces dividing America's third-largest city into different worlds." —*Pacific Standard*

"As questions and criticism about race in America rightfully continue to dominate the national conversation, this book brings the problem right to home. Moore, the South Side bureau reporter for WBEZ, explores how institutionalized segregation continues to keep predominantly black neighborhoods at an economic and educational disadvantage."

—*RedEye*

"An excellent work for all readers interested in knowing more about important, ongoing urban issues." —*Library Journal*

"Thoughtful and clarifying investigation . . . Moore refines our perception of the realities of segregation and the many possible paths to change."   —*Booklist*

"Moore has captured the rhythm of Chicago, its beauty and heartbreak, and its racial demons and activist angels with such vibrant prose and personality that she has achieved that rare literary feat: it is both a page-turner and magnum opus. By traveling to the South Side with her, we not only understand why it has been able to produce some of our nation's most exceptional African American leaders, but also how its ongoing racial segregation haunts and harms the vast majority of Chicagoans today."   —Salamishah Tillet, associate professor of English and Africana Studies, University of Pennsylvania

THE
SOUTH
SIDE

A PORTRAIT OF CHICAGO AND
AMERICAN SEGREGATION

NATALIE Y. MOORE

Picador

St. Martin's Press
New York

picadorusa.com • picadorbookroom.tumblr.com
twitter.com/picadorusa • facebook.com/picadorusa

Picador® is a U.S. registered trademark and is used by Macmillan Publishing Group, LLC, under license from Pan Books Limited.

For book club information, please visit facebook.com/picadorbookclub or e-mail marketing@picadorusa.com.

Map of the South Side of Chicago is by Chris Hagan and is used with permission.

Designed by Letra Libre, Inc.

The Library of Congress has cataloged the St. Martin's Press
edition as follows:

Names: Moore, Natalie Y., author.
Title: The South Side : a portrait of Chicago and American segregation / Natalie Y. Moore.
Description: New York City : St. Martin's Press, [2016]
Identifiers: LCCN 2015033955 | ISBN 9781137280152 (hardcover) | ISBN 9781466878969 (e-book)
Subjects: LCSH: African Americans—Segregation—Illinois—Chicago—History. | Segregation—Illinois—Chicago—History—20th century. | Discrimination in housing—Illinois—Chicago—History. | Racism—Illinois—Chicago—History. | African Americans—Illinois—Chicago—Social conditions. | Moore, Natalie Y. | Chicago—Race relations—History. | Chicago—Social conditions—21st century. | BISAC: SOCIAL SCIENCE / Sociology / Urban.
Classification: LCC F548.9.A1 M66 2016 | DDC 305.8009773'11—dc23
LC record available at http://lccn.loc.gov/2015033955

Picador Paperback ISBN 978-1-250-11833-2

Our books may be purchased in bulk for promotional, educational, or business use. Please contact your local bookseller or the Macmillan Corporate and Premium Sales Department at 1-800-221-7945, extension 5442, or by e-mail at MacmillanSpecialMarkets@macmillan.com.

First published by St. Martin's Press

First Picador Edition: April 2017

10 9 8 7 6 5 4

For Roddy

CONTENTS

Eight pages of photographs appear between pages 136 and 137.

NORTH SIDE

LAKE MICHIGAN

WEST SIDE

ROOSEVELT RD

ILLINOIS

Douglas

47TH ST   Grand Boulevard

Hyde Park

West Englewood

Englewood

79TH ST

Chatham

95TH ST

Beverly

Roseland

INDIANA

5 miles

Map of the South Side of Chicago

ACKNOWLEDGMENTS

TO MY AGENT, CHARLOTTE SHEEDY, THANKS FOR MAKING THIS PROJECT COME TO fruition and forcing me to see what was right under my nose. Thanks to my wonderful editor, Karen Wolny, who pushed and guided me, making this a much better book. And thanks to the entire St. Martin's Press team, including Laura Apperson, Gabrielle Gantz and Donna Cherry.

My formal education began with wonderful Chicago Public Schools teachers and I thought of them often during the writing of this book, especially in the schools integration chapter. Howard University taught me much about the bigger space in which it meant to be a black girl from the South Side of Chicago. Thanks to the history and journalism departments: Joseph Reidy, Arnold Taylor, Jannette Dates, Clint Wilson, Lawrence Kaggwa, Jeanne Toungara and Eileen Boris.

Chloe Riley pitched in with enthusiasm at every turn as my research assistant. Pablo Boczkowski, of my alma mater Northwestern University, put me on the right path for the media study, and thanks for lending me Miya Williams.

My research was bolstered by assistance from the National Archives at Chicago, Chicago History Museum Research Center, Harold Washington Library Center, the Woodstock Institute, Vivian G. Harsh Research Collection and Columbia College Chicago Library.

To all of those who read chapter drafts, thank you: Natalie Hopkinson, Chana Garcia, Nicole Tefera, Patrick Rivers, Badia Ahad-Legardy, Audrey Petty, Rick Kogan, Amanda Williams, Stephen Franklin,

Monica Eng, Linda Lutton, Brentin Mock, Afi-Odelia Scruggs, Ron Stodghill, Brandi Kenner-Bell and Mick Dumke.

Scholars and writers have helped me over the years as a reporter understand the policies around black Chicago and segregation through being a source, inspiration or mentor: my "play grandfather" Timuel Black, Gary Orfield, Janet Smith, Mary Pattillo, Steve Bogira, Barbara Ransby, Cathy Cohen, Mariame Kaba, Nikole Hannah-Jones, D. Bradford Hunt, Douglas Massey, Robert Sampson, Lawrence Vale, Isabel Wilkerson, Thomas Sugrue, Laura Washington and Arnold Hirsch. I'm indebted to your work and hope this book isn't reinventing the wheel but building upon your scholarship.

Thanks to Bill Healy, David Pierini, Francine Washington, Tamiko Holt, Sally Eisele, William Jelani Cobb, Krista Franklin, Jennifer Halperin, J. Nicole Brooks, Salamishah Tillet, Scott Smith, Janelle Thompson, Kimberly Henderson, the staff of Mollison Elementary, Niala Boodhoo, Ta-Nehisi Coates, Achy Obejas, Lance Williams, Maxine McKinney de Royston, Reggie Royston, Alice Kim, Jane Saks, Ben Austen, Tanya Triche, Esther Williams, Jessica Kimbrough, our Black Girl South Side Salon and "the Hot Links." Thanks to my colleagues at WBEZ, especially Cate Cahan, Ben Calhoun, Goli Sheikholeslami and Ira Glass.

My parents, siblings, aunts, uncles and cousins served as inspiration at various points of writing. Thank you for sharing your stories of our family.

And my own family expanded during the writing of this book. Sydney, Raven and Milan—your laughter and bubbling personalities were a welcome distraction when I should've been at my laptop. My life is richer with each of you in it. Rod, I'm eternally grateful for your love, counsel and patience.

INTRODUCTION

CHICAGO IS ONE OF THE MOST SEGREGATED YET DIVERSE CITIES IN AMERICA.
Chicagoans typically don't live, work or play together. Unlike many other major U.S. cities, no one race dominates. We are about equal parts black, white and Latino, each group clustered in various enclaves. Chicago is a city in which black people sue over segregation and discrimination, whether it concerns disparities in public schools or not being admitted into hot downtown spots. Some people shrug off segregation because they say racism and white supremacy will still exist. I concur. But segregation amplifies racial inequities. It's deliberate, ugly and harmful. The legacy of segregation and its ongoing policies keep Chicago divided.

Our mayors have touted and promoted Chicago as a world-class city. The skyscrapers kissing the clouds, billion-dollar Millennium Park, Michelin-rated restaurants, pristine lake views, fabulous shopping, vibrant theater scene, downtown flower beds and stellar architecture tell one story.

Yet Chicago is compromised by the specter of segregation, which is often swept under the rug. We can't honestly talk about problems such as violence and unemployment without addressing segregation. Throughout the twentieth century, black families faced white violence when they dared to move into white neighborhoods. Redlining, bad mortgages, racial steering and failed school policies led to the northern version of Jim Crow, all of which had a lasting effect. Today more than half of the black population in Chicago lives in only 20 of the city's 77 communities.[1]

Early on, I learned that the terms "South Side" and "North Side" were shorthand for "black" and "white." Before he became a South Side congressman, Jesse Jackson Jr. spoke to my public high school. He didn't use explicit racial terms, but he told the assembly that he wanted his community to look like downtown and parts of the North Side. The audience cheered; the tacit racial dynamic of which Jackson spoke resonated with black South Side kids.

Still, the South Side is a magical place. It's the heart of black America, with its miles upon miles of black middle-class neighborhoods and strong political and business legacies. In summertime Chi, the aroma of barbecue wafts from backyard grills and smoky rib joints onto the Dan Ryan Expressway. Chicago is a soulful city that gave us Sam Cooke and Common, Koko Taylor and Chaka Khan. Driving east on 79th Street toward Lake Michigan is a colorful trip: men sipping out of bottles on corners, vibrant businesses, bars, funeral homes, foreboding boarded-up structures, liquor stores, churches, Harold's Chicken Shacks and sounds of house music dancing in the air. This sense of place is special. I would never want to erase black Chicago.

I found value growing up in my black Chatham neighborhood, and those experiences make me a proud South Side black girl. Identity is wonderful whether you're South Side Irish, from Koreatown or from the largest Polish community outside of Poland. I wouldn't move to Chinatown or Little Village, a Mexican and Mexican American area, because I would feel my presence to be disruptive. I love the Indian food on Devon Avenue, Vietnamese noodles on Broadway and Swedish bakeries in Andersonville. The cultural diversity tucked away in Chicago's ethnic enclaves is worth celebrating. High-poverty black segregation is not.

And even though Harlem, Atlanta, Detroit and Washington, D.C., are home to prosperous black enclaves, it's Chicago's South Side that gave the country its first black president. Inspired by Harold Washington, the city's first black mayor, Barack Obama chose to move to Chicago so South Side politics could catapult him to the national scene. In native daughter Michelle Obama I see a woman a generation ahead of me who represents a legacy of high-achieving, confident South Side girls who deftly navigate white and black worlds.

Chicago's diversity and segregation aren't unique.

Nate Silver of the statistical website *FiveThirtyEight* has said that some of the nation's most diverse cities are also the most segregated:

> You can have a diverse city, but not diverse neighborhoods. Whereas Chicago's citywide diversity index is 70 percent, seventh best out of the 100 most populous U.S. cities, its neighborhood diversity index is just 36 percent, which ranks 82nd. New York also has a big gap. Its citywide diversity index is 73 percent, fourth highest in the country, but its neighborhood diversity index is 47 percent, which ranks 49th. . . . Most cities east of the Rocky Mountains with substantial black populations are quite segregated. There's not a lot to distinguish Baltimore from Cleveland, Memphis, Milwaukee, New Orleans, Philadelphia or St. Louis.

Sacramento is the most diverse city at the neighborhood level.[2]

Scholars at Brown University have documented residential segregation across the country. The average white person in metropolitan American cities lives in a 75 percent white neighborhood. Blacks and Hispanics live in neighborhoods with high minority representation. The Chicago metro area ranks number five in the top ten cities with the highest level of black–white segregation, behind Detroit, which claims the number one spot.[3]

In the Chicago region, segregation also exists because of people's preferences. According to University of Illinois at Chicago scholar Maria Krysan, who participated in a 2012 discussion on race produced by WBEZ, "Race: Out Loud," whites prefer no more than about 20 percent African Americans in their neighborhood while blacks prefer closer to a 50 percent split.

* * *

In 2007, I took a job at WBEZ–Chicago Public Media as the South Side reporter set up in a one-woman storefront. It's a dream job to tell the stories of my communities with the kind of nuance associated with public radio. In covering urban affairs and noticing disparities in my own neighborhood life, I always circled back to segregation as the common denominator. It was easy to connect the dots from housing to education to crime to food access: segregation is the culprit.

Black neighborhoods, regardless of income, fall prey to the perils of segregation. Retail redlining, the practice of businesses declining to come to black communities, is a nascent area of study, but a quick glance at black communities tells the story: businesses, despite high-earning blacks in many neighborhoods, apparently refuse to set up shop if too many African Americans live there. Research shows that this leads to billions of dollars in retail leakage: money doesn't stay in the black community. The patterns of segregation leave black communities with joblessness, few grocery stores, boarded-up buildings and disinvestment. And higher murder counts. Economic development proves elusive. The only conclusion is that hypersegregated, poverty-stricken areas don't get the resources that flood into more affluent neighborhoods.

Subprime lending and the foreclosure crisis undermined integration. During the housing bust, racial segregation grew. I don't believe white people have to be the saviors of communities, but there's no denying the disparities in the distribution of resources. Immigrants and white ethnics move out of their low-income neighborhoods with the assumption that another ethnic group will move in. The problem is that no other group wants to move into poor black neighborhoods. Well, except other blacks.

According to Princeton University sociologist Douglas Massey:

> It's not about black people wanting to live with white people. It's about access to all the benefits and resources of American society. Inevitably benefits and resources are unevenly distributed around the metropolitan area. To access them, you have to move. And historically in the United States, poor groups have come in, for example, and they settle in lousy neighborhoods as they move up economic ladder and seek to move up the residential ladder.
>
> African Americans have never been given those first few steps up the ladder because the residential mobility has been so constrained. People are coming around to seeing that as a critical issue.[4]

U.S. Supreme Court justice Ruth Bader Ginsburg says that public acceptance of blacks is slow, and she contrasted the public acceptance of gays because of familiarity.

> Once [gay] people began to say who they were, you found that it was your next-door neighbor or it could be your child, and we found people we admired. That understanding still doesn't exist with race; you still have separation of neighborhoods, where the races are not mixed. It's the familiarity with people who are gay that still doesn't exist for race and will remain that way for a long time as long as where we live remains divided.[5]

America learned a long time ago that separate is *not* equal. Racial uprisings in U.S. cities in the late 1960s revealed what many blacks already knew: The country was moving toward two societies: one black, one white, separate and unequal.

According to the famous Report of the National Advisory Commission on Civil Disorders, better known as the 1968 Kerner Commission: "Segregation and poverty have created in the racial ghetto a destructive environment totally unknown to most white Americans. What white Americans have never fully understood—but what the Negro can never forget—is that white society is deeply implicated in the ghetto. White institutions created it, white institutions maintain it, and white society condones it."[6] Not much has changed since then.

That same year the Fair Housing Act was passed to open housing and prohibit discrimination in the private housing market. The act has fallen short because it doesn't have enough teeth for enforcement. "The fundamental weakness of the 1968 Fair Housing Act was its reliance on individual efforts to combat a social problem that was systemic and institutional in nature. The resulting contest was inherently unequal, so that enforcement efforts were intrinsically flawed and structurally condemned to ineffectiveness," wrote Douglas Massey and Nancy Denton in *American Apartheid*. The legislation assumed people knew when they had suffered discrimination. "Conditions in the ghetto have deteriorated markedly since the 1968 Fair Housing Act was passed, and almost every problem defined by the Kerner Commission has become worse."[7]

Nikole Hannah-Jones, at the time a reporter for *ProPublica,* investigated how Democratic and Republican presidents over four decades declined to use billions of dollars in federal funds to fight segregation.[8] Despite the Fair Housing Act, no real dent has been made in residential integration. Rarely was money withheld from communities for violation of the act.

The report the Kerner Commission produced continues to be relevant, and we see evidence of it in cities across the country. Black residents in Baltimore and Ferguson, Missouri, have taken to the streets not just to protest the deaths of Freddie Gray and Michael Brown at the hands of police. Those two locales have something in common with black Chicago communities and other black urban areas: state-sponsored segregation.

* * *

The City of Big Shoulders. Hog Butcher for the World. Loving Chicago is like loving a woman with a broken nose. We Real Cool. And you say Chi City. The Jungle. Carl Sandburg, Nelson Algren, Gwendolyn Brooks, Kanye West and Upton Sinclair each imagined Chicago as their muse.

In 1871, the city famously burned in the Great Chicago Fire. Chicago bounced back, though, and grew bigger and better; the resilience of its residents a metaphor for the guts and moxie running throughout the Second City. Urban planner Daniel Burnham made no small plans when he developed the country's first skyscraper in downtown Chicago or beautified the city with an expansive park system. We have no east side; instead the border is Lake Michigan—the Great Lake so vast that the shores on the other side are invisible. Our skyline is magnificent, mile after mile. The city on a grid is easy to navigate, but it's massive— which is an asset as well as a deficit. Our wide geography perpetuates separation, physically and mentally.

Some people argue that segregation aids blacks economically. I'm not nostalgic for Jim Crow, the idea that segregation benefited blacks because of the misguided notion that we had our own and stuck together in intraracial harmony—we were "unified." But those feel-good images casually dismiss the horrors of Jim Crow. I don't think integration is the magic bullet either. But I ponder the future of Chicago given its acute segregation, which should be a relic of the city's well-documented past.

"In some respects, Chicago has exacerbated the problem of segregation, but it's important at the outset to note that this is really a national problem that goes to the roots of our country when it comes to race relations," Robert Sampson, a social sciences professor at Harvard University, told me.[9]

Daily headlines on race, police, black bodies and white privilege barrage us. Black bodies are under attack and viewed as walking weapons. The Black Lives Matter movement boldly confronts white supremacy, police brutality and a racist criminal justice system. An urgent conversation on race brews in a cauldron of vexation: I think about race every day. I see race every day. I see that the conditions of black neighborhoods are often the product of intentional segregation. This isn't a new topic, but it needs to be dissected and better understood, especially in the wake of protests in Ferguson, Baltimore and other cities faltering under the weight of segregation. A wider conversation about segregation seems to be happening in cities around the country. Ending segregation surely won't end racism, but its dismantling will provide better outcomes for black people.

This book, written a century after the Great Migration to Chicago began, attempts to showcase a sliver of the South Side by shining a light on contemporary segregation that is informed by history. Even though Chicago's black West Side wrestles with similar issues, I focus here only on the South Side.

This is also a story of northern racism.

Chapters 1 through 4 concentrate on housing policies in Chicago by explaining how we got to where we are and sharing my own experiences and those of my family. My parents bought a house in a black neighborhood, as did my Great Migration–era grandparents. I bought into the American Dream of home ownership in a black neighborhood and found the stakes are higher and the returns are lower. Black middle-class neighborhoods continue to be vulnerable to crime and bad banking policies. For poor black families, the vertical segregation of Chicago's notorious high-rise public housing developments, once the world's largest, has been demolished in favor of horizontal segregation. Chapter 5 examines school segregation through the lens of my busing experience and details the lack of political will to truly integrate Chicago public schools.

Segregation is typically studied through housing patterns and education. The rest of this book examines other ways segregation seeps into our consciousness and realms of our lives: food deserts, black politics and violence. Too often people argue that we have moved toward a class-based society; while race and class are linked, many policies and elements of inequity on the South Side are firmly rooted in race. Throughout, I repeatedly underscore the point of race over class.

As a post–civil rights generation baby, I, and many of my friends, wrestle with race in our fair city today. I love my Chicago. Though I'm polemic, I'm also prescriptive. I conclude the book with solutions from people who struggle with segregation in Chicago. Until we address segregation, racial inequities will prevail. A century of bad segregationist policies can't be undone in a generation. The lingering effects drag out in black communities and very much inform how neighborhoods still are shaped today. This portrait of the South Side can be applied in many urban milieus across the country. Fair housing laws must be enforced. Integration needs to be of a piece with public education. Low-income and affordable housing should be dispersed throughout metropolitan regions. Members of the real estate industry need better training.

It's all too easy to throw up my hands and accept the city, broken nose and all, for its designation as one of the most segregated places in the United States. Yet I know the city can treat its residents better. The City of Chicago sponsors the popular Summer Dance, where hundreds, sometimes thousands, of people turn out. Each week in downtown Grant Park a dance lesson is given—from flamenco to African to ballroom—and then it turns into a big DJ/live band party with a makeshift dance floor. In July 2011, the theme was "Soul Train." Earlier that year the founder of that groundbreaking Chicago television show, Don Cornelius, died. What emerged during the July tribute could easily be characterized as one of the world's largest *Soul Train* lines. The diversity, perhaps unremarkable in some other cities, stunned me. All races, homeless people, children, seniors waited their turn to do the robot, some 1970s moves or simply dance to the beat in the legendary *Soul Train* line. R&B music blared and the park swelled into a giant club scene that spilled out onto the sidewalks. As trite as this sounds, I was so proud of my city. Exuberance lingered in the air of that humid, sticky evening. As I headed back south that night, I couldn't shake my buoyancy. I witnessed Chicagoans of all stripes communing festively. I imagined Nelson Algren's quote about the City on the Make, "but never a lovely so real."

1

A LEGACY THREATENED

I AM A CHILD OF CHATHAM.

I grew up in black segregated Chicago. Not in a neighborhood deci-mated by the 1968 riots, blight, poverty, white flight and boarded-up buildings. My South Side black cocoon was a solid black middle-class neighborhood. Judges, teachers, lawyers, doctors and city, postal and social workers live in Chatham. The neighborhood has an assorted housing stock: ranches, Georgians, sturdy bungalows, bi-level chic mid-century moderns. An unusual showstopper mansion, modeled after the White House and built with robin's-egg blue bricks imported from Italy, stood on display around the corner where I grew up. Our family of five lived in a four-bedroom brick Cape Cod with an unfinished basement prone to flooding. The lower level had dark wood paneling, a bar and milk crates crammed with dusty records from my parents' era—from a Redd Foxx comedy album to the Ohio Players to Malcolm X's *The Ballot or the Bullet.*

When we were growing up, ice cream trucks jingled in the sum-mertime. We girls jumped Double Dutch rope—despite my occasional double-handed turns—on the sidewalks in front of our homes. We rode our ten-speed bikes to buy Jays Salt 'n Vinegar potato chips, Now & Later candy and dill pickles at the nearby Amoco gas station. We rotated having crushes on David, who lived around the corner and rode his bike incessantly up and down the streets. Pajama parties meant Jason and Freddy horror flicks on loop. We avoided the loose Doberman pinschers that would escape the gate of that big blue mansion. We jumped through lawn sprinklers in our swimsuits in backyards while our parents barbecued. We played makeshift baseball in the alley with tennis racquets. We blew out candles on pound cakes at our birthday parties. We had the kind of dramatic childhood fights that resulted in the silent treatment or smack talking. Posters of Michael Jackson, decked out in his yellow "Human Nature" sweater, decorated our bedroom walls. We walked the track and swung on swings at Nat "King" Cole Park, named after the Chicago-born crooner. The park's basketball courts hosted some of the city's best street players in the 1970s and 1980s. Former Illinois U.S. senator Roland Burris lived around the corner from our house (in gospel powerhouse Mahalia Jackson's former residence), and he exemplified the cliché "It takes a village" by cajoling my parents to let me attend his alma mater, Howard University.

In our backyard, before the term "organic" entered the mainstream culinary lexicon, my dad harvested vegetables. On Saturday mornings, my younger brother, sister and I pulled weeds to clear the way for him to plant cucumbers, zucchini, carrots, bell peppers, collard greens, eggplant, tomatoes and radishes. Every year he gently reminded me that Chicago weather wouldn't allow him to grow my favorites—watermelon and strawberries. My mother drove a red Camaro for the better part of the 1980s. Not fire-engine or candy-apple red; more like the color of smeared red lipstick.

It would be years before I realized that I grew up in kind of a cozy racial cocoon of black middle-class vivacity in a city otherwise torn by racial division.

My parents, Joe and Yvonne, were first-generation college graduates and South Side natives. Joe, a Vietnam veteran who worked at Shell Oil Co., first as a marketing manager and later as an area diversity veep, represented the post–civil rights wave of African Americans hired by

Corporate America. He never shaved his mustache and liked to say "It's Nation Time, time for all black people to stand up and be counted," in his version of middle-class militancy. Yvonne, with her pageboy hairstyle and freckles sprinkled across the bridge of her nose, taught special education/home economics at a public school two blocks from our home. It sometimes embarrassed me when her students recognized me walking with friends in the neighborhood. "Hey, are you Miz Moore's daughter?" As a child I looked so much like her, she joked that I sprang from her forehead like Zeus's daughter.

My grandparents—one who didn't make it past third grade, another a Pullman Porter turned Playboy Mansion bartender—moved to the South Side during the Great Migration, which lured blacks from the South to the land o' milk and honey up North. They worked hard, bought houses, two flats and later rental properties and sent their children to college.

My own immediate family mirrored *The Cosby Show*—to a degree. Sitcoms always sanitize life, right? And decades later, we know this television show was an artifact of the times, a fallacy constructed by the eponymous patriarch whose reported sexually predatory offstage life casts a shadow on his art. But our world brimmed with similar middle-class black families rooted in black identity. We were neither special nor an anomaly in Chicago. But the Cosby label stuck. In 1986, at the height of Huxtable fever, the *Chicago Sun-Times* did a feature story on local black and white families drawn to the transcendent television sitcom. A friend of a friend recommended our family, and a reporter and photographer came to watch the show at our house and afterward peppered us with questions. I was ten, my brother Joey, seven, and sister Megan, five. The article noted that my little sister bubbled like young Rudy Huxtable. But when she disobeyed my mother twice during the interview, Mommy quipped, "What would Clair Huxtable do?" Everyone laughed.

During the interview, my dad wore his corporate work uniform—crisp shirt and patterned, but not too flashy, with a tie. This was unusual; he always changed into sweats when he came home after his long suburban commute. Naturally, we children snickered and questioned him when he only removed the suit jacket that evening. He explained that he had to give a positive image of black people to the news media. The blanket Chicago South Side image in many white minds equals pathological ghetto. Reporters often enable that stereotype by only covering crime when they deign to venture to the South Side. Daddy was a man who went to work every day, provided for his family and wanted to project that image for readers of the newspaper. He was simultaneously routine and radical.

This existence embodied what being a child of Chatham was like. The ideals and values of the civil rights generation found a place to live. In the tradition of being a good, upstanding Negro, my dad wanted to present a positive image in the news media by showing how we lived accordingly in black middle-class-dom.

Blacks started moving into Chatham after the U.S. Supreme Court struck down racially restrictive housing covenants in the 1948 *Shelley v. Kraemer* decision. Once confined to the city's "Black Belt," African Americans finally could choose where they wanted to lay claim to the American Dream. Upwardly mobile blacks started moving into Chatham in the 1950s with their own aspirations after white families fled, faced with the specter of so-called outsiders.

The founders of the Luster hair care company lived in Chatham. The Johnson Products Company plant—makers of Afro Sheen—operated on the outskirts, as did the iconic Soft Sheen. The black-owned Baldwin Ice Cream had a shop near our house. Black-owned banks operated in the neighborhood. Catholic, Baptist, Presbyterian and A.M.E. churches boasted strong memberships. I didn't know "Ay-rab" wasn't a word until I attended college. Some Arab merchants, who lived outside of Chatham, owned stores in the neighborhood and had unsavory reputations of bad business practices and poor service. An Arab-owned, full-service grocery store that opened a few blocks from our house went out of business because the community refused to support it. Shoppers complained about the service and low-quality food. In my household, my father drilled into us not to shop at that store or patronize non-black-owned small businesses in Chatham. Honestly, it wasn't that hard; we had black dry cleaners, hair salons, barbecue joints, barbershops and soul food restaurants.

Everyone on our block knew each other and looked out for one another. Mr. and Mrs. Strong's granddaughter Aisha and I met at age seven. She lived in Philadelphia but spent every summer in Chicago. Aisha introduced me to Prince's first album, *For You,* and told of the bombing of the black liberation group MOVE in her hometown. Each spring I counted on Mrs. Lee to order a box of Thin Mints to support my Girl Scout troop. Mr. Henderson's family owned a popular shoe store. Mr. Montgomery retired from the Chicago Police Department. Mrs. Smith always kept her long silver hair knotted in a bun and tended to a sweet dog named Chug who rarely barked. Her son Brian went to school with actress Jennifer Beals. Three doors down, the Nolans owned an auto body shop, and every Fourth of July fireworks erupted during their backyard parties. Mrs. Peterson's daughter Pam and her bestie, Zenobia, gave me and my friends makeup lessons. A few blocks over I met Brandi at a young age; our fathers attended college together. She and I devoured books and discussed the likes of Gloria Naylor and the insipid Sweet Valley High series around her kitchen table.

Lest I construct Chatham as a black urban Mayberry, my father also instilled in us his self-efficacy. He volunteered with the Chatham Avalon Park Community Council. At his behest, my siblings and I canvassed the neighborhood putting flyers for community meetings in mailboxes. This level of activity protected Chatham's legacy. Residents attended block meetings and police community gatherings and knocked on the city council member's door. The neighborhood endured its share of crimes: robberies, break-ins, muggings and assaults. When I was in high school, an ominous "Chatham rapist" haunted the neighborhood. On more than one occasion, thieves broke into our garage and stole the tires off of my dad's 1984 brown Pontiac Bonneville company car. In 1981, just days before Megan was born, my mother discovered our Great Dane, Caesar, dead in the basement laundry room. Blood dripped from his mouth as a result of rat poisoning. To this day, my father believes Chicago police officers did the deed in retaliation for him reporting them sleeping on the job nearby in a squad car. Daddy and his nephew loaded the dog's body in a wheelbarrow to be picked up in an alley by whomever you call to dispose of animal carcasses. A thief stole the empty wheelbarrow.

Chicago boasts miles upon miles of black neighborhoods with high rates of home ownership. In South Shore, the Jackson Park Highlands district is a designated Chicago landmark, home to gorgeous architecture, the stately houses displayed on oversized grassy lots. Over in Pill Hill, the lawns are all so perfectly manicured it appears as if all the homeowners use the same landscaping company. Roseland may be one of the most troubled neighborhoods in the city, but a tiny affluent section has Tudor homes with Mercedes-Benzes in the driveways. Burnside, Avalon Park and Washington Heights are examples of uneventful, middle-class communities with single-family bungalows, ranches and frame homes.

Black middle-class neighborhoods are not immune from urban ills. As Chicago sociologist Mary Pattillo writes in *Black Picket Fences: Privilege and Peril Among the Black Middle Class*, the black middle class is not the same as the white middle class. Black middle-class neighborhoods are characterized by "more poverty, higher crime, worse schools and fewer services than white middle-class neighborhoods."[1]

At a time when the number of annual murders in Chicago was notably high, my parents fretted that Joey would fall into the hands of gang recruiters. Parental love and opportunity don't always protect black boys. A mile from our house, national high school basketball phenom and Chatham native Ben Wilson was gunned down across the street from his school in 1984; then age eight, that's my first memory of violence.

Crack may not have choked Chatham, but one neighbor on our block became addicted. I learned my first street lesson bike riding solo on 83rd Street. I was 11 years old and about to roll past a group of unfamiliar teen boys. The worry rumpled my face like a piece of wrinkled clothing. I was scared of getting jumped. As my wheels squeaked by, one of the teens said to me, "If you look scared, you get jumped."

Chatham may have been the beginning of my world, but it never confined me. On the heels of integration, a yellow school bus ferried

Joey, Megan, and me to a public elementary school in another South Side neighborhood called Beverly. Little did we know we were part of desegregated busing. By age 11, my neighborhood friends Donna, Brandi, Aisha and I ignored the closest mall on 95th Street and ventured downtown or to swanky North Michigan Avenue via public transportation. In high school, we ambled about in North Side malls and eclectic pre-gentrified neighborhoods, such as Wicker Park, to browse clothing, book and record stores. I unconsciously knew that Chicago's blacks, whites, Latinos and Asians generally didn't live together. I certainly never saw any non-blacks living in Chatham. But growing up in segregation felt like air and water—a constant, but something I never pondered until a small incident upended my detachment.

* * *

It was a hot summer day in 1990. Donna, Brandi, Aisha and I boarded the Chicago Transit Authority "L" train from downtown and headed back to the South Side to get dressed for an evening of dreamboat loveliness. We were 14 years old with tickets to see R&B crooner and New Edition front man Johnny Gill at the New Regal Theatre on 79th Street. I seriously crushed on him and had made my own fan button.

An easy visual clue to Chicago's segregation is watching who boards and exits the "L." Back then white people emptied off by downtown. A few intrepid riders may have stayed on until the Chinatown stop at 22nd and Cermak. But on this particular day, the white folk stayed on and packed the train shoulder to shoulder past 22nd Street. Talk about baffling. Yes, the South Side is synonymous with blacks, and yes, whites and Latinos live in ethnic enclaves in the city's largest geographic swath. But no way did this throng of white Chicagoans live off of my "L" line. Why was I so shocked? I felt my world pivot. I wasn't scared or angry, just disoriented.

Then, at 35th Street, all of the white riders unloaded from the train cars: the stop for Comiskey Park, the White Sox baseball stadium. Crisis averted! Mystery solved. Absolute relief. My little world was pieced back together, but that's when segregation became real to me.

* * *

I celebrate my upbringing. Chatham molded me. The environment nurtured me. A rhapsody in blackness. It's such a delicious reversal of privilege and entitlement that caused me to feel territorial in a space like public transportation.

But I understood the racial lines and demarcations of Chicago. I knew something was amiss in my neighborhood. There were fewer places to shop, and crime and poverty were closer. In my adult years, I realized that for all of their uplift and efficacy, black middle-class neighborhoods are by nature precarious. They aren't ghettos, but they exist because of segregationist housing policies designed to create ghettos. When housing opened up across the city and redlining wasn't as prevalent, white flight ensued. Black middle-class neighborhoods do their best to thrive in impossible, ugly circumstances. But like black ghettos, the black middle class, too, complains about policing, city services, investment and amenities.

By definition, the black middle class equates to the white lower middle class in America. Many white Chicagoans have no idea that a place such as Chatham exists and couldn't pinpoint it on a map. Everyday black middle-class life is invisible in America. People going to work, sending their children to school, living their lives, minding their business. When studying segregation, researchers typically concentrate on the urban black poor underclass. The black elite are more visible with the election of Barack Obama and his inner circle of friends coupled with familiar faces like Oprah. In a graduate school journalism policy class I took at Northwestern University, a professor rented a bus to give students a tour of different parts of the city. She let me narrate part of the South Side, and when we drove around Chatham my white peers gaped, remarking how the neighborhood looked better than some white areas. They were shocked and awed.

Chatham has long enjoyed an independent streak—namely by not voting for Mayor Richard M. Daley—and mightily protecting its black cocoon. The economic crisis and housing collapse that began in 2008 tested the limits of black efficacy and excellence, and Chatham continues to fight for its legacy. Although white flight is in the past, home values and investment reveal current fragilities. Research indicates that black wealth barely exists and black middle-class kids are downwardly mobile.[2]

The term "middle class" is hard to define in the United States. It's aspirational and nebulous, and people in a range of incomes, from low to upper, consider themselves in that social stratum. Social scientists measure income, occupation, education and wealth. Northwestern University sociologist Mary Pattillo told me, "Given those somewhat objective measures, basically what we find is on any one of those measures, the black middle class is smaller and somewhat more disadvantaged than the white middle class." For example, about 37 percent of whites have a college education, compared to 18 percent of blacks. Further, middle-class blacks are clustered in lower-class occupations, such as sales and administrative work, while whites are clustered more in higher-earning white-collar occupations.[3] Meanwhile, the backbone of the black middle class has been in the public sector—teachers, social workers and municipal jobs.

"Black middle-class neighborhoods across the country and surely in Chicago have two faces to them," Pattillo said. "I call this the privilege and the peril of the black middle class. The privilege comes with these being homeowners. Some of those perils are the result of racial segregation. We're thinking about Chatham situated within the larger South Side." That means higher crime and poverty rates and proximity to underperforming schools.

"I don't want to say all people in general are bad influences or living next to poor people is a peril in of itself. But there's no question that when you have higher poverty rates, you have fewer disposable resources, for example, for families to spend on businesses, for families to spend on institutions," Pattillo explained.

In a ten-year span, from 2000 to 2010, Chatham coped with massive change. The economy, housing values, median incomes and cultural

clashes with newly arrived public housing residents affected the neighborhood in stark ways. Those residents moved to Chatham on subsidized housing vouchers after the city demolished their buildings.

Table 1.1

Chatham	2000	2010
Population	37,275	31,028
Median household income	$41,845	$33,890
Unemployment	7.4%	19.0%
Residents in poverty	17.7%	24.5%
Owner occupied	6,481	5,332

Table 1.2   Chatham Median Home Sales

2003	$181,946
2005	$185,915
2008	$168,647
2010	$132,388
2012	$129,431
2013	$120,624

Source: Chicago Rehab Network, "Aldermanic Briefing: Chicago Community Area Fact
Sheets," October 15, 2013.

* * *

My parents bought the Cape Cod Chatham house in 1974, the year they
got married. Their search for a home never strayed from the South Side
since they were both natives. The pretty homes, postage-stamp lawns
and stability drew them to Chatham. Instead of a big-production wedding, my parents exchanged vows at City Hall, my mother outfitted in a
minidress, and they used their savings for a down payment on the house,
which they bought for $30,000 from an older widow, a stranger who
quickly became fond of my father. For a couple ready to start a family,

the house was perfect: a basement, family room extension and two-car garage. Once settled in the house, they held a belated wedding reception to which my mother wore a three-piece ivory silk pantsuit.

"Chatham was a neighborhood of excellence. It was a no-brainer," my father reflected about their decision.

"Chatham was just really the neighborhood of choice," my mother chimed in. "It was the black neighborhood, very stable middle-class neighborhood. Professional blacks and working people lived there too."[4]

They planted a metaphorical red-black-and-green flag. Immediately my father volunteered with the block club and greater neighborhood association. "If you wanted to live in a nice community, you had to be a part of maintaining that nice community. If you want good property values, you've got to have good people involved with the same values."

By the time my parents moved to Chatham, there were about as many whites in the neighborhood as one would find at a Louis Farrakhan revival.

But Chatham's origins actually go back to white immigrants—and it's a story similar to other black South Side neighborhoods. Many of them started off white.

In the late 1800s, Italian stonemasons and Hungarian and Irish railroad workers inhabited Chatham, which is about ten miles from downtown. The population quadrupled when new Swedish and other immigrants moved in during the 1920s, firmly shifting the neighborhood from working to middle class. When the U.S. Supreme Court struck down racially restrictive covenants in 1948, black families exited the hemmed-in borders of the Black Belt. Some went to Chatham, and whites quickly decamped. Some families moved in the middle of the night. In 1950, Chatham was 99 percent white. In 1960, its white population had dropped to 36 percent. By 1970, only 0.2 percent of the population was white.[5] White families didn't like the idea of living harmoniously next to black folk. Sometimes real estate agents ushered them out by playing on their fears that "the blacks" were coming. Racially motivated vandalism occurred; for example, in 1956 someone shot out the windows of gospel singer Mahalia Jackson's home.

Chatham maintained its middle-class character as the population shifted from white to black. And in our household, as well as in others, one of the unofficial mantras was to "buy black."

"We bought our gas in the community. We went to the cleaners in the community. We got our hair cut in the community. I would take the family on Sundays to dinner at restaurants like Army & Lou's and Izola's, and that's where we used to see Mayor Harold Washington with his bodyguard eating dinner. We tried to support the black businesses in the community," my dad said.

My parents never worried about a black cocoon limiting their children's existence and experiences in the 1980s. All the while, several events shaped Black America, a time when the post–civil rights era was in full effect. The Reagan era stripped cities of sorely needed federal dollars. At the same time, crack flooded the streets, spiking urban violence and renewing the so-called War on Drugs. A conservative backlash blamed black people for problems in black neighborhoods—ignoring segregation and turning back the clock on civil rights, such as when President Reagan vetoed the 1988 Civil Rights Bill. Historically black colleges saw dips in enrollment as black students applied to other institutions. Black Entertainment Television (BET) launched. The Nation of Islam rebooted and tapped into racial pride. Hip-hop matured with protest messages. Michael Jackson enticed us to all sing together. In Chicago, voters elected the city's first black mayor in 1983. Oprah brought her folksy talk show persona to the local ABC affiliate and syndicated it in 1986. Jesse Jackson Sr. pursued the White House twice.

"We did a lot of things outside of the neighborhood," my mother said. "I remember I would take the three of you on the 'L,' and I had some friends that would say 'You took public transportation?' But it was a way to show you more of the city, and you were exposed to different things other than this black middle-class neighborhood. Sometimes parents don't want to expose their kids to what they call 'the element.' And I never really felt that way. And I think with the attitude Joe and I had, we believed all people were equal and we didn't make a whole lot of class distinctions—at least I hope I didn't."

It's hard to make strong class distinctions in middle-class black communities because the definition is more elastic. In those areas, subsidized housing exists, as do multi-unit apartment rental buildings. And despite their higher incomes, black homeowners pay the cost of racial segregation.

"The black tax is more crime, and goods and services cost more. I remember grocery shopping in the neighborhood and when I wanted to pay by check I had to almost get out my birth certificate. I stopped going there," my dad explained. He went to the same chain in a white area on another occasion and wrote a check. "I never even had to show my driver's license. They didn't ask me any of the other things I had to go through. And their prices were lower."

Criminality loomed too.

"There was some crime [in Chatham], but nowhere near the kind of crime . . . as there was in other parts of the city. As the result of the solidarity in our community, we were not hit as hard with crime— and maybe because of the economics; the economics were a little better there," he said.

My mother recalled a spate of robberies targeting older women in broad daylight as they walked from their garages into the house.

Black neighborhoods tend to be class heterogeneous, a mix of poor, working and middle class. The iconic, picturesque images and ideals of Chatham can't always insulate the neighborhood from crime or lack of services/amenities. Compounding that experience is the fact that, plainly put, home ownership keeps black poorer than whites. The Chathams of this country suffer from good ol' fashioned racism. When these neighborhoods turned black after whites left, resources fled too. Negative racial impressions strengthened because blacks "invaded" white space. It doesn't matter if black neighborhoods score high marks on the typical things white middle-class families look for in their home search. According to Gregory Squires's 2007 study for the *American Academy of Political and Social Science:*

> Evidence indicates that it is the presence of blacks, and not just neighborhood conditions associated with black neighborhoods (e.g., bad schools, high crime) that accounts for white aversion to such areas. In one survey, whites reported that they would be unlikely to purchase a home that met their requirements in terms of price, number of rooms, and other housing characteristics in a neighborhood with good schools and low crime rates

if there was a substantial representation of African Americans. The presence of Hispanics or Asians had no such effect.[6]

My father spoke of a "black tax." It's real. Public safety concerns and higher-priced goods in black neighborhoods equate to what's dubbed a black homeowners' "segregation tax." According to the Brookings Institution, black homeowners receive 18 percent less value for their homes than white homeowners. Typically, black homeowners in metropolitan areas in the Midwest are subjected to a higher segregation tax than in other parts of the United States. Homeowners in black neighborhoods don't actually pay the government in cash with this tax. "'Tax' in this context can be considered similar to the high domestic prices for sugar and steel that result from import quotas and tariff barriers—what are often characterized as a 'tax' paid by American consumers," the 2001 Brookings report says.[7]

The reduced equity for homeowners in highly segregated neighborhoods reflects the impact of past and current public policies. Black isolation propagates the cycle of inequity. Conversely, home values in poor white neighborhoods are higher than in poor minority neighborhoods. Homes in black neighborhoods are poor long-term investments because it's difficult to build equity in them since they are valued lower: the more segregated an area, the wider the black/white gap in home value per dollar of income; the less segregated an area, the narrower the gap. According to Brookings, the worst metropolitan areas for the segregation tax besides Chicago include Buffalo, New York; Milwaukee; Baltimore; Detroit; Philadelphia; Gary, Indiana; Ft. Lauderdale–Hollywood–Pompano Beach, Florida; and Toledo, Ohio. The best include Boston; Providence, Rhode Island; Honolulu; Tulsa and Oklahoma City; and Albuquerque, New Mexico.[8] The antidote to better housing values is stable integrated neighborhoods.

We're taught that home ownership is a requisite for accessing the American Dream. For black families, that idea can be a cruel joke.

Emory University professor of tax law Dorothy Brown knocks down this wealth-building American Dream premise. "Historically, this is how wealth has been built in the white community. This is not how wealth has been built in the black community," Brown told me. The home ownership market works differently if you're black. According to Brown, if a neighborhood is more than 10 percent black, the value of the home goes down. "Most whites want to live in homogenous white neighborhoods. They don't want to live around lots of blacks. And I define lots of blacks as 10 percent."[9]

People in all-black neighborhoods aren't necessarily aware of the financial consequences associated with buying a home in a majority-black neighborhood. They may be first-time homeowners lost in a reverie of black picket fences.

"I would argue part of the reason we have this racial wealth gap is because most Americans have most of their net worth tied up in their homes, and if you're white and you're living in a predominantly white neighborhood, that's actually not a bad financial thing to do. If you break it out to race, you're going to see far less equity in black homes. It's worked for whites; it hasn't worked for blacks," Brown told me.

Brown isn't advocating that people shun diverse or even black neighborhoods when buying a home. Rather, she advises people not to put all their eggs in the home ownership basket but to invest in the stock market, mutual funds and retirement accounts. Her message is especially haunting, given that the housing collapse wiped out a generation of black wealth.

*   *   *

In academic parlance, Chatham qualifies as a middle-market neighborhood—stable, majority owner occupied. It's also the kind of neighborhood where block clubs are visible before you step on a street. Black South Side neighborhoods are riddled with welcoming signs plopped on corners announcing their presence plus instructions for what not to do: for example, no loitering, no drugs, no car washing or loud music. These messages, perhaps even read as conservative, disrupt rampant stereotypes about blacks tolerating disorder in their communities.

The 1990s onward brought a flush of cash and capital to places like Chatham that had been starved for decades. Then, in 2008, all of that crashed. Hard.

"The foreclosure crisis cannot be underestimated, and the way it has been particularly concentrated in black neighborhoods is not at all random," sociologist Mary Pattillo told me. "We shouldn't . . . say that the housing crisis just happened to be black neighborhoods hardest hit. It didn't happen that way at all.

"We have lots of data that show that black families making the same amount of money and the same amount of credit risk as white families were still disproportionately sold [more] subprime loans than white families. And that has devastated the black community in terms of wealth possession and in terms of now-vacant boarded-up homes. It's opened up increased renters. In areas with high home ownership, that undermines the kind of block club mentality that many of these neighborhoods have fostered over the decades."

In 2013, Illinois attorney general Lisa Madigan and the U.S. Department of Justice announced a $335 million settlement with Bank of America after suing its subsidiary Countrywide for abuses, discrimination and misconduct that led to discriminatory lending in African American communities and contributed to the financial crisis. From 2004 to 2008, approximately 15,000 black and Latino Illinoisans were steered into subprime loans and charged higher interest rates and fees on mortgages than their white counterparts.

University of Illinois at Chicago professor Phil Ashton examined the transformation of neighborhood housing markets and the challenges of recovery. Chatham was one of the three South Side neighborhoods studied that "are also 'stuck' with potentially long-term ramifications resulting from concentrated subprime lending." Many homeowners were left underwater, meaning they owed more than the value of their houses. In the mid-1990s, the bulk of lenders in Chatham were Federal Housing Administration loan products and small savings banks. Conservative underwriting standards of the day kept home buying relatively steady. According to Ashton, however, from 2004 to 2007, large mortgage companies specializing in subprime lending were responsible for most of the Chatham loans.[10]

Another important element differentiates the black middle class from its white peers: The black middle class is newer and just starting to get into the second and third generation. A person new to the middle class may have grown up poor and as a result foots the financial obligations of their parents, who may not have money to keep up with bills. In addition, a person new to the middle class would not have had parents to help with a home down payment or a college education. The recency of the development of the black middle class compared to that of the white middle class contributes to the fragility of the former.

According to Gregory Squires, who wrote the 2007 *American Academy of Political and Social Science* report on racial discrimination, in housing markets, 28 percent of whites receive an inheritance averaging $52,430 compared to 7.7 percent of blacks with an average bequest of $21,796.[11]

Barack and Michelle Obama—pre-presidency—symbolize the fact that race trumps class even for this upper-middle-class family. Dorothy Brown, the Emory University professor, analyzed the Obamas' tax returns from 2000 through 2004 in a paper titled "Lessons from Barack and Michelle Obama's Tax Returns." Their combined annual income fluctuated; the lowest was $207,647 on their 2004 tax return, and the highest was $272,759 on their 2001 tax return. With that level of income, the Obamas did not resemble their financial peers, who are disproportionately white. They more closely resembled their racial peers, who disproportionately have much lower incomes. And in their investments, the Obamas appeared more like households earning less than $100,000, because they didn't diversify their portfolio in the stock market.

The South Side Obamas, who lived in Hyde Park, paid more in taxes than their financial peers. There are several explanations for this. The couple had lower itemized deductions than their higher-income financial peers. And there are two race-based explanations: the marriage penalty and stock ownership.

"As a result of their household income levels, the Obamas would have been subject to significant marriage penalties if either spouse contributed close to 50 percent of household income," Brown wrote in her analysis, and continued:

Michelle [contributed] an ever-increasing amount of household income. For each year, however, the Obamas are subject to the greatest penalty because the lower-earning spouse contributes between 40 and 50 percent. In 2002 Michelle Obama contributed 43.67 percent of wage income to the household. In 2003 she contributed 48.63 percent to the household. In 2004 Michelle Obama contributed 58.80 percent to the household. Between 2002 and 2004, the median contribution to household income by wives was approximately 35 percent. . . .

Black wives have historically worked outside the home more than white wives. . . . Married black couples were more likely to pay a penalty than married white couples, largely because married black husbands and wives were the most likely to contribute roughly equal amounts to household income.

The second potential reason why the Obamas paid higher taxes than their financial peers is because of their lack of stock ownership and income eligible for capital gains treatment. During the examined tax years, the Obamas received no capital gains or dividend payments. According to Brown:

Tax Policy Center data for 2005 indicate that greater than 75 percent of all capital gains and dividend income flows to households with income above $200,000. According to IRS data from 2003, the percent [*sic*] of capital gains and dividend income as a share of all income is 1.4 percent for the average household making less than $100,000. For households making between $200,000 and $1 million, this income accounts for 12.2 percent of total income. Again, the Obamas do not resemble their financial peers—they appear more like those households making less than $100,000, which is less than half of their household income. . . .

While many may assume that once blacks earn more money, their stock ownership will mirror that of their equal-earning white peers because they believe stock ownership is a class issue, the Obamas' tax return data proves that assumption to be false. Higher household income has not allowed the Obamas to transcend race.[12]

*   *   *

Chicagoans cling to neighborhood identity, and for many of its residents, Chatham is a state of mind. The foreclosures, subprime lending and recession weren't the only influences threatening the collective efficacy for neighborhood stability. Crime has always been an issue in Chatham—even if traditionally it has been lower than in other black neighborhoods—but the media glare and perception of lack of safety have changed how the neighborhood is widely viewed.

"Unfortunately, predominately black neighborhoods in Chicago, whether poor, working class, or middle income, have always faced spatial vulnerability to crime to an extent that white neighborhoods of all kinds simply have not," writes Robert Sampson in *Great American City: Chicago and the Enduring Neighborhood Effect.*[13]

In recent years, there has been an uptick in robbery and aggravated battery in Chatham. The causes are drugs, fragmenting gangs, stores illegally selling loose cigarettes, muggings outside of bars.

In 2010, the murder of an Iraqi war veteran in front of his parents' home shook the neighborhood, and the story reverberated around the city. Thirty-year-old Thomas Wortham IV—whom my brother and sister knew as children—was an off-duty police officer shot to death. He died on the street he grew up on. On the fatal night, he was about to leave his parents' home on a motorcycle when two men tried to steal it.

Given the distress of crime, Sampson wonders whether Chatham will "become the newly truly disadvantaged as the black middle class flees, more houses are foreclosed, and poverty rises with the influx of families displaced by the city's [public] housing authority?" The answer, he discovers, is no. "The data tell a story of resistance to crime, challenge-inspired collective efficacy, and a long-term stability to the area in its social character, despite underlying structural vulnerabilities." Sampson defines "collective efficacy" as the process of activating or converting social ties among neighborhood residents to achieve goals. According to his research, Chatham ranked second in collective efficacy among black Chicago neighborhoods and ranks eighth in the entire city.[14]

Fighting for a legacy shouldn't be so hard when the community is engaged. Chatham residents attend community policing meetings—when blocks are calm and when blocks are hot. Block clubs abound, as do local community groups. One example is the Chatham Avalon Park Community Council.

Council president Keith Tate's family moved to predominantly white Chatham in 1955. His father loved the neighborhood so much that he convinced his sisters to buy nearby. Then his aunt and uncles on both sides of the family bought too. The tight-knit community led Keith Tate to return to the neighborhood to raise his own family.

"One of the biggest challenges is the lack of continuity and connectedness within the community," Tate told me.[15] He's not harkening back to a mythical Mayberry existence of back-in-the-day stories. A real problem in Chatham is that it's an aging community—not with vibrant senior citizens but with people in their 80s and 90s who either no longer can contribute to neighborhood efficacy or have moved to senior facilities and left their homes to children not as invested in the property.

Tate recognizes that fear cripples the neighborhood. "Now we have what is called a fear complex. Parents are afraid to let their kids come out and play, afraid to take them to the parks, afraid to let them cross the street—which is an ideology they brought to this community," he said. "It's a perception, and in some cases, your perception is your reality."

Monthly community meetings, supporting small business owners and cultivating relationships with police officers are standard practices for Chatham. Tate told me that a marketing blitz must be done to attract families to the historic bungalows—and not just black families. Even though I believe that Chicago segregation can't continue as it is, I was surprised to hear a dedicated Chatham leader take such a view on race when the identity of the neighborhood has been so wrapped up in blackness.

"We're marketing to nonblacks because the nonblacks that come through the community, they look and say to me 'Oh, these people don't know what they have,'" Tate said, referring to cheaper housing prices compared to areas of the North Side. And economically, Tate said, the presence of other races could help retail development.

A NEW FORM OF REDLINING

Bridget Gainer is a white North Side politician who grew up on the South Side. She's a Cook County commissioner and chair of a local land bank formed to address the overwhelming inventory of vacant property.

When she talks about places like Chatham, Gainer puts into perspective the changing needs of residents in changing neighborhoods. It's not a sexy, hip neighborhood on the edge of downtown but instead a silent victim of the financial crisis.

"There might be vacancies, but people are cutting their neighbor's grass and they're taking the papers off of the porch and making it so you can't really tell that it's vacant. The vacancies aren't really driven by crime so much as it's driven by an aging population. Those are the things I think about when I think about Chatham because to some degree, it's a victim of its own success. It was such a stable place that produced so many successful people. But like lots of neighborhoods, you're not getting the same kind of return, of people moving back there and still having some of those things that still bring people there in the first place," Gainer told me.[16]

The land bank acquires some of that vacant housing, holds it, makes sure it's safe and then finds developers to rehab it for a reasonable amount of money. The land bank clears the red tape on taxes and water bills, and it tries to find alternative lending products for buyers.

But the whole financial meltdown gave Gainer a different view on how the system isn't working. "The whole appraisal system in my mind got totally upside down, and that's a massive area for reform. You could argue there's quasi redlining when it comes to appraisal," she explained. For example, how can a suburban appraiser understand a black Chicago neighborhood when that person knows nothing about the community and may bring the baggage of stereotypes? You wouldn't use an uninformed realtor so why use an uninformed appraiser?

"Everyone's afraid of overestimating the value of homes; they're lowballing their estimates. So you saw that appraisers started to over-compensate for mistakes they made in the past but because there was greater scrutiny on evaluations, you started to get this really wide and unconnected group of people doing appraisals who may not have a lot of community knowledge. And so the appraisal system I think was fatally flawed," Gainer said.

This idea dovetails with the work of Dorothy Brown, the Emory University professor. She said racism could consciously or uncon-sciously be embedded in how appraisers value properties when they are in black neighborhoods. Brokers play a crucial role too. "Brokers decide what neighborhoods to send their clients to. If a broker thinks that showing black prospective homeowners a house in neighborhood X is going to annoy the neighbors, then the broker's not going to do it. The broker works for the neighborhood and the broker wants more referrals."

Brown laughed as she told me her radical idea for upending the way home ownership functions around race. "Let's reconfigure the mortgage interest deduction. Let's not allow it across the board. We know there's this racial disparity and the impact of home ownership based on the percentage of black neighbors you have. We know it's not a level playing field. Why don't we use the tax deduction to disrupt it?

"Why don't we say no one gets a mortgage interest deduction un-less they live in an integrated neighborhood? We realize you're taking a penalty in the market, and we want to compensate you by lowering your taxes." If your neighborhood is 10 percent or more black, you get the deduction, Brown explained.

Brown thinks this plan could work because the Constitution says you can't take account of race except when you can show intentional discrimination. For her, the government's past policies on home owner-ship, such as the Federal Housing Administration's redlining practices, should qualify as discrimination. The government allowed redlining to take place in black neighborhoods by not offering home loans and helped subsidize the growth of the suburbs in the mid-twentieth century.

* * *

In the fall of 1996, my junior year of college, I called home for a regular check-in. I asked my mother what she was doing. "Packing," she replied. "Where are you going?" I asked, assuming she was taking a trip. "We're moving," Mommy answered.

Silence.

"Moving where?"

"To Beverly."

Silence.

Tears.

Click.

Yes, I had a flair for the dramatic. I overreacted because I couldn't say good-bye to the home I grew up in. Come Thanksgiving, I'd be in a new house. In my immaturity, I focused on waves of nostalgia and attachment to Chatham. I was silly and selfish. My siblings had their own reactions. Joey, then a senior in high school, was upset about leaving his friends. Megan, a sophomore, had more friends in the new neighborhood and could walk to high school, unlike my brother.

For years my parents had house hunted in Beverly, a family-friendly South Side integrated neighborhood with a gorgeous and bigger housing stock. It's the area where we Moore children attended a public elementary school through a busing program. I figured house hunting was a hobby. Some couples play cards; others golf; mine spent several years dropping by open houses. I never took seriously their desire to move beyond what they referred to as a starter home. My father explained that it was a bigger house with a bigger backyard—although I still had to share a room with my sister when I visited.

"I miss Chatham. Chatham is my first love," my mother admitted. "We just wanted a larger home." It's about one and a half times bigger, with two family rooms and many more bathrooms.

"We should've moved earlier. We had outgrown the house but we were so committed to the community," my dad added.

A decision based on square footage turned out to be a sage financial move. Moving to an integrated neighborhood provided my parents a long-term cushion, as the research of Emory professor Dorothy Brown indicates. In 1996, they sold the Chatham home for $130,000, clearing close to $100,000 in profit that they put into the new house, which was just shy of $300,000. Nearly 20 years later, the Chatham median home sale price is $129,000 as the neighborhood scales out of the postrecession haze. Of course, if my parents had stayed, the house would've been paid for, but the 2008 housing collapse would have undermined their investment and demolished their nest egg. They bought in the South Side Beverly/Morgan Park area, which is about 60 percent white. That house is now paid for. No obvious foreclosures or board-ups mar the neighborhood. The area is safe and residents take pride in its village feel.

According to Brown, homeowners pay a price for living in an area 10 percent or more black. There's also an integration penalty. Edison Park is a neighborhood comparable to Beverly. It's about as far north as Beverly is south. In 2010, 34 blacks out of more than 11,000 people lived there. Beverly's median income is higher, but its median home sale price at the market's peak was about $40,000 lower.[17]

My 20-year-old self moved on from the emotional attachment of Chatham, and I'm happy that, in quasi-retirement, my parents made prudent financial decisions. The home is a source of family joy for backyard July 4 barbecues, Christmas by the fireplace and weekend afternoons when my dad fires up the grill for cheese-stuffed hamburgers and roasted vegetables.

It took me years to realize how smart my parents were.

I am one of the people who didn't return to Chatham. When it was time for me to buy in 2008, I wanted that hip, sexy new thing. I was single and didn't want a house. I ended up buying in an area formerly known as the Black Belt, a move that turned out to be a financial bust for me.

I, too, am now part of the black ownership cautionary tale.

2

JIM CROW IN CHICAGO

*The ache for home lives in all of us, the safe place where we can go as
we are and not be questioned.*

—Maya Angelou, *All God's Children Need Traveling Shoes*

JOSEPH MOORE SR. HATED THE SOUTH.

Born in 1911, my paternal grandfather was the fourth of eight children born to Odelia Richardson Moore and William Moore of Nashville, Tennessee.

Granddaddy witnessed enough episodes of racism to cause him to flee his birthplace.

In the early 1920s, his eldest brother, William, was riding a streetcar when a white woman boarded and demanded that a black woman give up her seat in the colored section. William erupted. Police arrested him, and he served a 30-day chain gang punishment for being an uppity nigger.

Another time William galloped on his horse, Punch, when a group of white boys chased him home. William ran into his house and grabbed a razor blade to protect himself. The boys banged on the front door and accused William of trying to rape a white girl earlier that day.

William's mother, Odelia, paid a visit to the accuser because she knew the family. The girl professed in front of her mother that teenage William tried to rape her. Incredibly, given the era, the girl's mother turned to her daughter and said William couldn't possibly have done so because she had never left the house that day.

Another Moore child, Granddaddy's older brother McCurtis, faced white brutality and ditched Tennessee out of necessity. After he fought a bunch of white boys, they wanted to kill him. The family hustled McCurtis out of Nashville for New York before the gang showed up on the doorstep. He never returned to live in Tennessee.

Fed-up teenage Joe Sr. ran away to Chicago while in high school to escape the oppressive South. He moved in with Aunt Florence, his father's sister, and his grandmother Bettie. They were pre–Great Migration migrants, although no one in the family knows why they made their way to Chicago. Joe Sr. worked odd jobs, including at the White Sox ballpark.

Three of my late grandparents voyaged to Chicago as part of the Great Migration, a wave of black Americans who left the South in search of opportunity and a better life. The Goodwins and Moores contributed to building a sturdy black middle class on the South Side. Their family journey is like that of so many black Chicagoans who moved north. Some fled out of fear of southern racial violence, others joined relatives who had already completed the trek or bolted to avoid a life of sharecropping.

Political and economic wealth grew along with culture, and Chicago became the heart of black America. The Great Migration also set the stage for lingering hypersegregation, a division between black and white that has shaped the Chicago experience. It's as much a part of the city's legacy as the guitar wailing of Muddy Waters, the powerful words of Richard Wright and the rhythm of the poetry of Gwendolyn Brooks.

Frances Harlow Moore, my paternal grandmother, was born and raised in Springfield, Illinois, the Land of Lincoln. Her family had migrated there from Virginia. She ended up in Chicago after visiting an aunt and cousin. After bouncing to Chicago as a teenager, Joe Moore Sr. went to live with his brother in New York but eventually settled back down in Chicago. Joe married Frances and worked as a Pullman Porter and greatly admired union leader A. Philip Randolph. For 40 years he was a member of the Brotherhood of Sleeping Car Porters. Granddaddy preferred toiling the longest routes, such as Chicago to Seattle, because it gave him the opportunity to earn more tips, which his daughter, my aunt Joyce, looked forward to counting as a child. The money made a difference in their household. Labor runs in our family, and the practice of good tipping is a result of Granddaddy's career.

In his later years, Granddaddy served up drinks at the Playboy Mansion, a job he got through the Chicago Urban League. In the 1980s, he took up acting, nabbing roles as a movie extra or in commercials.

On my mother's side, my grandfather James Goodwin determined after he returned from unloading planes in the South Pacific for the Army in World War II that he wanted to live in either Harlem or Chicago. He represents the second wave of migration, when African American men returned from overseas and didn't want to suffer segregation down South as they had in the military. During the 1940s, black leaders and the black press demanded equal rights in the Double V Campaign—victory abroad, victory at home. James grew up in Harris County, Georgia, which looks straight out of a set from the film *The Color Purple,* with its red clay dirt and rural white church accompanied with a backyard family cemetery. The decision to leave came easy because his childhood love, Nina, also a Harris County native, had already moved.

"My father came to Chicago because my mother was here," my mother, Yvonne, said, laughing. "He was following her. She came because her cousin was here and they were like sisters."[1]

This is how the black migrant story worked; it was similar to the immigrant story. Nina's cousin Clara Kennebrew and husband, L.C., wanted to flee Georgia. L.C. had an aunt in Chicago, so that naturally led the couple to the South Side. They easily enticed Nina up to the Promised Land. An only child whose parents had died, she had nothing to keep her in Georgia.

"My mother said the minute she stepped off the train, she knew where she was and she was happy here," my mother explained. The feel of the big city, the crackle of the concrete beneath her feet welcomed her.

Nina found home when she debarked the train at 12th Street, the beginning of the Black Belt. Concrete must have felt different on her feet than spongy red clay dirt. The bright streetlights and crowds mesmerized the country Georgia woman. Lake Michigan's ferocious waves clapped against the shoreline. Cold winters allowed her to save up for fashionable wool coats from Marshall Field's. Public transportation, jitneys and my grandfather in his Buicks or Cadillacs ferried Nina about the South Side, and she never saw the need to get her driver's license.

My two sets of grandparents bought homes and two-flats in South Side neighborhoods that opened up to blacks in the mid-twentieth century. At one point both families owned additional properties as real estate income. My grandmothers weren't June Cleavers. Like other black women in their generation, they worked.

The Goodwins lived in Woodlawn, just south of the University of Chicago, and across the alley from Emmett Till, the black teenager killed by white men for allegedly flirting with a white woman while visiting family in Mississippi in 1955. James Goodwin hailed from a family of eight brothers and one sister—he was the only one of his siblings to leave Georgia. Every summer my mother, her parents and younger brother journeyed down South to visit relatives. Sometimes those trips proved a culture shock to young Yvonne, who refused buttermilk in her cereal. (I've often wondered what our life would have been like had I been raised in Georgia, where almost everyone in the family goes by a nickname. My grandfather was born Jimmie Lee, but his nephews called him Jake. Chicagoans called him James or Jim. Nina's people called her Dale. She had three first cousins named Nook, Nump and Gump. Don't ask how people get these names. I figured I'd probably be christened "Peaches.") As children in Woodlawn, my mother and her next-door neighbor and cousin, Harriette (the daughter of Clara and L.C.), often walked to the nearby Walgreens on 63rd and Cottage to eat in the nice restaurant with booths. The girls enjoyed gazing out the window and saw this experience as a step up from White Castle. But the duo went there, too, with the kids next door to listen to the jukebox.

Granddaddy Goodwin drank Old Style beer and occasionally played the numbers. He loved Mahalia Jackson. He watched the White Sox and Cubs on television. We're among the rare families that root for both teams and ignore the South Side–North Side rivalry—except when the teams play each other. Then we're South Side all day. Every day Granddaddy read the *Tribune* and often called legendary columnist Mike Royko a racist bastard, even though he kind of looked like Royko and they wore the same glasses. Granddaddy was six feet tall and occasionally mistaken for white. Right after I was born, he retired from RR Donnelley, which printed the first known telephone directory, as a printer. I could always count on him to be a real-life Tooth Fairy or kindly slip me $10 just because.

Grandmommy Goodwin worked as a cook in a Chicago public school and, knowing the conditions in which food was prepared in kitchens, consequently hated eating out in restaurants. At home, she cooked delicious oven-baked short ribs and pound cakes. Grandmommy and I rode the "L" train downtown to her favorite store, Marshall Field's. In 1980, she and my grandfather left Woodlawn for Park Manor, a ten-minute car ride from our Chatham home. I used to love spending the night at their flat, which boasted plastic covers on the living room furniture, pea-green shaggy carpet, Jesus and MLK on the walls. I stayed up late to watch Johnny Carson's *Tonight Show* and drink Hawaiian Punch.

Grandmommy Moore, who retired as a secretary for a federal agency, picked me up from elementary school and offered me a hot dog on a toasted bun with Grey Poupon before running me to different beauty shops on the South Side to hot comb my thick hair. That was our special time together. She taught me how to make a lemon meringue pie and called me her pride and joy. My paternal grandparents first lived with their three children in Princeton Park, rental town homes on the South Side that were a step above public housing. Then they bought a house in a South Side neighborhood that had transitioned from white to black. Those railroad tips helped them to home ownership.

By migrating to the South Side, all of my grandparents had good lives. At the time, they likely didn't contemplate the patterns of housing segregation firmly ensconced in the city. Some of the area's shoddy housing already had been torn down by the time of this second-wave migration. The fact that they were able to buy their own homes enabled them to avoid some of the violence and horrible discriminatory practices that kept blacks in manufactured black ghettos.

But the housing ills still remained on the South Side, deliberate and repeated. Blacks had choices yanked away from them. Housing policies rewarded people for acting in racist ways and offered few incentives to change. As soon as those black migrants disembarked the trains from Mississippi, Alabama and Louisiana, white Chicago conspired to keep them in their place in the Jim Crow North.

BLACK METROPOLIS

Chicago's black history begins well before the twentieth-century movement of blacks from southern farms to northern factories. It was a black man who founded the modern-day city. Jean Baptiste Point DuSable, a Haitian fur trader, set up a trading post around 1779 on the banks of Lake Michigan. Quinn Chapel A.M.E. Church served as a station for the Underground Railroad. Ida B. Wells brought her radicalism to Chicago in the late 1800s, a time when black institutions such as churches and hospitals began to thrive.

But the Great Migration forever changed the face and fabric of the city. Between 1916 and 1970, Chicago gained more than 500,000 African Americans.

"Over time, this mass relocation would come to dwarf the California Gold Rush of the 1850s with its one hundred thousand participants and the Dust Bowl migration of some three hundred thousand people from Oklahoma and Arkansas to California in the 1930s. But more remarkably, it was the first mass act of independence by a people who were in bondage in this country for far longer than they have been free," Isabel Wilkerson writes in *The Warmth of Other Suns: The Epic Story of America's Great Migration.*

In Chicago, the black population soared from under 44,103 at the start of the Great Migration to more than 1 million by the end.[2]

But the city didn't embrace its new residents and consciously confined them to a black ghetto, the Black Belt on the South Side.

Whites didn't want to live with blacks, much less beach with them.

On a hot summer day in 1919, a Negro boy took a dip into Lake Michigan to cool off and swam in the "white" part of the waters. A race riot broke out, and the boy drowned during the clash. White youth involved in the rioting belonged to so-called athletic clubs, a gentler, race-friendly way to describe white gangs. Future mayor Richard J. Daley belonged to the Hamburg Club, made up of a bunch of tough white boys. His membership wouldn't stop him from running the city for two decades; in fact, Daley used his leadership in the club to play Democratic politics and get his pals jobs. Violence swept over Chicago for several days, leaving 38 people dead, 537 injured and 1,000 homeless.[3]

Two years before the riot, the Chicago Real Estate Board appointed a committee to figure out how to deal with the "Negro Problem." It adopted a report that recommended each block be filled solidly with buildings, with further expansion confined to contiguous blocks to prevent blacks from resettling in white areas.[4]

But the U.S. Supreme Court had struck down such a segregationist practice in a 1917 Kentucky case, *Buchanan v. Warley*. Although that decision didn't result in a general rollback of de jure segregation or lead to integration, it did stop state and local governments from passing more pervasive and brutal segregation laws like those enacted in South Africa.[5]

Meanwhile, the court case meant little in Chicago, where the color line may not have been as barbarous as in the South but where blacks still suffered their share of housing inequity and ugly racial strife. The northern land of milk and honey at times was sour.

In the 1920s, the real estate profession incorporated restrictions into its code of ethics and added restrictive covenants to property deeds. Racially restrictive covenants prohibited the sale, lease or occupation of a property by African Americans. These covenants would have a long-lasting effect and shape black neighborhoods for decades to come. The Supreme Court upheld this form of segregation with its 1926 dismissal of *Corrigan v. Buckley*, a case in which a white woman sold her house to a black family in Washington, D.C. Another white homeowner blocked the sale on the grounds that it violated the restrictive covenant.

By 1930, blacks were spatially isolated to a high degree in American cities, with Chicago leading the way. The Home Owners' Loan Corporation was formed in 1933 as part of the New Deal and provided funds for refinancing urban mortgages in danger of default.[6] But the Depression-era government program institutionalized redlining, a practice that excluded blacks by color coding black neighborhoods based on loan risks. The lowest color was red, where blacks lived. Redlining influenced lending practices of the Federal Housing Administration and the Veterans Administration of the 1940s with regard to blacks.

Chicago blacks experienced a complicated relationship between the metaphorical two homes—the North that was supposed to be the promised land and the South from which they escaped. As Richard Wright observed in an ethnography of Chicago's Black Belt for the Works Progress Administration:

> In the eyes of millions of Negroes the North has long been a haven of opportunity and justice. Many of those who came north did so to escape the sharp competition of southern white labor, to avoid the persecution of petty officers of the southern law and the persecution of the southern press, and to gain the long-denied right of franchise. . . . The above causes of Negro migration existed long before any exodus of Negroes took place. The more immediate and pressing causes were economic and social. The living standards of southern Negroes were abnormally low. Wages were as low as 50¢ per day. Added to this were the boll weevil pests, floods, storms, all of which augmented the hazards of rural life. Other contributing factors were vicious residential segregation and a lack of school facilities.[7]

Throngs of blacks traveled North to a vibrant metropolis of the 1920s. The black *Chicago Defender* newspaper encouraged migration and opposed segregation while stealthily having the publication delivered in the South. Thomas Dorsey birthed gospel music inside the city's Pilgrim Baptist Church in the 1930s. Chicago's literary and arts renaissance attracted painter Archibald Motley Jr. The South Side Community Arts Center cultivated Gwendolyn Brooks, Elizabeth Catlett and Gordon Parks. Chess Records cranked out R&B hits, and the blues scene boomed. Black-owned banks and other institutions opened and supported the community.

A running narrative about life in the Black Belt romanticizes segregation. Even today people who didn't live in that era wax poetic about how it was good for the black community because doctors lived next to janitors; we had our own institutions and we existed outside of white people. While all of that is true, it doesn't provide the complete picture of the insidious nature of segregation. Black people didn't *choose* to be separate. White people forced them into second-class citizenry. And that led to substandard housing, overcrowded schools or even white hospitals rejecting black patients. Chicago didn't have visible "white only" or "colored only" signs glued to public places, but the city designed a way for blacks not to fully participate in the freedoms of the North.

In 1945, St. Clair Drake and Horace Cayton published *Black Metropolis: A Study of Negro Life in a Northern City*, a landmark sociological account of black life and the color line on Chicago's South Side during the 1930s. Drake and Cayton recognized that the Black Belt wasn't an accident. Poverty, low-wage jobs, juvenile delinquency and high death rates existed because white people did not want blacks in their neighborhoods.

Drake and Cayton wrote: "Black Metropolis has become a seemingly permanent enclave within the city's blighted area. The impecunious immigrant, once he gets on his feet, may . . . move into an area of second-settlement. Even the vice-lord or gangster, after he makes his pile, may lose himself in a respectable neighborhood. Negroes, regardless of their influence or respectability, wear the badge of color. They are expected to stay in the Black Belt.[8]

The ghetto created music, nightlife and faith communities but also abnormally high rental costs, blight and overcrowded housing. This wasn't unique to Chicago.

Decades later, East Coast sociologists Douglas Massey and Nancy Denton observed that black segregation is not comparable to segregation experienced by other racial and ethnic groups in the United States. Sustained levels of black residential segregation is not happenstance. "This extreme racial isolation did not just happen; it was manufactured by whites through a series of self-conscious actions and purposeful institutional arrangements that continue today. Not only is the depth of black segregation unprecedented and utterly unique compared with that of other groups, but it shows little sign of change with the passage of time or improvements in socioeconomic status," they write.[9]

* * *

When Lorraine Hansberry, the first black woman to have a play produced on Broadway, penned her groundbreaking *A Raisin in the Sun* in 1958, she no doubt drew from her experiences as a daughter of the South Side of Chicago. When the playwright chronicled how the Younger family sought to leave their black ghetto for white Clybourne Park, Hansberry understood the trouble of integrating a neighborhood. When Karl Linder of the white home improvement association tried to foil the Youngers' home purchase, Hansberry wrote with authority, for this was the Hansberry family's story.

In 1937, her father, Carl Hansberry, purchased a home at 6140 S. Rhodes in the white Woodlawn neighborhood, just south and west of the University of Chicago. Supreme Life, one of the largest black-owned insurance companies in the country, located on the South Side, gave him a loan. When the family moved in, white mobs flung bricks through the windows, and one almost struck eight-year-old Lorraine. Her mother, Nannie, a schoolteacher, patrolled the house at night with a gun.

A white woman named Anna Lee brought a lawsuit charging that a restrictive agreement forbidding sales to blacks in the neighborhood had been violated. Lee filed on behalf of the Hyde Park–Woodlawn Improvement Society, and the circuit court and the Illinois Supreme Court upheld Lee's assertion. The Hansberrys were forced to move.

The Hansberrys nurtured politics and culture. Lorraine's uncle taught African history at Howard University. Paul Robeson, Duke Ellington, W. E. B. Du Bois and Walter White visited their home.[10] Carl Hansberry, a prominent real estate businessman, was no stranger to civil rights. He filed a lawsuit in 1938 against Santa Fe Railway, alleging that the company charged African Americans first-class fares but put them in third-class passenger cars. Hansberry lost. After the Illinois State Supreme Court decision upholding the right of white property owners in the Hansberry case, the official student magazine of the University of Chicago, *Pulse*, published an editorial about the college's support of restrictive covenants, arguing that Negroes wouldn't profit from their dissolution "for chiseling landlords would take over in most cases, returning housing to the previous situation, and if not, 'vigilante' committees of whites would precipitate riots and force the Negroes from their community."

Horace Cayton, coauthor of *Black Metropolis*, responded in the *Defender:*

> Your statement that Negroes would not profit by a dissolution of restrictions because "chiseling landlords would take over in most cases," is not sound. The entire Negro community is characterized by "chiseling landlords," but this does not obviate the fact that nearly 200,000 Negro citizens are forced to live in an area which has housing facilities for only 150,000. I might suggest that the "vigilante" committees of whites whom you assume precipitate riots are the same groups which have been organized and financed by the University of Chicago. If that support was withdrawn neither the continued resistance to the expansion of the area, not the possibility for a riot would in all probability obtain.[11]

Hansberry v. Lee went to the U.S. Supreme Court in 1940. Rows of blacks sat in the session to hear arguments.[12] Prominent black attorney Earl Dickerson represented Hansberry. The court ruled in favor of Hansberry and invalidated the racial covenant—but the judges didn't adduce the unconstitutionality of restrictive covenants; the ruling hinged on a technicality. Anna Lee claimed more than 500 land owners had signed the restrictive agreement, which stated that it would be ineffective unless signed by 95 percent of the area owners. According to Dickerson, the required percentage did not sign the agreement, thus violating the contract. He stated that only 54 percent of the owners had signed.[13]

Nonetheless, the court decision was a welcomed win, and 500 homes in the contested area opened up to blacks. The overcrowded Black Belt was rupturing, and this small victory allowed blacks to move; this is in part why my grandparents were able to move to Woodlawn in the 1940s. In a *Defender* column, Carl Hansberry reacted: "I feel that the decision will be of tangible and practicable value to both the white and colored citizens of Chicago, and it gives me the courage to continue to fight for the full and complete citizenship rights of the colored citizens of Illinois."[14]

The weight of racism reportedly took its toll on Hansberry. He died a month before his fifty-first birthday in 1946 of a cerebral hemorrhage in Mexico, where he had planned to move the family.

Despite the Supreme Court ruling, restrictive agreements continued in Chicago and elsewhere in the United States. But the debate and fight raged on. Blacks organized and whites garrisoned their communities.

The Hyde Park Property Owners, Inc. created a pamphlet on restrictive covenants in 1944 in conjunction with the Federation of Neighborhood Associations, which opposed housing integration. The South Side neighborhood group within University of Chicago borders encouraged property owners to read up on the subject. The group argued that restrictive agreements were:

1. Valid and legally enforceable. Your contractual rights as a citizen are guaranteed by the U.S. Constitution
2. Morally justified and not motivated by prejudice!
3. Absolutely essential to the future well-being of Hyde Park and the City of Chicago

According to the pamphlet: "Race restrictive covenants do not segregate negroes. They segregate whites. These covenants do not connote prejudice. They have been signed by persons in industrial and professional life whose activities provide employment for thousands of negroes. The living space of negroes is not confined by these agreements."[15]

The property owners rested their logic on case precedent. The pamphlet stated:

Race restrictive agreements give protection to a neighborhood, encourage residents to remain in it, stimulate new construction and maintain community morale. They offer permanency of investments, safeguards against the deteriorating influence of undesirable neighbors and good environment for the establishment of homes. They are private contracts between the owners of private property in which the parties agree not to rent or sell such property to certain classes of people. They have been sanctioned by the highest courts of the United States and Illinois.

The pamphlet also listed differences in property values—high on the white North Side, low on the black South Side—to make its case for the restrictions. The association basically endorsed separate but equal. "There may be a city in the United States where negroes are better situated than Chicago but we do not know where that place is. The colored belt on Chicago's south side occupies as fine a section, geographically, as there is in the city."

The white property owners saw themselves as sympathetic and altruistic. The pamphlet also talked about new public schools that had been built and how migrating children from the South "have been provided with the same educational opportunities available to all other Chicago children." As if they weren't U.S. citizens.

In 1945, the NAACP convened a restrictive covenants conference in Chicago with lawyers from Detroit, Los Angeles and St. Louis in attendance. A year later, the Council Against Racial and Religious Discrimination gathered in a downtown Chicago hotel to figure out how to eliminate restrictive covenants. The two-day summit brought together a wide array of players: the Chicago Urban League, the American Council on Race Relations, members of the Illinois General Assembly, the American Civil Liberties Union, the NAACP, the YWCA, the Japanese American Citizens League, rabbis, ministers, labor groups, postal workers and lawyers. Earl Dickerson, the black attorney who represented Carl Hansberry, participated.

Conference registration cost $1, and attendees were asked what churchmen, voters, property owners and organized labor could do to end restrictive covenants.

Dickerson, whom J. Edgar Hoover, head of the Federal Bureau of Investigation, called a communist in 1943,[16] instructed the audience on what lawyers could do. Dickerson said that lawyers needed to dwell on the broader aspects of segregation, a social evil, and how restrictive covenants perpetuate the cycle. He argued that the covenants weren't merely private contracts but powerful tools that threatened the city as a whole because of their unconstitutionality.[17]

Henry Kohn, an attorney and panel chairman, beseeched property owners who opposed restrictive covenants to educate other property owners. "If, then, all work together to maintain the occupancy standards of the neighborhood, and the physical conditions of the properties, the creation of new slums will be prevented and friction and ill-will between the white and colored residents will be minimized if not eliminated."

Lawyers and civil rights groups in Chicago and elsewhere kept up the pressure about the appalling nature of housing segregation. They kept pushing the issue of covenants, and in 1948 a case went before the U.S. Supreme Court. The justices finally struck down the restrictive covenants in *Shelley v. Kraemer*. In this case, the Shelleys, a black family in St. Louis, bought in a white neighborhood controlled by a restrictive covenant. The high court ruled the Fourteenth Amendment's guarantee of equal protection applied in this case to prohibit the enforcement of the covenant, therefore ending this crushing form of racial discrimination. A forerunner to the civil rights movement, the court's decision had an enormous impact on black America. No longer could white neighborhood groups or powerful institutions endorse or enforce restrictive covenants.

All over the country, neighborhoods opened up. In a mass exodus, black Chicago families left their cramped quarters for South Side neighborhoods that once purposefully excluded them.

But another set of housing obstacles awaited them.

WHITE FLIGHT

If my maternal grandparents had moved from Woodlawn to Park Manor decades earlier instead of in 1980, they undoubtedly would have suffered racial violence.

On July 25, 1949, Roscoe and Ethel Johnson entered their new Park Manor home on 71st and St. Lawrence as the first Negroes on the block. Neither a welcome wagon nor a neighborly pie greeted them. A mob immediately gathered and tried to set the Johnsons' furniture on fire, burning two mattresses in the process. By nightfall, 2,000 rioters had stoned every window in the house. They hurled oil-soaked burning rags and gasoline-filled containers inside. The Johnsons crawled on their hands and knees to dodge bricks. White people spat on the street, saying "It's a shame the niggers movin' in . . . property values will go to hell."[18]

Scholar Arnold Hirsch suggests the violence against Roscoe and Ethel Johnson served as a turning point for Park Manor. "Soon thereafter, the First Federal Savings and Loan Association and the Chicago City Bank decided the neighborhood was 'gone' and became 'major lenders' for blacks entering Park Manor."[19] That change accelerated succession. A white resident said it was easier to move out than to stay. Real estate agents called to see if families wanted to sell. Whites resisted Chicago Urban League efforts to organize block clubs, packed their bags and left en masse. At the same time that black families exited black ghettos, white families refused to be their new neighbors.

The Johnson family tragedy followed a trend. In the late 1940s and 1950s, white mobs rioted when black families moved into white neighborhoods. Arson and vandalism occurred frequently.

The Chicago Commission on Human Relations responded to attacks but influenced the press to not report on them. "The mayor's Commission on Human Relations has consistently tried to keep racial violence quiet, thus providing protecting for the mob and offering no insurance that it will not happen again," some young Roosevelt College progressives charged.[20]

Elsewhere, as the South Side neighborhood Englewood transitioned from white to black, the city discovered that the way black and white families purchased properties differed.[21] Speculators bought homes cheaply from whites who panicked at the idea of living in a racially changing neighborhood. Black families bought houses for a low down payment but had to sign an installment contract that left the title to the house in the speculator's name. Speculators found a shield with land trusts in which the owner's identity could be hidden from public record. Later the speculators would jack up the contract price, and monthly payments were high. Sellers never gave buyers a grace period if they missed a payment. Contract buyers were responsible for repairs and didn't reap the benefits of tax deductions from owning a home. Contract buying happened more frequently on the West Side of Chicago, and in the 1960s, black buyers organized to take action against the exploitation.

During this same period, from 1950 to 1960, many South Side neighborhoods swiftly turned over from white to black. White flight received a boost from the public and private sector. Underhanded real estate agents adopted "blockbusting" and "panic peddling" practices to trigger the turnover of white-owned homes to blacks. Agents would scare whites into selling before it was "too late" and "the blacks" lowered their property values. Sometimes agents might hire black subagents to walk or drive through a changing neighborhood to solicit business or behave in such a way to exaggerate white fears. In turn, worried whites would sell their homes cheaply, and panic peddlers would inflate prices to sell the homes to black families, thus hastening white flight. Racial steering, where agents discouraged white buyers from considering racially integrated neighborhoods or steered blacks away from viewing homes in white suburbs, came next.

Whites indeed sought racial refuge in the suburbs. After World War II, suburban areas received preference for residential investment. In the 1950s, Federal Housing Administration financing favored loans in suburbs, which expedited white flight and the decline of cities.

In the decade and a half after World War II, builders constructed 700,000 new houses in the Chicago metropolitan area. Between 1940 and 1960, suburban acreage doubled. Expressways opened in the region to facilitate travel to the new lily-white suburbs.[22]

Chicago activists pushed for better housing. In 1963, Mayor Richard J. Daley foolishly declared "there are no ghettos in Chicago." When Martin Luther King Jr. went to Chicago in 1966 to take on the North, Daley recoiled. He disliked the civil rights leader and scoffed at a "Negro" outsider trying to fix his city. King led rallies against the discriminatory housing market, but he realized that his tactics of peaceful nonviolence didn't work in the brutal North when whites physically attacked him. Daley and King drafted a summit agreement that had no legal standing. King's housing activism failed in Chicago, and a gleeful Daley let the door slam behind him.[23]

Meanwhile, other housing efforts started and sputtered.

In the late 1960s, the U.S. Department of Housing and Urban Development began to support open housing experiments. In response to Chicago-area racial residential segregation, the Leadership Council for Metropolitan Open Communities conducted an experiment with a goal of providing a link between black inner-city brokers and white suburban real estate boards.

In 1979, appointed monitor Brian J. L. Berry pretty much summed the project up as an abject failure. He concluded that the well-intentioned program did not achieve its primary goal of transforming a dual housing market into one in which the entire stock of housing in the metropolitan area was available to all citizens regardless of race. Scores of white city residents refused to share their neighborhoods with blacks and retreated to the suburbs. Middle-class black residents found a variety of housing at attractive prices in the city and tossed out the idea of becoming pioneer integrationists in the suburbs.[24]

One far South Side neighborhood did buck the trend of white flight. In 1970, Beverly was 99 percent white. In 2013, it was 62 percent white. Blacks didn't migrate there in the 1950s after the *Shelley v. Kraemer* verdict likely because the housing stock cost more in that Irish-Catholic neighborhood than elsewhere on the South Side. Some whites living in Beverly had already fled neighborhoods that had changed over from white to black, and Beverly signified the end of the road for them.

Some white homeowners feared Beverly's fate as a new black ghetto if integration happened, but other residents recognized the inevitability of integration. One resident completed flip-chart presentations around Beverly with that very message.[25] The community banded together to quell white fears, welcome its new black neighbors and battle the crafty real estate industry. The head of the Beverly Area Planning Association (BAPA), which adopted a new mission statement that celebrated diversity, said, "White families in urban areas must realize they can't run away from blacks. And they must realize that middle-class blacks and whites both want the same things—good schools, good services, low crime rate. At the same time, blacks are realizing that a neighborhood that is all one race increases the process of deterioration."[26]

BAPA convinced homeowners to sign "letters of agency" to prevent unauthorized solicitation from real estate agents. These letters asserted that homeowners had no intention of selling. BAPA kept the letters on file and served "uncooperative" real estate firms with notices to cease solicitation. Homeowners also refrained from putting for-sale signs in their yards. In 1977, my aunt and uncle were among the first black families to move to Beverly and were the first on their block. That year, there, someone threw rocks through the living room window of their tri-level home. They assumed the action was racially motivated.

Beverly isn't perfect or without racial turmoil. I have a friend whose family moved there in the 1970s, and someone scribbled "nigger" on their garage. The family left the word up for a while to rattle their neighbors into understanding racism. Black boys recall stories in the 1990s of being bullied by white boys and police officers. Nonetheless, Beverly has maintained integration and is viewed as a model in the region. My parents moved to the area in 1996 because they wanted a bigger house and a healthier investment.

In the mid-1980s, Beverly, and a dozen integrated southern and western suburbs, conducted a testing program in which black and white couples of comparable incomes posed as potential home buyers to see how real estate agents treated them. According to BAPA, white testers were discouraged from racially integrated areas and black testers usually were steered away from homes in predominantly white suburbs. My Beverly aunt and late uncle participated as testers and experienced steering firsthand.[27]

BAPA sued four southwest suburban real estate firms for steering blacks to Beverly only. White clients were told they wouldn't want to live there because they'd be uncomfortable in an integrated neighborhood. BAPA lost the first case and settled the other four. Real estate agents went through training on better practices and struck back, suing BAPA and accusing the organization of trying to keep suburban brokers from doing business in Beverly and Morgan Park. BAPA prevailed against the lawsuit.

It seems that fear guides housing attitudes in Chicago every decade—a potent combination that leads to bad government policies.

When voters elected Harold Washington as the city's first black mayor in 1983, many white ethnic communities panicked. The white working-class bungalow belt of the Southwest and Northwest Sides feared blacks would be their new neighbors and cause a decrease in their property values.

In response, they created a program to prevent white flight in the form of three home equity districts in which taxes are collected. The money goes into a fund that functions as a kind of insurance program—homeowners could file a cash claim if the house value dropped upon selling. Initially, Washington supported the tax program, but he changed his mind once black aldermen objected.[28]

Very few claims have been filed, and most were related to the housing crisis of the late 2000s. But, curiously, the program still exists amid changing neighborhood demographics that include a surge in Latino home ownership. Some communities have a tiny black population. But the home equity districts still collect cash and are flush with it—with little oversight or imagination on how to spend the money. I wouldn't mind paying a few extra bucks on a tax bill to go into a community pot that could help economic improvement, streetscaping or other neighborhood needs.

* * *

My family doesn't have many relics of its journey to Chicago. Relatives in Nashville preserved a stack of faded and some illegible letters between them and Chicago loved ones in the 1920s, '30s and '40s. Family members penned correspondence divulging home remedies for sickness, drama with a cousin's health, wedding announcements and sometimes banalities of life. One letter mentioned my grandfather Joe. His grandmother Bettie Moore and aunt Florence moved from Nashville to Chicago before the official start of the Great Migration. When Bettie didn't receive a response from her son William and daughter-in-law Odelia, she sent a pleading letter.

> May 10, 1927
>
> Mrs. Odelia Moore
>
> Dear Son & Daughter
>
> I thought I would write to you all again. This is my 3rd letter I have wrote to you all and I haven't heard from you all yet. Why don't you all write to me. This leave me not feeling so well. But I do trust that this will find you all well and doing well. Well Odelia Sunday was Mothers Day and Joe Edward came to see me. I know him as soon as I looked up and saw. He has eyes so much like William Jr. He gave me 50 cents. . . . [29]

Bettie Moore actually had been in Chicago at least ten years when she wrote that letter. She was dying in a nursing home when my grandfather came to see her. Her letter asked for home remedies because she was too poor to pay for the doctor, which speaks to how blacks were living in poverty in Chicago.

My great-aunt Martha Pratt is my family's oldest living relative in Chicago. She's a retired public high school math teacher who came to Chicago in the late 1940s when her husband sought greater opportunity for his pediatric dentistry practice. They had been living in Hot Springs, Arkansas—a place too slow and sleepy for an ambitious black couple.

After a bad fall in 2013, Aunt Martha moved into a rehab facility. Her memory is a bit hazy, but she's alert and aware. "I'm an old chicken," she told me, laughing.[30] "Don't you hope you get this old." Silver hair in a French braid, few wrinkles on her smooth peanut butter skin.

On one of my Sunday visits, Aunt Martha greeted me with "Give me a little sugar, girlfriend" before asking me to flip the television to the Chicago Bears football game. I wanted to jog her early memories of the South Side.

In 1935, Martha, then 14, stayed the whole summer with Aunt Florence, a devout Catholic.

"I just wanted to come to Chicago. Chicago sounded big to me—a country girl from Nashville, Tennessee." Martha didn't remember what neighborhood her aunt lived in. I imagine how Chicago must have looked to her, a place where she could roam freely in a way she could not in her native Nashville. Plus she was only 14. For Martha and others who came North, Chicago offered emotional freedom.

Martha did remember spending her days walking around a shopping area. "I'd window shop and look at myself in the mirror in the windows and say 'here I am in big old Chicago.' I was very proud of that trip."

The city and family influenced her. Martha returned to Nashville a Catholic, changed her middle name from Ritter to Rita after the saint and declared herself no longer a Baptist. But Martha never thought she'd one day live in Chicago.

By the time she moved to Chicago as an adult, Martha believed the city offered her greater opportunity. In Hot Springs, Arkansas, she was offered only middling teaching positions or the opportunity to work in the bathhouses. "I don't think I'd be nearly as far along. The opportunities were greater here. I lived better," she told me.

Martha still owns her house in a formerly white neighborhood on the South Side—"I never thought of living in a white neighborhood. You don't ask for trouble"—has a handsome retirement and played tennis and bridge for years.

Despite its benefits, the North presented its share of problems and, at times, angered my grandparents.

In the 1960s, my grandmother walked my teenage father to a neighborhood store to apply for a job bagging groceries. The store would not provide an application because they were "not hiring colored." Dad ended up working as an usher at Orchestra Hall. Our cousin Roberta, well-traveled and sophisticated, sang with the symphony choir and got him that job. Once on a family vacation to Michigan, Joe Sr. pulled over to a roadside cafe to purchase a cup of coffee. When they wouldn't serve him, his children thought he was going to blow up. Anger puts it mildly. He had to be calmed down, my father recalled.

Granddaddy Moore and Grandmommy Goodwin didn't particularly care for the South and eventually either limited their visits or stopped going altogether. I never once knew my grandmother to travel back. Once my mother and Granddaddy took the three of us children to Georgia for a Goodwin family reunion. When we pulled up to Grand-mommy's old house, which was dilapidated by then, my mother advised me not to take photos because Grandmommy wouldn't be interested in traveling down memory lane.

Joe Sr. continued to visit his mother and take his family to Tennes-see. When he did return, he couldn't shield his children from second-class citizenry that repulsed him.

One Nashville summer during the 1950s, my father and his younger brother wandered out of a five-and-dime store. They were old enough to read but younger than ten. "We were thirsty and we saw these two water fountains. One said 'colored' and one said 'white,'" my father remembered. The brothers looked at each other and asked what that meant. "And I said 'I don't know. But remember, Mama said things are gonna be different down here and we're used to drinking white water.'" They interpreted the Jim Crow signs to mean white water as clear and shunned the "colored" water. As their lips touched the "white" water, "that's when Uncle Johnny and Daddy picked us up from the back and held us," my father recalled. "And I must admit, looking back, that was the first time I've ever seen fear in the eyes of my father and my uncle. They were looking around and we had no idea what was going on. They took us home and I remember Grandma Moore said something like 'were you followed?'"[31] Odelia Moore had plenty of experience shep-herding her sons out of the South because of white violence and didn't want that for her young northern grandsons.

My grandparents lived the American Dream. The Great Migration provided opportunities for their progeny not afforded to them. Their children were first-generation college graduates, and their legacy trick-les down to their grandchildren.

When I graduated from Howard University in 1998, Granddaddy Goodwin was the only grandparent who attended. My grandmother Nina had Alzheimer's and my other grandfather was too sick. My pater-nal grandmother, Frances, had died of cancer in 1988. James Goodwin flew to the ceremony and said he would have walked to Washington,

D.C., to see me graduate. Afterward, I heard him brag to neighbors back in Chicago about all the black people he saw walk across the stage. My diploma meant the world to a man who never finished third grade.

He died in 2004, almost a year after my grandmother Nina. Joe Sr. died in 1999.

All four of my grandparents are interred at the historic Oakwood Cemetery on the South Side. Jesse Owens, Ida B. Wells and Harold Washington are buried there, in the largest Confederate burial ground in the North. Granddaddy Goodwin would have preferred to be buried in the Georgia cemetery behind the white church in the country with his siblings and parents, but my grandmother didn't want her remains in the South. Georgia was no longer her home. Chicago was.

3

A DREAM DEFERRED

ON A MARCH MORNING IN 1962, CHICAGO MAYOR RICHARD J. DALEY DEDICATED A
spanking new public housing high-rise development on the South Side.
The Robert Taylor Homes shined—clean buildings, polished elevators.
In a lobby ceremony, Daley presented keys and flowers to tenant James
Weston, a 32-year-old married glass inspector and father of two.

"This project represents the future of a great city," the powerful
mayor intoned. "It represents vision. It represents what all of us feel
America should be—and that is a decent home for every family in every
safe community."[1]

Indeed, the Robert Taylor Homes contrasted with the previous
housing in the Black Belt. Families up from the Great Migration often lived in slummy, overcrowded one-room kitchenettes—cut-up, run-
down, fire-gutted structures.

Taylor replaced those slums and became the world's largest public housing development with 28 buildings and 4,300 units, stretch-
ing nearly two miles. On that winter morning in 1962, the high-rises
symbolized new opportunities for black families yearning for suitable
affordable housing.[2]

Decades later, jackhammers flattened the last Taylor tower to a pile of rubble. Over the years, the high-rises had morphed from housing two-parent working families to housing unemployed single mothers and became a playground for vicious gangs and open-air drug markets. Government and housing officials branded Taylor a national failure, emblematic of mammoth social problems. Unemployment soared, public assistance provided income for the majority of families and the poorly managed buildings decayed.

In time, policy makers engineered a second slum clearance. In 1999, the Chicago Housing Authority (CHA) devised the ambitious and controversial $1.5 billion Plan for Transformation, a blueprint to deconcentrate poverty by rehabbing or developing 25,000 units across the city. The man responsible for the biggest public housing redevelopment program in the country happened to be Chicago mayor Richard M. Daley, the son of Richard J. Daley.

The latter Daley received special permission from Washington, D.C., to tear down the high-rises and construct new mixed-income communities that assembled poor, affordable and higher-end households under a banner of unity on the very footprint of the former projects. In 2008, the mayor stood in front of Parkside of Old Town—a North Side development that replaced Cabrini-Green public housing—flanked by public officials, cameras and residents. "When I said I was going to do this, most people thought that I lost my mind. Someone said 'why are you going to do this—it's the federal government, nothing's going to change. People don't want change there.' But I said to myself when you drove through the city and public housing was on one side of the street, the other housing on the other . . . why is it that we always look to the other side and never look to public housing?" Daley stated.[3]

The Daleys, father and son, have a public housing legacy wrapped in symbolism. One built the high-rises. The other tore them down. Both ceded to political pressures of how and where to house poor black people, and by so doing affected tens of thousands of public housing families. But essentially both men perpetuated the ruthless cycle of segregation. The Plan for Transformation allowed only a small percentage of families to move back to their original communities in those new mixed-income neighborhoods. Thousands of families were relocated with subsidized housing vouchers to live in poor, underresourced black neighborhoods—the antithesis of the plan's expressed goal.

The vertical segregation of the high-rises mutated to horizontal segregation.

* * *

Lobeta Holt was one of the last residents to leave one of the remaining Robert Taylor buildings in 2002.

She moved in at age 18 and left at age 30.

"I loved it. It was like a home to me. People respected me. You could knock on the door and ask for sugar and bread, and it was like a family," Holt, 41, told me wistfully.[4]

Holt had a rough childhood in which she was bounced around homes. She struck out on her own at 14, when she had her first child. As much as she laments about the good ol' days at Taylor, life demanded a lot of negotiation, including convincing drug dealers and gangbangers to leave her sons alone.

In the 12 years since her Taylor building closed and our interview, the mother of seven lived in five apartments on her subsidized housing choice voucher—commonly known as Section 8—around the South Side.

At first CHA denied Holt a voucher under a one-strike rule because of a drug charge against her then-14-year-old son. Authorities dropped the charges, and Holt says CHA tried moving her into two other CHA properties. Holt rejected those choices because one was too far, isolated at the city's southern edge, and the other wouldn't have been safe for teenage boys vulnerable to street gangs. Under pressure and a looming deadline, Holt says she regretfully selected the voucher as her final CHA housing choice.

"I let them [the CHA service provider] really convince me. I am real weak when it comes to talking to somebody," Holt said.

Each apartment in which she used a voucher presented a barrage of problems: failed inspections, red ants biting her children, malfunctioning appliances. One of her more recent homes flooded, and she lost everything.

"Who wants to move every year or two—especially when you don't have the money?" Holt said. She can't remember all the schools her children attended. "They did very poor because they were so used to that school then they have to transfer. They started dropping out."

None of her children finished high school. All but one has a criminal record.

When I visited her at her new apartment in a South Side neighborhood near the closed steel mills, Holt surveyed her sparse current living quarters. "I heard it's a bad area to live in. They shoot. I haven't seen it yet because I'm fresh in the hood. I don't socialize at all. I keep to myself," she told me. Almost a third of the residents in the neighborhood live in poverty. She moved in two weeks earlier with two of her children, ages 7 and 21.

Holt has severe asthma and is disabled. At times she's had to breathe through a tube in her neck connected to an oxygen tank. Holt admits to psychological problems, and in 2001, she was shot at a bus stop when visiting family on the West Side.

"I drink now. I drink too much, and I'm on psych meds. I have depression, anxiety. This ain't how I wanna live. I want a beautiful home. And a job. That's my goal," Holt said. "I wish I could find my dream home. I wish I could find a home where I could stay for years. I want a house with [a] big pretty yard. A home with a washer and dryer.

"I'm way over Section 8," Holt said of the subsidized housing voucher she uses to rent.

* * *

Chicago's public housing developments have inspired pop culture and incensed policy makers. The Near North Side's Cabrini-Green is arguably the best known. The 1970s television sitcom *Good Times* portrayed a black family living there and keeping their heads above water. The acclaimed documentary *Hoop Dreams* followed a high school star basketball player from Cabrini. A serial killer haunted residents in the horror flick *Candyman*. Students from the movie *Cooley High* lived there too. On the West Side, journalist Alex Kotlowitz's 1991 nonfiction *There Are No Children Here* heartbreakingly captured the childhoods of two brothers coming of age in the Henry Horner Homes living in the "other America." (Oprah Winfrey turned it into a TV movie.)

Before the city's public housing stock gained the "notorious" epithet, lofty goals gave hope to struggling families. Decades of mismanagement, bad policies and state-sanctioned segregation, however, made it a case study in how *not* to treat the black urban underclass.

At its inception, the CHA represented a new era of affordable housing to supplant blight. Formed in 1937 under President Franklin Roosevelt's New Deal, CHA provided shelter for war-industry workers during World War II. Subsequently, developments served as transitional postwar housing, and by the 1950s, the agency was the biggest landlord in the city, with more than 40,000 units.

In the backdrop, other dynamics shaped the racial composition of housing around Chicago. As mentioned, some black families exited the Black Belt for some white South Side neighborhoods that opened up after the U.S. Supreme Court struck down racially restrictive housing covenants in 1948. White flight began promptly, and the chance of integrated neighborhoods on the South Side greatly diminished. Public housing ended up as just one casualty of anti-integration forces.

CHA built its initial housing developments—Jane Addams, Julia C. Lathrop and Trumbull Park Homes—in white neighborhoods. Cabrini's first buildings opened in the 1940s, replacing an Italian slum dubbed "Little Hell." The task of integrating CHA developments met stern resistance. Angry white mobs rioted in 1948 when eight black families moved into Fernwood Homes in the South Side Roseland neighborhood.[5] White Southwest Side neighborhoods protested that the mayor had the nerve to suggest that public housing welcome blacks in their community. City Hall killed any proposals to build public housing for black tenants in white wards (and to build any senior public housing, because old blacks might show up). Council members elbowed out the progressive CHA head, Elizabeth Wood, who pressed for racially mixed housing, and fired her in 1954.

A new adversary to progressive housing policy emerged when voters elected Richard J. Daley mayor the following year. He sneered at integration and famously said that Chicago had no ghettos or segregation. Daley made sure the Robert Taylor Homes were built in a black ward.

Robert Taylor himself would have been irate that the infamous high-rises would bear his name. As the first black CHA commissioner, and later chair, he served from 1943 to 1950. Taylor grew up in Tuskegee, Alabama, and earned a banking and finance degree from the University of Illinois–Champaign. He worked for black-owned banks and dedicated his career to securing home loans for blacks. Although his family lived comfortably in the Black Belt, Taylor understood the surrounding inferior housing. After joining the CHA board, he traveled throughout Europe to study public housing and subscribed to the theory that low-rises accompanied by grassy space were the best housing for poor families. Like Wood, he championed integrated housing.

However, Chicago aldermen refused to support racially mixed housing, so Taylor, feeling politically deflated, resigned from CHA's board in 1950. He died of a heart attack in 1957. The Taylor family considered the high-rises a mockery, not a salute, to his legacy.[6] (Taylor's granddaughter is Valerie Jarrett, close friend and adviser to President Barack Obama.)

The honeymoon at the Robert Taylor Homes was short-lived, and families like that of James Weston, who received flowers and keys from Daley at the 1962 grand opening, didn't stay long. Many scholars say the 1969 Brooke Amendment, while good intentioned, crippled public housing and pushed out families like the Westons by mandating that public housing authorities rent to the very poor, thus replacing working-class families. The law required families to pay no more than 25 percent of their income for housing; as a result, 8,000 CHA families received rent reductions in 1970.[7] CHA collected less rent income, impacting operations and property maintenance.

Every decade reflected a shift in family status and income at CHA properties.

- In 1963, 51 percent of residents had two parents in the home. By 1983–1984, that number had fallen to 6 percent.
- In 1972, 54 percent of families received some sort of public assistance. By 1992, just 10 percent of families had employment. At Taylor, the rate was only 4.3 percent.[8]

The underground drug economy flourished in the 1970s as a substitute for the formal economy. Neglected residents watched the red-and-beige Taylor buildings deteriorate. The high-rises built in the mid-twentieth century to replace Black Belt slums had become their own slums.

Decades earlier, Elizabeth Wood had argued against high-rise housing, saying that families wanted low-rises with yards for their children. A good chunk of CHA high-rises were gallery style, meaning their exterior hallways were partially exposed to the outside, dubbed "sidewalks in the sky." The design politics invited piercing criticism about warehousing poor families on top of one another. But high-rises aren't inherently deleterious. Chicago's lakefront bursts with high-rises on the North Side, and pockets of high-rises dot the South Side. The New York City Housing Authority had built high-rises for low-income families that were successful. So why did Chicago's towers evoke anguish and surrender to a bureaucratic mess? Roosevelt University professor D. Bradford Hunt suggests that one of the misguided strategies that tripped up CHA was a seemingly innocuous one: housing too many children.

Hunt says the decision to develop projects with high proportions of apartments with multiple bedrooms to accommodate large families was a fatal error. The high-rises had higher youth–adult ratios than other public housing developments—and than other Chicago neighborhoods, for that matter—leading to social and fiscal disorder. By 1965, Taylor already had 2.86 youths for every 1 adult; in the city as a whole, the number was less than 1 youth to 1 adult. It's not about blaming families for having too many children, Hunt explains. But the number of children living in high-rises hampered the ability of adults to mind the children, resulting in higher crime and vandalism. Pragmatically speaking, too many youths caused elevator breakdowns.[9]

Black children and adults in public housing lived out of the mainstream. Greater Chicago blamed them for their condition: Anonymous poor high-rise dwellers. Trifling black folk mooching off the government. Politicians and policy makers asked themselves: Where do we put poor people? Local and national pressure to solve the problem surged.

By the 1990s, Washington tired of CHA, which often was declared the worst public housing agency in the nation. The U.S. Department of Housing and Urban Development took over CHA in 1995, citing dangerous conditions, dysfunctional management and an aging housing stock that concentrated the very poor in high-rise ghettos. Department of Housing and Urban Development (HUD) secretary Henry Cisneros testified before a House committee that nearly half of CHA's residents were children. "The problems in Chicago have accumulated over decades. Discrimination was part of the problem. Low-income African-American families were segregated in huge projects and deliberately isolated from white neighborhoods," Cisneros said.[10] "The architectural designs of the past, dense high-rises, contributed to the isolation. . . . Of the 15 poorest communities in the nation, 11 are in CHA public housing communities." He vowed to turn CHA around. A year later, CHA apartments failed a national viability test, and the agency lost more than $100 million.

Richard M. Daley waged a political gamble and wrested back control of CHA in 1999. Ethan Michaeli, publisher of the *Residents' Journal*, the award-winning publication produced by CHA residents, succinctly described Daley's political quagmire. "He had half of the people in the city wanting to tear the buildings down because they thought the residents were welfare queens living in high-rise palaces, and other half of the city wanting to tear the buildings down because they felt residents were incarcerated victims oppressed by a cruel government bureaucracy," Michaeli said in a 2012 televised interview.[11]

The solution: Tear down the high- and mid-rises.

Demolition began erasing the city's second skyline in the late 1990s, and the Plan for Transformation began.

THE OVERHAUL

The plan rolled out before it had an official name. A first grader's 1992 death became known as the shot that brought down the projects.[12]

Dantrell Davis held his mother's hand one fall morning as she walked him to Jenner Elementary, a Cabrini-Green neighborhood school. From a vacant tenth-floor Cabrini apartment, a sniper fired at rival gang members but struck seven-year-old Dantrell. The little boy with apple cheeks was the third Cabrini resident from Jenner Elementary shot to death that year.

Outrage exploded internationally. The city's establishment rallied around Dantrell's murder, and conversations about overhauling public housing hit a fever pitch. Then–CHA chief executive Vincent Lane used the bully pulpit to advocate for a mix of poor, working and professional families at CHA properties. Lane had already flirted with promoting economic diversity in some South Side lakefront buildings.

Now, against a backdrop of tragedy, his idea gained traction and financing.

In 1994, the federal government awarded a $50 million HOPE VI grant to facilitate redevelopment of the Cabrini Extension North site, which included Dantrell's building. The Housing Opportunities for People Everywhere program aimed to break up racial and economic segregation in public housing developments around the country. More federal money flowed to Chicago under President Bill Clinton after Daley received approval to expand this strategy of redevelopment, now formally known as the $1.5 billion Plan for Transformation, which officials submitted for HUD approval in 2000.

In CHA's own words: "The guiding principle behind the Plan is the comprehensive integration of low-income families into the larger physical, social and economic fabric of the city."[13]

The crux of the plan involved razing the high-rises for happily-ever-after mixed-income communities where a third of the apartments rented or sold at market rate, a third were affordable for working-class families and a third were public housing. No social science research informed

CHA's mix of housing. Officials argued that higher-income families could be good role models for poor families. CHA also wanted to break the cycle of intergenerational poverty; families shouldn't feel that signing a lease to an apartment guaranteed they'd have it for life. Global powerhouse advertising firm Leo Burnett created a slick pro bono campaign called CHAnge to spread messaging among the public, philanthropists and civic leaders.

Most public housing residents refused to embrace the Plan for Transformation and argued that CHA spurned their input. They skeptically viewed the demolitions as land grabs and unequivocal gentrification designed to push them off of prime land. North Side Cabrini—minutes away from the city's tony Gold Coast and in the shadow of the most affluent Chicago communities—tested the waters of CHA's newfound direction. From 2000 to 2007, nearly $1 billion in residential property had been sold near Cabrini. Grocery stores and other amenities didn't open in the neighborhood until monied white residents moved in. Although CHA buildings publicly had failed national standards, vocal residents accused the agency of purposely letting the high-rises decline so demolition became the only option. For example, in 1991–1992, Taylor had a 21 percent vacancy rate. In 1999, CHA owned 38,000 units and promised to demolish thousands of obsolete units so it could concentrate on rehabbing/redeveloping 25,000 units. That added up to a net loss of 13,000 apartments. The CHA believed there was no other option.[14]

The number of units is important because it determined how many leaseholders at the start of the Plan for Transformation had the "right to return." CHA borrowed refugee-style language to describe lease-compliant residents who dwelled in a unit on October 1, 1999 and were thus eligible to move back into the refurbished homes. These residents were classified as 10/1/99 residents, and there were 16,846 10/1/99 families when the plan began.

Originally, the Plan for Transformation had a 2010 date of completion. That date was extended to 2015. CHA missed that deadline too. Table 3.1 gives a snapshot of where those families are living—or not living—in 2013.

Based on CHA's articulated mission of deconcentrating poverty and incorporating residents into the larger physical landscape of Chicago,

Table 3.1

59% of CHA residents satisfied their right of return by making a final housing selection

    18% live in traditional CHA public housing
    17% live on a Section 8 housing voucher
    9% live in mixed-income housing
    11% are living without a subsidy
    2% were housed then evicted
    2% were housed then died

7% of CHA residents have not made a final housing selection

    1% live in traditional and CHA mixed-income housing
    4% have a Section 8 housing voucher
    1% live without a subsidy

35% CHA residents are no longer eligible to return to CHA housing

    19% have lost their right to return
    9% were evicted/non-lease compliant
    7% are deceased

Source: Author's compilation from data presented in "Relocation Status Report," Chicago Housing Authority, September 30, 2013.

the agency did not live up to its promises. Out of 16,000-plus families, only 1,468 permanently live in mixed-income communities with names like Legends (Taylor replacement), Oakwood Shores (Ida B. Wells replacement) and Park Boulevard (Stateway Gardens replacement).

*   *   *

Geographically, I didn't grow up too far away from the Robert Taylor Homes, but the mental gulf stretched far beyond those miles. I observed the cinder-block wall along the Dan Ryan Expressway, those anonymous ashen towers occupied by people locked out of society. My segregated world never intersected with that hypersegregated island. By the time I enrolled in graduate school at Northwestern University's Medill School of Journalism in 1998, I used the beat of urban affairs in one of my classes to explore public housing within the beginning of the Cabrini

teardowns. When I moved back to Chicago in 2006 to be an urban affairs reporter, I observed the rapid dismantlement of traditional public
housing.

The *Chicago Reporter*, a local investigative magazine on race and
poverty, assigned me a cover story on the history of the Robert Taylor
Homes months before the 2007 demolition of the very last tower. I set
up an interview with one of the last handful of families at the building.
Initially my middle-class assumptions guided me. As I walked toward
the infamous project, the ugly, faded-beige building begged to be torn
down. Graffiti-strewn hallways led to a rickety elevator. I just *knew* the
people longed to exit the dank place and move to greener pastures.

Sixty-five-year-old Barbara Moore (no relation) disabused me of
that perception. She moved to Taylor in 1967 from one of those despi-
cable Black Belt kitchenettes with her two young sons, basking in her
beautiful apartment equipped with new appliances. Moore said as the
years passed, management ignored work orders and the buildings fell
into disrepair while she bounced from one low-wage job to the next.

She fully understood how society viewed her and her neighbors.

"Women have been degraded," she told me. "It seems as if people on
the outside believe all of us are whores, bitches, dropouts, have babies.
Like we smell, don't take baths."[15]

Moore's observations about how society views public housing residents are spot on. Implicit in her statement is that she's seen as nothing
more than a Reagan-era welfare queen gaming the government in her
high-rise ghetto palace. A recurring theme I've witnessed in my reporting of low-income communities is this: People don't like poor people.
They don't deserve public assistance. They don't deserve our sympathy.

Despite the dilapidation of Taylor, Moore clung to the cliché there's
no place like home. The ache of home knows no income or class limita-
tions. I walked into that interview thinking that Taylor residents surely
wanted to leave. I walked out curbing my own biases to appreciate that
the cliché of home is real. I thought about how it would feel if an outsider unsentimentally ordered me and my family out of our home. No
one wants to be told that where they live is fucked up. Home isn't where
the hatred is. For public housing residents, bouts of pain or institutional

neglect may have colored their experience. But so many of them wanted to return home, to their new-and-improved address.

Over the course of the Plan for Transformation, CHA residents fought and sued to stay. Sometimes they achieved victories. Federal judges ruled that a detailed plan for residents had to be in place before CHA demolished buildings at Cabrini and Henry Horner. On the South Side, less litigious Taylor and Stateway Gardens residents moved out more quickly because of an aggressive demolition schedule; therefore, more empty tracts of land dotted the corridor.

Public housing residents have floundered under this massive plan. Those thrust into the private housing market struggled with new bills for heat and electricity, which previously were covered by public housing. Children shuffled from school to school during multiple moves. Between 1999 and 2015, CHA had eight different chief executives. Even CHA admits it underestimated the breadth of executing the now billion-dollar Plan for Transformation. Although leaders may have wanted families to go forth and thrive in a brave new Chicago world, that wasn't easy. The resident population included people with substance abuse problems, spotty work histories and little education. CHA housing is often the housing of last resort for such families.

But some residents have literally been left behind. CHA couldn't keep up with all of the 10/1/99 residents and hired a private firm in 2008 to the tune of $900,000 in a quest to track down residents.[16]

CHA could not have predicted one of the biggest blows to the Plan for Transformation: the housing crash of 2008, which slowed down the pace of private developers building the mixed-income communities. Market-rate housing sales slumped, and private foundations invested in CHA's success offered down payment assistance to jump-start home buying. A number of for-sale units switched to rentals.

Resistance among public housing residents sometimes boiled down to a reluctance to change. Mothers in Taylor had learned how to survive. Families relied on each other. Neighbors built close communities in tough circumstances. A lack of a formal economy produced a thriving underground economy through the bartering of food, services or child care. To this day Facebook groups wax nostalgic on what it was like to live in those fallen buildings. ("Remember Mrs. Walks who ran the laundromat?" "When you on punishment and your friends live one floor up or down on the same side as you and you still get to talk to them hanging out the window!!" "Mrs. Mattie King baking everything . . . her cupcakes were better than hostess lol I loved that lady & so did my mom.") Former residents post family pictures and use the social media site as a bulletin board to find friends. YouTube videos lament Taylor's demise with grainy footage of demolitions. I've heard over and over again people say they wept when the moving vans pulled up. Many people who lived in high-rises didn't consider them an inner-city prison. Life was more than a ghetto.

In one conversation, Alaine Jefferson, 40, told me half a dozen times that she wished CHA would rebuild Stateway Gardens the way it was. "There was a lot of love in Stateway," Jefferson said. "You know how they say it takes a village to raise a child? Stateway was that village."[17]

The young mother raised her three school-age children in Stateway from 1993 to 1999 and shared memories with me. If her daughter got in trouble, Jefferson said neighbors flooded her with phone calls. Jefferson volunteered at the local park district and coached the Stateway girls in jump rope competitions. Her children took gymnastics and hockey and did art projects that turned juice boxes into checker pieces. In the summer, Jefferson helped monitor a free summer breakfast and lunch program for youths. One day every week, neighbors collectively cleaned their gallery-style porches. On hot days, Jefferson and friends sat under the building in the breezeways to cool off.

"My favorite time was just the togetherness of the building," Jefferson said. She attended early Plan for Transformation meetings and said no one ever asked residents what they wanted. When I asked if she wanted to live in Park Boulevard, the mixed-income development that replaced Stateway, Jefferson shook her head no. "It looks terrible. You have a lot of empty space."

To some critics, the Plan for Transformation is sarcastically judged a success if the standard is based on demolition. The State Street corridor is more bare than settled. Miles of vacant land make it look like an urban prairie. In fact, in 2012 CHA said it controlled 400 acres, an area bigger than Chicago's downtown showpiece Grant Park.

SUBSIDIZED HOUSING IN THE PRIVATE MARKET

Most 10/1/99 residents rent in the private market with a Housing Choice Voucher, the program that replaced Section 8. This move dovetails with a national trend of more voucher management by public housing authorities. Underscoring the need for affordable housing in the city is the fact that CHA has a ridiculously long wait list of tens of thousands of people.

Table 3.2 Total CHA Vouchers

1999	25,431
2012	38,002

Source: Chicago Housing Authority response to a Freedom of Information Act Request.

MIT professor Lawrence J. Vale writes in *Purging the Poorest: Public Housing and the Design Politics of Twice-Cleared Communities:* "Of even greater concern, in comparison to others in the CHA system, those who relocated with vouchers between 1999 and 2008 exhibited stagnating employment rates, lower earnings, higher rates of need for Temporary Assistance for Needy Families and food stamps, marking them as more vulnerable than those who remained in conventional public housing or moved to mixed-income communities."[18]

In March 2005, CHA settled a class-action lawsuit in which CHA relocates claimed they had been resegregated in the private market with vouchers in violation of fair housing laws. The agency modified its programs to encourage former CHA residents to move to economically and racially integrated communities. Families received access to social services. The public housing agency implemented a resident service program in 2007 to address the trauma of poverty. The Urban Institute, a Washington, D.C.–based think tank, found that residents who received wraparound services and intensive case management had increased family stability.

CHA likes to boast that vouchered-out public housing residents are not the majority in any of Chicago's 77 community areas. Of course not. That would be impossible in a city of almost 3 million. But numbers reveal that the largest cluster of voucher holders live in segregated black neighborhoods. Those neighborhoods have a good number of residents living below the poverty level and have 1,000 or more voucher holders living within their borders.[19] Meanwhile, the whitest, and some of the most affluent, neighborhoods in the city have the fewest number of voucher holders.

Kimberley McAfee, 42, is satisfied with her Woodlawn duplex, for which she currently uses a voucher. A Chicago Public Schools lunchroom attendant and mother of five, McAfee grew up in Stateway Gardens and got her own apartment when she turned 18. In 2001, at the beginning of the Plan for Transformation, she reluctantly left. Over the years, she's had a long journey with multiple moves.

The first was to South Shore, a black lakefront neighborhood where pockets of affluence abut poor, multi-unit apartment buildings. South Shore is home to the largest number of voucher holders in Chicago.

"We was trapped in four different kinds of gangs," McAfee recalled. "[The apartment] balcony was kind of weak and the kids couldn't play on it. They were playing out front and we heard gunshots. Two of my daughters hid under a car." The girls were 10 and 11 years old. Fortunately, no one was hurt during the daytime shooting.[20]

After a year, the family moved to Englewood. "That block was kind of decent," McAfee told me. "No, let me take that back." She recalled that a group of young boys shot at her neighbor. No one was hurt. She lived there for two years. "The reason I moved from there was the apartment was in foreclosure in 2003. The landlord had told us we had to move because he couldn't take care of the building."

Move number three led the family to a house in Roseland on the South Side.

"It was all right," McAfee said. "My girls kept getting into it with the grown people on the block because the boyfriends of grown people were trying to holler at my daughters who were in high school." They lived there two years. The bathroom ceiling caved in, and the house went into foreclosure.

Then the family moved back to Englewood, which didn't work out either.

"They just stayed in shoot-outs over there. Some boy got shot with an Uzi in front of our house. I didn't know him. My kids were there." After two years, the family left and moved to the Woodlawn duplex in 2010.

Unsurprisingly, McAfee loved Stateway. I asked her about the difference between the violence there and the violence she'd experienced in the voucher world.

"I was more protected in the projects than anywhere else out here," she explained. "When they [the Gangster Disciples gang] were at war, they let everyone know so all your kids would be in the house. I always felt safe in Stateway."

McAfee brushed off violence as if it were lint on her pants. In a cruel twist, she got shot in the leg in 2007 while attending a Robert Taylor Homes reunion on State Street, in an empty field a mile south from the former development. "I was an innocent bystander," she said. The bullet is still lodged in her buttocks, and there's a rod in her leg. During that shooting, a boy was killed.

When the Plan for Transformation was in draft form, resident activists from the Coalition to Protect Public Housing predicted voucher mayhem. "The coalition also thought that the plan's reliance on having public housing residents take Section 8 vouchers to find housing in the private rental market was unrealistic. The criticism was based on the regional rental market study's documentation of the tight rental market. Consequently, many relocated CHA families were using the vouchers to move to areas that were as segregated as the CHA communities they were leaving," writes Patricia A. Wright in a chapter in *Where Are Poor People to Live? Transforming Public Housing Communities.*[21]

CHA is not solely responsible for families' individual housing choices. Families with vouchers seek welcoming areas or ones near their social/familial/job networks. Landlords discriminate against voucher holders. HUD says it wants families to live in better neighborhoods, but what the federal government is willing to pay is, by and large, insufficient for market rental rates in low-poverty areas. Finding a two-bedroom apartment for $800 in, say, the North Side's yuppie Lincoln Park area is virtually impossible. CHA did experiment with "super vouchers," putting people in apartments where rents can start at $2,300, but political pressure quashed that policy.

Meanwhile, several other black South Side neighborhoods have absorbed more than 1,000 voucher holders each. These are not poor communities, but 20 percent or more of the population lives in poverty. Homeowners make up Chatham, Greater Grand Crossing and Auburn Gresham, but the proximity of these areas to lower-income black neighborhoods renders them vulnerable to outside forces, such as crime. These black middle-class and working-class areas thrive with strong block clubs and efficacy, but they also teeter and could use more city and private resources. Certainly, the dispersal of public housing families rocked these communities, and the timing of the Plan for Transformation inflamed instability. Every single community that received a large number of voucher holders declined in tangible ways between the 2000 and 2010 census. Median household incomes and home sales plummeted. Poverty markedly increased. Whenever spikes in crime occur on the South Side, mutters about the "project people" can be heard. There's a nugget of truth in those complaints.

The drug trade has relocated, and the criminal spillover has distressed Chatham and Auburn Gresham. Open-air drug markets prospered at public housing developments, but it's important to note that drug dealers weren't necessarily CHA residents. Dealers plied their trade in a vibrant criminal setting at neglected high-rises. If an open-air drug market collapses because of closed buildings, displaced dealers relocate in new areas, and turf wars break out. Freelance drug crews seek corners to continue their illegal enterprises. A police commander in Auburn Gresham told me in 2009 that half of the drug dealer offenders arrested in his district had arrest histories around public housing.[22]

CHA persistently and rightfully defends the majority of its residents as law-abiding citizens. To shed light on the impact of relocations on neighborhood crime, the Urban Institute released a study in 2012. Researchers found that crime was worse from 2000 to 2008 in neighborhoods where former CHA residents used vouchers. Violent crime was 21 percent higher in neighborhoods with high concentrations of voucher holders than in neighborhoods with no relocated households. Violent crime dropped about 26 percent across the city during this same time period. According to the Urban Institute, areas inhabited by voucher holders experienced less of a decrease of crime than occurred in areas without clusters of voucher holders.[23]

Relocation might affect crime for three reasons: a disruption in social networks, which puts residents at risk of committing crimes or becoming victims; new residents disrupting the communities' sense of mutual trust and social cohesion; or residents and their associates engaging in criminal or drug activity when they lived in public housing and bringing similar activity when they relocated.

However, stereotypes allow voucher holders to be scapegoated and stigmatized. Just about anything that goes wrong in black Chicago neighborhoods gets blamed on "those people from the projects tearing up our neighborhoods." Intracultural conflict is real but can be less about violent crime and more about quality of life. Former high-rise residents occupied public space at their developments because there was no backyard to fire up a grill, no back porch to set out lawn chairs, no patio for entertaining. When voucher holders move to a neat block with bungalows and two-flat apartment buildings, putting a weight bench on front lawns, selling potato chips on corners, playing cards on the street or barbecuing on the sidewalk fails to endear them to neighbors.

"They had to get educated to us and we had to get educated to them," Keith Tate, president of the Chatham Avalon Park Community Council, told me. Tate said that, over the years, Section 8 administrators from CHA have come to community meetings at the request of homeowners. "Initially, we said we will embrace people coming from Section 8 but we need them to understand we have a community with standards and values."[24]

When problems surfaced on blocks, homeowners checked to see if problem renters had vouchers.

"Unfortunately, [CHA] would saturate a particular block by bringing in a number of voucher individuals, and they all knew each other. One block we had seven houses that were all identified [as being rented to voucher holders] and they all destroyed the block. We got all of them moved. That connectivity gave them control of the block. When you have that kind of scenario, it becomes chaotic," Tate explained.

In response to the chaos, neighbors formed phone trees to let an absentee Section 8 landlord know of trouble brewing. One home housed four mothers with 12 children among them. "It was off the chain," Tate said. "Every weekend a party. Kids were everywhere. We had to bring it to the owner of the house, and he was like it couldn't be a problem. Every time there was a problem, we called. We didn't care if it was one, two, three a.m." Eventually the landlord tired of the barrage of calls from multiple neighbors and got new tenants.

At a monthly Chatham community meeting in 2015, a CHA representative answered questions from residents and ended up busting assumptions. He told the homeowners that if they suspected a troubled property was Section 8, they should call CHA. In his experience, 70 percent of complaints do not pertain to Section 8 properties. Within the communities, however, bad behavior, criminality, prostitution, barbecuing on front lawns and pit bulls fighting are what people associate with Section 8.

The Urban Institute's Sue Popkin has studied CHA for more than two decades. She says that, for the most part, people are living in better housing in safer neighborhoods. But she notes that relocation has been extremely hard on children and CHA hasn't given them enough support. Youths struggle academically and exhibit the effects of growing up around violence. "I worry a lot about the kids," Popkin once told me. "The services that helped the adults do better don't seem to have helped the kids. It's an urgent issue. These are kids who have grown up in families who've lived in chronic disadvantage for generations, and it's going to take more than just moving to slightly safer places to help them on a better trajectory."[25] Other research shows that public housing residents say their stress level is down since moving into mixed-income neighborhoods.[26] Larger structural issues in Chicago around employment, discrimination and access to opportunity must be addressed in tandem with putting families on a path to self-sufficiency.

The lives of many CHA residents did improve. Although Alaine Jefferson missed her tight-knit Stateway community terribly, she was climbing the economic mobility ladder. When I interviewed Jefferson, she was a Chicago Public Schools part-time bus aide while she worked on a master's degree in accounting at Robert Morris University. In 2013, she earned a degree in human services from the University of Phoenix. Jefferson told me that Stateway was a stepping-stone. "I didn't have direction. I was all over the place. I didn't know what I wanted to do [at] that time. I knew I wanted to graduate from college and get a good job. I gained a lot of experience in Stateway with the park district," she said. "If I hadn't gone through Stateway, I wouldn't be as strong as I am today. I've been encouraged and been blessed."[27]

At the time of our interview, Jefferson used a voucher to live in a rehabbed apartment in Washington Park on the South Side and was taking advantage of CHA self-sufficiency programs, where she was learning financial literacy and job-interviewing skills. Next, Jefferson wanted to go through the home ownership program at CHA.

"I don't want to pay rent; I want to pay a mortgage. I'm building up money to be financially stable. I couldn't pay for a furnace if it went out. That's my reason for staying in the voucher program at this time." Jefferson's goal was to move to the western suburbs, where there are an abundance of jobs and more resources, opportunities and amenities.

Those who live in mixed-income apartments experience less crime and less stress in prettier surroundings. But just 9 percent of 10/1/99 families are afforded that opportunity. To qualify, residents go through a rigorous background check, counseling, rules orientation, social services assessment and training before they move in. Not everyone qualifies to get to or makes it beyond that point. Housing counselors bark like drill sergeants when they lecture on social behavior, such as how often to dust and do chores.

Race and class flare-ups pose complications at these properties. Condo owners have blamed building wrongdoings on CHA residents only to find out a fellow owner put the trash in the wrong place. All mixed-income renters—CHA, affordable and market rate—are required to take yearly drug tests.

Cultural clashes run the gamut.

Cabrini public housing residents have told stories about holding a postfuneral repast (reception) in an apartment. White homeowners who now live on the former Cabrini footprint called the police, not knowing this is a common black ritual. One public housing renter received an eviction notice when an annual inspection turned up a cluttered closet. Lawyers intervened and the woman got to stay.

Westhaven Park Tower is a building with mostly white condo owners and black CHA renters on the footprint of the former Henry Horner Homes. Owners wanted CHA to provide 24-hour security to prevent their public housing neighbors from having unwanted guests. They complained about late-night noise and that thorny issue of loitering in the lobby, going so far as to remove standard apartment building lobby furniture, which later was put back.

In demonizing the so-called undeserving poor, mixed-income homeowners forget that they too benefit from subsidized housing. The new communities are built on federal land, which CHA received for free and allowed developers to construct properties and sell units more cheaply than if they had to purchase the land. One Westhaven resident said he expected "everybody to live in the building like I live in the building."[28]

These incidents touching on the cultural polarity in mixed-income developments are simply how people live. Upper-middle-class condo owners enjoy socializing in their units. Public housing residents see benefit in communal living that's more indicative of true city dwelling. One person's loitering is another's hanging out.

* * *

Accusations of purposeful segregation are nothing new to CHA.

In 1966, black residents accused CHA of violating their rights by building public housing exclusively in black neighborhoods and creating racial quotas to limit the number of black families in white public housing when there were white developments. In 1969, in the landmark *Gautreaux v. Chicago Housing Authority* case, a federal judge found that CHA had deliberately engaged in discriminatory housing practices.[29] One of the many outcomes was that new public housing was to be located in nonblack neighborhoods. It was a very slow process to build, for example, three units (hence, scattered-site housing) in white census tracts. The other major initiative was to use the Section 8 program to place 7,100 families in predominantly white suburbs. The results were mostly positive for the families.

Today it is impossible to desegregate family CHA public housing because the overwhelming number of CHA residents and applicants are black. The federal court can't order minority families to white public housing sites because there are none. Due to high costs and political opposition, CHA no longer builds scattered-site housing, though it could be a solution. Faced with those problems, CHA relied on vouchers and the mixed-income model when the Plan for Transformation began.

I don't regret that the city knocked down the public housing highrises. Nor am I unsympathetic to the fervent pull of home residents continue to feel. Love, family and community flourished at public housing dwellings despite the realities of crime, disorder and disinvestment.

But the disappearance of those structures from the city's skyline has also erased the visibility of public housing families in Chicago, and the Plan for Transformation's public policy has benefited and also failed thousands of families.

CHA's Plan for Transformation is woefully behind schedule due to broken promises, a housing collapse and bureaucratic paralysis. CHA has been operating outside the sphere of real political accountability to speed things along or rethink how to house residents. The use of subsidized housing vouchers in the segregated private market has failed the expressed plan of breaking of concentrated poverty.

When I learned about a small program dubbed "super vouchers," I thought CHA had figured out a way to reverse the Section 8 paradigm of putting families in neighborhoods with high segregation and poverty. The mobility program allowed families to live in areas with fewer than 20 percent in poverty and low subsidized housing saturation.

CHA spends extra federal money to make up the difference in higher rents in those areas. Only 10 percent of the voucher holders were in this program.

In 2014, I interviewed a black working woman who lived downtown on a super voucher, which allowed her to receive up to 300 percent of fair market rent. She wanted better schools for her two children. Finding an apartment wasn't easy; at first she faced discrimination from landlords who didn't want to take her voucher. She filed a complaint against the city.

As word spread about super vouchers, criticism heated. Landlords hated the federal program. The public didn't understand why even just a few low-income people got the chance to live in some of the most exclusive buildings in the city at taxpayer expense. Then Aaron Schock, a white Republican congressman from a small Illinois town who later resigned from his seat as a result of other controversies, stepped in with outrage. And *poof*, CHA altered the program to exclude luxury high-rises, a change that was perfectly legal. CHA changed the policy from 300 percent to 150 percent of fair market rent; 260 families were affected, a mere fraction of the tens of thousands of people on vouchers.

I was stunned by CHA's swift policy change. This was one of the rare times when a politician exerted pressure on CHA, and officials jumped like circus animals. Although this congressman had no ties to Chicago or CHA, the agency acquiesced anyway.

Clearly, race and stereotypes about voucher holders informed the public outcry. Most of the people in the opportunity areas didn't live in a building with a doorman. Yet the public didn't think the few families that had been moved to such buildings belonged in any luxury high-rise in Chicago. They didn't deserve a "high-rise palace" that didn't mirror something like the Robert Taylor Homes. They didn't belong in a place that wasn't a segregated black ghetto.

This incident recalls Barbara Moore, one of the last Taylor residents, and her observations about poor black women being degraded for living in public housing. A simplistic notion often guides us: Society doesn't like poor people.

4

NOTES FROM A BLACK GENTRIFIER

MY LONGTIME FRIEND ERIN CONCOCTED A SIGNATURE DRINK FOR MY HOUSE-
warming—the Prairie-tini, a play on my new address, Prairie Avenue.
Pear vodka supplied the martini portion of the wordplay.

In May 2008, I'd officially joined the ranks of homeowners with a
1,100-square-foot three-bedroom, two-bathroom condo in the up-and-
coming South Side neighborhood of Bronzeville. A few months later,
friends and family joined me in celebration of dark hardwood floors and
a stainless steel kitchen. Pans of jerk chicken fed guests in one of the
bedrooms I had permanently converted into a dining room. The second bedroom, my office filled with books, served as a secondary lounge
space. Folks enjoyed the breeze on the back deck, speaking louder every
time the Green Line "L" train zipped by behind the building. We par-
tied until about 3 a.m.

I felt proud and accomplished at age 32, a single woman who did
this on her own with savings and financial austerity. Occasionally I sat
in my living room simply to absorb the space that I bought and created,

from Tiffany blue–painted walls in the master bedroom to artwork hung in the long sage-colored hallway. I had achieved the American Dream. Or so I thought at the time.

On the hot September night of my housewarming, I didn't feel or quite know the extent of the financial crisis and economic recession soon to mire the nation. Even before the housing crash hit me personally, I had to reconcile what it meant to be black and to buy in a black Chicago neighborhood.

* * *

I am a so-called gentrifier.

My building was bought and rehabbed by a developer and turned into a condo structure.

"Gentrifier" is a complicated label for a black person, and I say it tongue in cheek because black Chicago neighborhoods don't gentrify. The definition of gentrification is rooted in class and the displacement of poor people. What does that look like in a black-on-black context? How is the notion of gentrification complicated by the fact that services don't come to communities when black folk with money take up residence?

Five years after I signed on the dotted line, I, like many others, re-financed. I had never wanted to know the value of my property as long as I still lived in the condo. I figured it was best to avoid that headache and cross my fingers. But alas, the appraisal came back as part of the refi process. In 2008, I paid $172,000, parking space included. In 2013, the place rang in at $55,000—a figure I had never ever imagined, even in my worst-case-scenario reverie. After I picked myself up off of the floor from the news, I had to listen to local and national reports about the comeback of the housing and condo market. All I could do was sulk and hope.

Hood fatigue is real. The trash, the drugs, the prostituted women. The vacancies, the broken glass, the poverty. Originally, women owned all of the condo units in our three-story redbrick walk-up. We mockingly referred to ourselves as "the Women of Brewster Place," living our dream deferred while battling an underhanded developer and unscrupulous drug dealers on the block.

I bought in Bronzeville because it was supposed to be the Next Big Thing. One of Chicago's grandest boulevards runs straight through the neighborhood. Maple trees and comely greystones line Dr. Martin Luther King Jr. Drive. Bronzeville is close to downtown, Lake Michigan, an expressway and ample public transportation. It is sandwiched between two vibrant neighborhoods—the South Loop and Hyde Park, home to the University of Chicago. But weedy lots mar Bronzeville, and miles of vacant tracts plead for economic development. As early as the mid-1980s, black middle-class professionals repurposed the neighborhood with hammers to begin a journey of housing rehabs. By the 1990s, the neighborhood known as the low end was rechristened Bronzeville, a throwback to a bygone era of black segregation in which yarns were spun about black uplift. In the 2000s, the city bulldozed the concrete wall of public housing high-rises in the neighborhood. Momentum continued with shady developers buying and gutting wherever they could. This spangled new neighborhood seemed ripe for all of the accoutrements any gentrifier's heart would desire. Organizers predicted that by 2010, the new Bronzeville would be up and running.

But, alas, not enough emerged besides a glut of condos and disappointed homeowners. Some signs of retail hope emerged: A press conference for a Starbucks grand opening in 2007. Another indie coffee shop. A couple of places to eat a sandwich without Plexiglas separating customer and employee. Black-owned galleries. No grocery store until a 2015 groundbreaking. The big, flashy development under way in 2013 was Walmart, hardly the splash more residents envisioned.

I represented the wave of young black professionals moving in during the 2000s, buying in to a historical legacy (my condo is blocks away from Ida B. Wells's former residence) and the chance to usher in an urban resurgence. The opportunity came with a lot more square footage and granite countertop space for the money than I could have afforded in the North Side neighborhoods. New neighbors held their breath for the wine shops, artisan olive oil markets and white-tablecloth restaurants. Old-timers, though, knew the drill.

Bronzeville seemed destined to forever be on the cusp. "Potential" is the word everyone uses to describe the neighborhood. Eventually, though, the patina wore off for many. Even before the economic downturn, the housing crisis and the failed 2016 Olympic bid that promised Chicago an economic shot, Bronzeville lagged when money flowed.

Some whites moved into the area, but most of the new residents are black, and the neighborhood name Bronzeville celebrates that identity. Bronzeville is overwhelmingly black. In 2010, the white population hovered around 2,600; the black population neared 40,000.

Uneven development is a hallmark of Chicago and is most acute in black neighborhoods. Failed political leadership, back-burner city status, racial perceptions and the capricious ways of capitalism have left Bronzeville as empty as some of the greystones along King Drive.

* * *

Bronzeville is a social construction.

Though it's a real place, it borrows heavily on a once-upon-a-time era.

You won't find Bronzeville on the City of Chicago 77 official neighborhood map. It's a state of mind, racial identity wrapped in racial utopia harkening back to the beginning of the last century. Douglas (named after U.S. senator Stephen A. Douglas) and Grand Boulevard (the stately street first known as South Park Way and then King Drive) are the original neighborhoods. Today Oakland and North Kenwood sometimes are lumped in Bronzeville, whose borders are the Dan Ryan Expressway to the west and Lake Michigan bordering the east, 26th Street to the north and 51st Street to the south.

But the story of the communities that make up Bronzeville goes back to the late nineteenth century. White millionaires lived in Italianate, Tudor, Queen Anne and Romanesque mansions in the Douglas neighborhood. In 1890, 10,000 blacks lived there and on Grand Boulevard. Then came the Great Migration after World War I, when southern blacks journeyed to Chicago to escape the brutality of the cotton fields. Between 1916 and 1920, more than 50,000 blacks came to Chicago. By

1925, the area that contained blacks was known as the Black Metropolis, and it was the second-largest African American community after Harlem in New York.[1]

In 1930, James "Jimmy" Gentry, a theater editor for the black *Chicago Bee* newspaper run by cosmetics king Anthony Overton, proposed an idea to his boss. He suggested that they use the word "Bronzeville" to describe the community since that depicted the skin tone of most denizens. Overton, also black, agreed, and the newspaper sponsored an unsuccessful Mayor of Bronzeville contest. Gentry took his idea to the *Chicago Defender,* and it became a promotional tool for the influential newspaper.[2]

During Bronzeville's heyday, black voters elected Oscar De Priest, the first black congressman since Reconstruction. Archibald Motley portrayed vibrant urban life in his paintings. Vivian Harsh, the first black librarian in the Chicago Public Library system, hosted salons attended by the likes of Richard Wright and Margaret Walker. The South Side Community Arts Center is the oldest such African American center in the United States. Johnson Publishing Company founder John H. Johnson attended Wendell Phillips High School in Bronzeville with Nat King Cole and Redd Foxx. Gwendolyn Brooks wrote "A Street in Bronzeville" in 1945. Joe Louis, Louis Armstrong and Dr. Daniel Hale Williams, the first person to conduct successful open-heart surgery, each spent time in Bronzeville. Sam Cooke grew up in Bronzeville. Duke Ellington and Count Basie performed there. Famed architect Louis Sullivan designed what would become Pilgrim Baptist Church, originally a Jewish synagogue. Black History Month was born at the Wabash YMCA.

Luminaries aside, Bronzeville suffered from overcrowded housing conditions due to state-sanctioned segregation. When the Supreme Court ruled against racially restrictive housing covenants in 1948, black families packed their bags for opened-up neighborhoods, which, in turn, ignited white flight. Meanwhile, the 1950s ushered in urban renewal, aka Negro removal. This included the construction of the Dan Ryan Expressway, which destroyed neighborhoods. The Lake Meadows highrises were apartments built to attract young middle-class whites, but middle-class blacks flocked to them instead. White city council members fought against public housing being constructed in their wards, so high-rise public housing was erected in the Black Belt. In the 1970s and 1980s, unemployment hit 90 percent. Bronzeville had morphed into the "low end."

With nowhere to go but up, middle-class blacks paved the way for a nascent resurgence. The bubbling began in the mid-1980s in an area called the Gap, part of the Douglas neighborhood. Buppies bought cheap nineteenth-century mansions on deserted blocks. Slowly, more families trickled in with hopes of restoring the luster of those grand homes. They kept coming in the next decade.

Leana Flowers, 63, made a boomerang return to the neighborhood. Until age seven, she lived on 45th and Forrestville and recalls a vibrant shopping area, a fancy Chinese restaurant for a family night out and pennies along with apples plopping into her trick-or-treat bags on Halloween. Her parents moved to Chatham after the restrictive covenants were lifted. In 1996, Flowers bought a 7,700-square-foot home on King Drive, gutted it and lived her dream of watching the black Bud Billiken Parade from her porch. The black back-to-school parade, sponsored by the *Chicago Defender*, supposedly is the second largest in the nation. And it is peak blackness since 1929. Bass thumps on the floats sponsored by local urban radio stations and corporations. High school band and dance teams juke in the streets. The climax is the South Shore Drill Team twirling flags in sync. Every politician seeking reelection rides in the parade. President Harry Truman once participated. Ethiopian emperor Haile Selassie did too. Barack Obama, Oprah Winfrey, Muhammad Ali and Spike Lee are among notables who have joined in on the second-Saturday-in-August fun. Spectators participate too, with neighbors selling everything from sunflower seeds to barbecue from their lawns. "I was drawn here because my father had a dancing school at Parkway Ballroom and two of his sisters, his older brother—they all owned homes in the 1950s," Flowers told me.[3] She's been active in Bronzeville community groups since she returned, trying to achieve the promise of the area. "It's very difficult and very hard not to get discouraged. I'm in a discouraged mood right now. This sort of gets to race. I don't know how to recruit development, retail to this corridor. It just seems it is so much to overcome."

THE BATTLE FOR RETAIL

Under the "L" train station on 47th Street, there's usually some tomfoolery going on. You can buy loose cigarettes from hustlers with a side of catcalling. Corner boys stand in their white T-shirt uniforms. Functional drug users pace up and down the blocks. Strewn litter flecks the sidewalks.

Forty-Seventh Street is the commercial heartbeat of Bronzeville. It was also the heart in the area's so-called halcyon days. It was once said that if you stood long enough on the corner of 47th and South Park, you'd run into whoever you were looking for.

Today the thoroughfare is often the source of middle-class angst. Although the newcomers expected more appealing retail to their tastes, what's there instead are hallmarks of black inner-city retail: beauty supply stores and takeout food joints with rolling shutters.

Abundance Bakery smells like thick frosting. The sweetness of vanilla and nutmeg fill the air of the small storefront where every dessert is made from scratch. At midnight workers arrive and bake until sunrise.

Mornings are the busiest time at Abundance. Customers gush over glazed doughnuts. The glass case displays pineapple upside-down cake slices, sweet potato squares, chunks of caramel cake, brownies and bread pudding. Abundance isn't a handsome space on east 47th Street. Empty white cake boxes fill a cracked window display. Owner Bill Ball sits in the kitchen—where signs instruct employees not to overmix the raisins in oatmeal cookies—until the door jingles to signal a patron.

Ball, 64, shuffled through the bakery wearing a black White Sox cap and a white apron on the day I visited to interview him. In 1990, Ball, armed with his mother's recipes, opened the bakery as a black man's escape from Corporate America.

"Business is okay. Things were better when the projects were here," Ball told me.[4] "Our monthly gross had declined since the time of public housing—between 15 and 20 percent."

Ball said his bakery flourished when public housing residents lived nearby. Poor people kept Abundance afloat. Never mind the retail truism that says higher-income households are needed to sustain a business. A bakery that rings up $2 for a coffee and doughnut isn't as inaccessible as Crate & Barrel would be in a low-income community. A slice of caramel cake isn't a cost along the lines of an overpriced yuppie cupcake shop.

Once upon a time, the world's largest public housing development was just a few blocks away from Abundance. The Robert Taylor Homes housed tens of thousands of families in 28 high-rises until the last tower came down in 2006. Across the street from the bakery is an empty, ghastly building unaffectionately nicknamed "the Carter," a pop culture nod to the apartments that drug kingpin Nino Brown bum-rushed in the movie *New Jack City*. Taking up an entire city block, the Rosenwald Court Apartments once housed hundreds of families.

All of those families eventually dispersed by 2000. In 1990, the Bronzeville area population—the Grand Boulevard and Douglas neighborhoods—was 66,000. By 2010, the population had dropped to 40,000.[5] Black professionals moved in, but the new residents didn't make up for the loss in Ball's customer base. The income of Bronzeville's new residents is not enough to call the entire neighborhood affluent. It truly is a mixed-income community where households earning more than $75,000 have grown exponentially despite the median income being lower than the city's $46,877. But the median housing prices before the housing bust were higher than the city median (in the $200,000 range) and higher than in many neighborhoods with even higher median incomes. In 2005, for example, the median home sale in Grand Boulevard was $281,737; $395,000 in Oakland in 2003; and $227,481 in Douglas in 2003, according to the Chicago Rehab Network.

"Forty-Seventh Street still has that stigma of being the ghetto. A lot of the buppies as soon as they come on 47th Street they want to get off 47th Street. It's still somewhat of a crime element around here. People get shot on 47th Street. I can't tell you how many times we've seen yellow ribbon stretched across the street over the past 20 years," Ball told me.

In his first decade of operation, when crime was higher, Ball fought off two thieves. "I'm sort of crazy," he said without a grin. The first time he was robbed, the bandit got caught and went to jail. The second time, Ball realized the gunman's weapon was unloaded, so he seized the gun. That fellow went to jail too.

Still, Ball always felt 47th Street was the perfect location for Abundance. He knew the demographics would eventually change. The neighborhood was too close to downtown, too close to the lake, to hold off gentrification for long. "It's slowly changing. It ain't gonna change fast," he said. Ball isn't antsy like nearby condo and homeowners gasping under the weight of sinking home values.

Ball's pretty matter-of-fact when explaining why things haven't changed more quickly: "The reluctance of the Europeans to move this way," he explained. He paused before adding an asterisk. "I'm not gonna say white folk. I'm gonna say people of economic means."

The Bronzeville Retail Initiative works to bring in more businesses while making the corridor more aesthetically appealing. Although many amenities are lacking, 47th Street does have much more beyond the surface such as the bakery and a number of clothing stores. It's hard to escape the retail tension between what is currently there and what people want. Certainly, there's a dearth of diverse retail, but that's also subjective.

In 2013, I classified the businesses between State Street and Lake Park, a 1.7-mile stretch, to really understand a portion of Bronzeville's commerce (see Table 4.1).

As long as I have lived in the area and driven back and forth on 47th Street, the number of clothing stores surprised me. These aren't cheap knockoff boutiques. They're known as hip-hop clothing stores, and some sell expensive brands like True Religion jeans.

There are plenty of one-offs: livery, nail shop, pawn shop, day care, shoe shine, graphic design, Harold's Chicken Shack, party store, bakery, a hardware store.

"We have to shift the way we think about supporting businesses. We've got a lot of businesspeople, but navigating the corridor isn't a pleasant experience. That's a big part of what we've got to do. We've

Table 4.1   Businesses on 47th Street (Bronzeville)

Services	*Retail*
3 cell phone stores	21 clothing stores
3 banks	
3 real estate/appraisals	
4 tax services	*Hair and Beauty*
3 clinics	10 barbershops/salons
	2 African braiding shops
	6 beauty supply stores
Food and Drink	
11 fast-food eateries	*Unused Space*
3 liquor stores	
2 corner stores	31 abandoned buildings
4 sit-down restaurants	14 vacant lots
(not all had servers)	

got to clean it up, make it attractive," Leana Flowers, who is part of the Bronzeville Retail Initiative, told me. She said residents also complain about the nonblack business owners who don't seem to be responsive to the community. Dollar stores hang their mattresses on building exteriors as displays, and would-be patrons are concerned with their safety.

Yet there are some business owners catering to a new Bronzeville clientele and bringing community comforts.

On a chilly October evening in 2012, visitors packed Blanc Gallery on King Drive for the opening night of the exhibition "Dreams in Jay-Z Minor." An outdoor patio, outfitted with heating lamps and hot chocolate stations, accommodated an overflow. The two artists featured in the exhibition didn't create an homage to Young Hova but a rumination on hip-hop culture and the fantastical nature of excess from a decidedly female perspective. The following summer, Blanc hosted free multiracial comedy shows—stand-up ranging from dry British humor to black male angst. The liveliness of Bronzeville was evident in the energy and laughter at those two events.

Cliff Rome coruns/owns Blanc, the Parkway Ballroom and H-Dog, a gourmet sausage restaurant all within walking distance of one another. Chef Rome has been working in and improving the neighborhood since the late 1990s. The historic Parkway often hosts black political fund-raisers and parties, but Rome said he has a tough time attracting the black middle class into H-Dog. Bus drivers, garbage collectors and other blue-collar workers get lamb sausage, Pellegrino and Chicago-style hot dogs to go. Rome said the educated folk sometimes look down on the area.

"Those of us in the community say they want to support the businesses but don't because it doesn't have all the lush or plush options as downtown, they're disappointing to me," Rome told me. "Black people are scared of black people for so many different reasons. If you move into a neighborhood that already has everything, what are you contributing? Your money. If you go into a community with no amenities that you like or creature comforts and you don't support it with your money, it'll never happen."[6]

My philosophy has been that if we don't support existing businesses, will new ones come? I've gotten my nails done, ordered from Harold's Chicken, bought from Abundance. There are other notable retail corridors in Bronzeville. Illinois Service Federal, a longtime black-owned savings and loan, is on the same block as Jokes & Notes, the comedy club that opened in 2006. A chicken-and-waffles restaurant is a draw on King Drive. But residents need to rethink retail and not just focus on what's lacking. And the newbies should give some of these retailers a chance, not just sigh in exasperation. It's easy to get frustrated when there's no decent grocery store. For me, it's not about pushing out the gym shoe stores or weave shops. A variety of businesses can thrive, not just coexist. My favorite example is Steve, the Greek owner of 200 Cut Rate Liquor on 47th Street. He's found a way to appease the various populations by keeping olive oil and Frappuccinos on the shelves. He also sells enough brands of moscato for cloying palates; across the aisle he stocks South African wines. From Carlos Rossi to Sophia Coppola, 200 Cut Rate carries wine for all.

The question frequently asked is: When will Bronzeville turn? That question continues to induce headaches for residents, some of whom are 25 years into the revitalization game. Resident and activist Dhyia Thompson wrote an essay in a Bronzeville newspaper about why the

community has produced little economic revitalization. She recounted a
health club salesman telling her his business wouldn't invest south of the
Loop because there isn't a market. Thompson wrote:

> His answer is not surprising and is the usual excuse given for the dis-
> play of anti-investment from corporations. Young working Blacks
> aren't moving to this community for boutique coffee shops or high
> end grocery stores; hell, they don't exist. We aren't seduced by super-
> ficial housing development billboards that display images of "happy"
> Asians, Whites, and Blacks. People stay, move into and/or open busi-
> nesses in Bronzeville, because of its potential; the vision of a successful
> community.[7]

Chalking up Bronzeville's lack of redevelopment to race matters may
come off as simplistic, but research proves otherwise.

A 2012 study by a Montana State University professor compared
Bronzeville to Pilsen, a South Side Mexican and Mexican American
neighborhood. While Pilsen has benefited from development and suffered displacement of lower-income residents, the *Urban Affairs Review*
paper noted that Bronzeville struggles to redevelop because of stereo-
typical conceptions of blackness. Pilsen is treated as a more viable site
of ethnic consumption in the form of tasty tacos and margaritas. The
subtle variations of the two racial conceptions open up a different set of
redevelopment possibilities, according to the paper's authors.[8]

Basically, the residents of Bronzeville are handcuffed to stigmatiza-
tion because redevelopment hinges on overcoming negative racialized
meanings.

According to a separate study conducted by University of Illinois at
Chicago researchers, several black South Side neighborhoods, including Bronzeville, experienced change in the 1990s and 2000s but did
not actually gentrify.[9] No infusion of capital and amenities followed
when new black middle-class homeowners bought into the neighborhood, therefore confirming the theory that green (as in money) doesn't
trump black (as in race). Robert J. Sampson, of Harvard University, also

wrote a paper on gentrification in 2014. He found that in black Chicago neighborhoods, gentrification stopped in places where the population was 40 percent black.[10]

The South Side dollar has long been undervalued, as has black spending nationally. Each year South Siders spend billions of dollars outside of their neighborhoods in what is known as retail leakage. According to some reports, $150 million is leaked annually from Bronzeville.[11] A *Chicago Reporter* analysis found that the whiter a neighborhood in Chicago gets, the more supermarkets it gets. "A lot of it boils down to how race still dictates, in many cases, what kind of development occurs in black communities," Robert Bullard, director of the Environmental Justice Resource Center at Clark Atlanta University, told the magazine. The *Reporter* found that two gentrifying areas were black by a slim margin, but most of Chicago's majority-black community areas didn't gain supermarkets.[12]

Retailers may chase dollars, but density doesn't always play a role for big business. The buying power of middle-income families can be greater than that of smaller suburban, affluent families, which is why the example of Abundance Bakery thriving in a low-income milieu is so telling: Race counts more than class.

At the 2013 American Planning Association annual conference in Chicago, the village manager of Olympia Fields, an affluent suburb of homeowners with a large black population of which the average annual household income is $77,000, revealed that quality restaurants are reluctant to move there.[13] The village manager cited cultural bias in the form of retail redlining because of the difficulty in attracting businesses to the community.

TOBACCO ROAD DREAMS

One of the difficulties with Bronzeville as a social construction occurs when residents view the neighborhood through sepia-toned filters. A common trope among some African Americans is that integration ruined the black community. "Segregation benefited us!" "Poor people lived next door to doctors!" "We supported black businesses!" This starry-eyed wistfulness about intraracial harmony is flawed.

"Black Metropolis: A Study of Negro Life in a Northern City," the groundbreaking study of race and urban life in Chicago released in 1945 by St. Clair Drake and Horace Canton, revealed that Negroes resented being compelled to live in a segregated Black Belt. White folk didn't want them, and Negroes understood segregation was an isolation tactic. Negro civic leaders opposed enforced segregation and attacked the forces that created an overcrowded Black Belt ghetto in which rates of disease and death were higher than in white areas.

During the Great Migration, businesses grew, but not always in blacks' favor. In 1938, Negroes in Bronzeville owned and operated 2,600 businesses; whites had 2,800. But most of the Negro businesses were smaller and older, and they received less than a tenth of all the money spent by Negroes within the area. Negro businessmen complained they couldn't compete with white businesses when it came to securing capital.[14]

Segregation myth-busting must put racial pride in perspective. There's a danger of harkening back too much to the good ol' days, because it can actually stunt revitalization. In "Jim Crow Nostalgia: Reconstructing Race in Bronzeville," Michelle R. Boyd takes the black middle-class leadership to task. New homeowners and boosters who repurposed the neighborhood during the 1990s saw a blank canvas and filled it in. The vision sometimes obfuscated a Jim Crow past of slum housing, black exclusion from unions, poorly paid jobs, racial violence and sanctioned segregation. Political elites wanted a noble black story that by and large ignored low-income needs, Boyd argues.

According to Boyd, promoters of Jim Crow nostalgia reframe racial identity and

> have defined contemporary black identity by describing it as an extension of a reimagined past. Their vision of the past, like all visions of the past, is a partial one—gilded by fond memory, embroidered by fable and tinged by contemporary concerns. Thus, it depicts the segregation period generally, and the Great Migration era in particular, as characterized by

class harmony, collectivist middle-class leadership, and vibrant black culture. Douglas/Grand Boulevard leaders have attempted to revitalize the neighborhood without sparking racial displacement, and in doing so, they have institutionalized Jim Crow nostalgia, both in their organizations and in the built environment. This reinterpretation of the segregation era is therefore not an accident; nor is it the national result of the passage of time. Rather, it is a political artifact, a strategic rendering of race, space, and history that political elites have used to both challenge and reproduce contemporary racialized urban inequity.[15]

In a segregated city with lopsided development, it's understandable that black folk wanted to stake their claim before white city elites did. But too much nostalgia has jeopardized Bronzeville.

* * *

Lou Rawls crooned a bluesy song in the 1960s titled "Tobacco Road." The lyrics describe a downtrodden black southern town: dead mother, drunken father, filthy town.

One politician fostered this fantasy for Bronzeville.

Third Ward alderwoman Dorothy Tillman gave 47th Street the Tobacco Road designation on street signs in the late 1990s. The imagery clashed with the olden neighborhood days by imposing rural poverty onto a busy urban thoroughfare. "In a sense it prostitutes the street historically," revered historian Timuel Black, who grew up in the area, told the *Chicago Reader* in 2000. "They're just looking for revenue for the city and whatever nomenclature they can give the area. They're trying to revitalize it through historical falsehood, and it's not fair to the community and the history of the neighborhood."[16]

Tillman was elected to the city council in 1983 and was a large presence with signature hats as big as her mouth. She sowed a base, won reelections and fast-tracked/oversaw Bronzeville's reawakening, although there were allegations of cronyism, nepotism and mismanagement on her watch.[17] Her bluesy concept for the neighborhood failed to gain widespread community backing.

There was also controversy surrounding the teardown of Gerri's Palm Tavern, a bar on 47th Street established in the 1930s.[18] Duke Ellington, Dinah Washington, Miles Davis and Count Basie played at the joint, and over the decades, owner Gerri Oliver dished up her signature red beans and rice for entertainers. Petitions flooded City Hall to save the dilapidated building, but the city evicted Oliver in 2001 under eminent domain power. A developer with ties to Tillman proposed to build an upscale jazz and supper club on the land.[19] It never happened.

Less than a block away, in 2004, Tillman did usher in a 40,000-square-foot performance and cultural center, but it was marred by controversy amid delayed construction and financial questions. The center received at least $4 million in federal and state funds. It was originally to be named after Lou Rawls, a native son and supporter of Tillman's project, who had donated hundreds of thousands of dollars before a reported falling-out with Tillman.[20] The center lost twice as much as it grossed in its first year, and controversy has dogged it during the time it was managed by Tillman's Tobacco Road nonprofit.[21] Mayor Richard M. Daley handed the keys over to Chicago City Colleges in 2010.

Tillman's revitalization plans for Bronzeville hinged on creating a 47th Street musical blues district that never materialized. Blues is a rich part of Chicago's South Side history, but projecting that cultural aesthetic as the driving force for redevelopment didn't fit. At the time, some detractors pointed out that jazz was a bigger factor on 47th Street during its heyday than blues. Maybe another street should have had the blues. To be fair, the legendary Checkerboard Lounge on 43rd Street attracted intrepid white blues lovers/tourists for decades (and famously the Rolling Stones) despite its location in the middle of the ghetto. The Checkerboard's last call at that location was in 2003. Tillman failed to provide forward-thinking development for Bronzeville, and the blues became a reality as abandoned lots continued to dot the neighborhood. In a mocking twist, the blues district streetscaping—bronze sculptures of musicians hanging from lampposts—remains.

"Tillman was not the right person because she held everything very close to the vest. She didn't collaborate," resident Leana Flowers told me. "She could not succeed in the vision because she couldn't work with people, and she was very resistant to gentrification." African American professionals were the so-called gentrifiers, not whites, and many felt Tillman was hostile to them. Public housing residents made up Tillman's base.

Flowers gave the example of planning for Mandrake Park near the Ida B. Wells public housing low-rises in the 1990s. This was shortly before the new mixed-income development Oakwood Shores replaced Wells. "When there was an idea of having tennis courts, she [Tillman] was resistant. She said, 'It's not for us; it's for the new people.' The underlying sentiment was it was white people because it's always race with Dorothy, but it's professional African Americans who wanted those amenities." These days, I sometimes play tennis at Mandrake Park, which has what are probably some of the sorriest public courts in the city.

In 2007, newer residents, worn out by the rudderless feel of the neighborhood, didn't give a shit that Tillman had marched with Martin Luther King Jr. Daley and Barack Obama had endorsed her, but it didn't matter. Antsy and aching for a big splash in Bronzeville, not to mention wanting a few potholes fixed, voters replaced her with Pat Dowell, an urban planner.

But Tillman's hollow leadership isn't the only political factor that hampered Bronzeville.

* * *

In the early 2000s, Bronzeville and Harlem appeared to be two trains on the same track toward rapid development. The iconic neighborhoods have much in common, as each competes for the title of the Capital of Black America because of literary, economic and intellectual legacies. Both conjure feelings of romanticism for black life back in the day. Both had plummeted into extreme disadvantaged areas that housed a black urban underclass when the black middle class fled after the abolishment of racially restrictive housing laws. Both marshaled a second renaissance in the 1990s appealing to a black middle class that snapped and spruced up bare greystones and brownstones. Both buckled over concerns surrounding gentrification pressures. National chains from Old Navy to MAC Cosmetics opened on 125th Street in Harlem. Chicago demolished high-rise public housing complexes. But Bronzeville stopped in its tracks. And so goes the question: Why did Harlem boom commercially and Bronzeville slump?

Several key differences about the neighborhoods must be understood. There are obvious reasons for New York City—more capital, Wall Street, an international metropolis. Harlem's public housing population essentially stayed put amid the rebirth. Manhattan's expensive property values and small landmass were bound to encroach onto Harlem and create a housing demand. Further, racial and socioeconomic segregation isn't as pervasive in New York as it is in Chicago. But there's no bigger explanation than the polar differences in political landscapes between the two cities. New York City is a pluralistic government system, and Chicago is the storied Democratic Machine. In "The New Urban Renewal: The Economic Transformation of Harlem and Bronzeville," Derek S. Hyra sheds light on how city politics affected community development and weighed local residential input.

President Bill Clinton established Empowerment Zones (EZs) in 1993 to help neighborhood revitalization with tax incentives and block grant money. Harlem and Bronzeville saw those dollars. (Clinton famously moved his postpresidency office to 125th Street in Harlem.) "In Chicago, Daley's hegemonic control over resource allocation allows him to fund political allies and co-opt others, such as social service groups and black churches. This strategy helps the mayor politically but is less beneficial to Bronzeville's employment rate," Hyra writes.[22] Daley created an EZ coordinating council with authority from his rubber-stamp city council to approve funding. Money got doled out to lackluster city programs or agencies tied to the city. Disgusted resident leaders watched the co-opting from the sidelines. Harlem's transformation hasn't been perfect either. Residents complained that money benefited global corporations instead of mom-and-pop businesses. A growing white monied population has created racial tension and rapid gentrification. But Chicago dropped the ball with EZs. According to Hyra, out of several cities that had EZs—including New York—only Chicago had no job growth because the funds didn't support economic development initiatives. And residents complained about the distribution of EZ money. A *Chicago Tribune* editorial in 1996 scoffed at the assertion. "One can moan . . . that the so-called 'Black Metropolis' revitalization plan should be getting more attention from City Hall and more dollars from the city's federal empowerment zone fund. . . . The public sector can help, but only Chicago's black civic and business community can bring back the glory that was Bronzeville."[23]

Naturally, that attitude rankled residents who felt that Chicago's political system resisted bottom-up planning and development in favor of employing old-school methods that favored cronyism.[24]

Bronzeville increasingly seemed to be a renaissance deferred.

But in the beginning, the potential gleamed.

Restoration efforts began as early as 1984, when the Chicago Landmarks Commission recommended that key structures be declared landmarks. The Illinois General Assembly appropriated $2 million in 1989 to rebuild the Eighth Regiment Armory, the first all-black regiment in the United States. Bickering among black politicians over who was in charge led to the money being rescinded.[25] Then in 1993, Bronzeville lost out on $6.5 million in Illinois rehab funds after a legislative dispute.[26] Eventually the armory was turned into a military academy in the Chicago Public Schools.

Back then, neglected public housing high-rises still formed a concrete wall on the western outskirts of Bronzeville. Preservationists fretted over neglected historic buildings. Boosters wanted to ensure the Black Metropolis–rich history developed under the Bronzeville moniker. In 1990, the McCormick Tribune Foundation gave a grant for a commission to come up with a blueprint to deliver to the city. Obama confidante Valerie Jarrett was the city planning commissioner. By 1993, the Illinois Institute of Technology, located in the neighborhood along the State Street corridor, hosted meetings for the Mid-South Planning Group, comprised of residents and activists.

A year later, the group released the comprehensive Mid-South Strategic Plan, known as Restoring Bronzeville. It heavily relied on tourism, boosting home ownership, promoting commercial activity in conjunction with the new McCormick Place Convention Center, emphasizing job growth and maintaining the historical character of the area. The plan also highlighted proximity to the expressway, downtown and a blues district. The assumption was that the community could comfortably accommodate 100,000 people. In 2010, Grand Boulevard and Douglas had a population of about 40,000—mirroring a citywide trend of black population loss. But the plan failed to address funding for the ten-year, $1 billion effort.

"We are a suffering neighborhood. But there are a lot of opportunities here and we want to encourage people to return and help us bring this community back," Mid-South Planning and Development Commission chairman Angelo Rose told the *Chicago Tribune*. "If our people don't do it for themselves, who will?"

Rose also said: "We need to be unapologetically African-American in planning. We need to understand that we, as African-Americans, have a value and a richness. In Chinatown, they make no apologies for how (Chinese) their community looks. If you walked into Little Village or Pilsen and went into businesses, they make no apologies for speaking Spanish."[27]

In May 1996, Daley formed two committees to figure ways to redevelop Bronzeville, but questions bubbled about the city's commitment. Two months later, Daley responded to criticism about the speed of the plan with an editorial for the *Chicago Sun-Times* by defending his record in Bronzeville. He touted the $36 million spent on infrastructure projects that included work on the public transportation train line and reconstructing a major thoroughfare. "Given that the two committees I appointed include about 30 people, along with elected officials, three to four weeks is not a long time to wait for the first meeting. Suggesting these committees are merely 'buffers' is an insult to the civic-minded members. . . . The 'Restoring Bronzeville' plan is projected over a 30-year timeline. It is only three years old, yet we have already acted on many of its key recommendations."[28]

Critics viewed the mayor's blue ribbon committee as stacked with political insiders. They felt development should have been from the bottom up, not the top down—the way the city typically does things.

Indeed, some capital improvements—newly paved streets, new sewers—came as well as restoration of historic black landmarks. Former slave Anthony Overton ran the *Chicago Bee* newspaper and a cosmetics line, and the building that originally housed the *Bee* became a library. The Overton Hygienic Building, which opened in 1922, is ready for small businesses, and the Supreme Life Building, built in 1921, houses the Black Metropolis tourism group. But then suddenly, the call for "Restoring Bronzeville" faded into the dusty City Hall archives, and in the 2000s, public mentions of the plan ceased.

In hindsight, one area that the plan banked on backfired and was questionable in the first place. Organizers wanted to promote Bronzeville, or the Black Metropolis, as a tourist and visitor center. In 1996, a new McCormick Place Convention Center opened, then the nation's largest. The aim was for the facility to serve as the official gateway to the Metropolis district and help tourist-oriented businesses influenced by the influx of conventioneers. As part of the $1 billion McCormick expansion, Daley negotiated a $10.5 million beautification project on King Drive from the convention center to south on 35th Street.

At the gateway to Bronzeville is a 15-foot bronze male statue called *Monument to the Great Northern Migration*. The man holds a tattered suitcase held together by rope.

The new McCormick Place faces downtown, and the southern border is an expressway, which is a wall or dividing line. There's no connection between McCormick Place and Bronzeville. It's the end of the line for many white people.

* * *

A month after I moved into my Bronzeville condo, someone gunned down a young man directly across the street as I entertained two visiting friends with old-school music videos and beer.

I met my next-door neighbor Randy Price on that warm spring night. We stood in front of the yellow tape asking police questions after the shooting. Blood from the uncovered dead body streamed onto the street.

Randy, a 58-year-old suburban transit bus driver, moved into his five-bedroom, A-frame house in 1982, during the "low-end era." Randy reminds me of the *In Living Color* television show character Benita Butrell, the nosy neighbor who spotted everybody's business on the block. When Prairie Avenue withered during the low-end days, Randy said he knew the building owners, the drug dealers, the mothers of drug dealers and drug users.

"They used to shit behind my garage. Prostitutes would sell themselves behind my house. No lights in the alley. This alley was drive-in city. When crack came, that changed everything. The cops didn't care back then. On the weekend, it was so much sex sold around here."[29]

His most harrowing stories stem from my building, pre-condo, in the 1980s and '90s.

"Your building—it was so bad these guys on the second floor were shooting, bam bam bam every night. I used to have used diapers in my yard every morning. Beer bottles. Needles. More beer bottles. They put speakers out on the balcony. The fat girl got killed. Her and the boyfriend were arguing. We heard them arguing and he stabbed her in [the] boobs with a knife. But that didn't kill her. He kicked her down the stairs and the knife punctured her chest cavity. Then [the landlord] had a whole bunch of drunks, Lloyd and them. Nice-looking sister. She drank so much it really took her looks away. Nobody was neighborly. Then they moved a hoodlum on the first floor. He walked around with his gun." Randy demonstrated the gun-wielding guy's strut on his newly shellacked floors. "I didn't park in front of ya'll building in them years because every time something happened in that building, it spilled into the streets. There was always loitering in front of building. I'd pick up paper, bottles. I stopped picking up the needles. Stray dogs ran through the neighborhood. I didn't barbecue on a holiday. I barbecued the next day to have peace and quiet. We wasn't the low end by choice. People treated it like the low end. I had to stay. I put money in it. My money is in this house."

In the early 2000s, condo conversions popped up on the block, people moved out or got displaced and Randy savored a bit of peace and quiet.

"The changes are positive. I was so thankful when you guys came. I haven't heard a peep in years. It's still rough but it was rougher," Randy told me. "Since we got that name Bronzeville, the changes came: They don't burn rubber, lights in the alley, new lights on the block. We're getting paving on the street. Police respond more aggressive now since the Bronzeville label has been laid on us. People don't call us the low end."

The neighborhood, and block, is still fragile, and while Randy doesn't spew anti–poor people rhetoric, he fears an influx of new low-income housing will reverse any gains. His antisegregation vision is a multiculti neighborhood. "I came up with a plan: All these empty apartments, flood them with Jamaicans. Bring Mexicans, Africans, Filipinos, Iraqis."

In spring 2013, a construction crew began rehabbing an abandoned multi-unit apartment building across the alley from me, much to Randy's chagrin. "We do not need more affordable housing. We've done it. Put them in Mount Prospect or Barrington. Been there done that!" he exclaimed. The areas he named are well-to-do majority-white suburbs. "I've paid my dues," he said of Bronzeville, and that's why he expressed weariness, perhaps unfairly, about the jackhammering behind us and the new neighbors to come. The new neighbors haven't caused any trouble since they moved in, and there's one less abandoned building in the neighborhood and on the block.

Those successes matter little because a vocal portion of Bronzeville denizens resent what they feel is an inequitable dispersal of affordable housing across the city. A few blocks away, that urban porn *New Jack City* Rosenwald building irks nearby homeowners. When city councilwoman Pat Dowell announced a plan in 2012 to rehab the imposing structure into affordable and senior housing with retail on the first floor, the opposition was ignited partly by hood fatigue, and the plan has unfairly been painted as the return of the projects.

I often questioned whether I committed class suicide by buying a home in Bronzeville. Moving into the fabled Black Metropolis initially kindled warm feelings and a sense of racial purpose. But mostly my bank account dictated my purchasing power. If my income had been higher, perhaps I would have bought elsewhere. I've encountered comments from black folk who never considered Bronzeville or any black community, much less one on the brink. They glance at me with slightly judgmental faces and make strong assumptions about my financial status. It's a condescending middle-class version of asking why poor people just don't move out of their poor neighborhoods. White folk have also informed me that no one made me buy in my neighborhood. By 2013, many of my friends packed their bags, defecting from Bronzeville for the concrete pastures of the South Loop and downtown. I felt stuck; moving wasn't economically feasible for me. I *thought* I did the right thing by literally buying into the so-called home American Dream, yet I became burdened by a financial albatross.

As the country coped with the housing crisis, many homeowners walked away from their worthless properties. Despite my $100,000 underwater status, that never seemed to be a personal option. My sense of responsibility—conceivably misplaced, given the role of banks during the economic catastrophe—kept me paying the condo mortgage on time. After all, I told myself, my expenses are low, I refinanced at one point, and I rationalized that eventually the unit could be a long-term rental investment.

Then life caught up with me.

My boyfriend, Rod, and I decided to get married. By spring 2014, I'd been dating the father of three daughters for three years. At that stage of our lives, a white-frosted cupcake wedding matched neither our sensibilities nor our practical natures. Finding a place big enough to live emerged as priority number one because neither of our homes could accommodate a blended family. We both were jaded by condo experiences and debated renting versus home ownership. At first, we searched for a great foreclosure deal in South Side lakefront neighborhoods and didn't find anything that worked for us. We scoured online real estate listings and quickly found a dreamy three-bedroom, four-bathroom apartment.

Before deciding what to do with my condo, we took a field trip to my bank. I asked for a loan reduction for the principal to be more aligned with the condo's value. Nope. Another refinance? Nope. My clever partner—always the resourceful one—even suggested we purchase one of the bank's foreclosed properties, sell my place at whatever

I could get and wrap the unpaid balance in with the new mortgage. Not my ideal scenario, but the bank rejected that too. On one of my many phone calls to the bank, I explained that we were both culpable in this morass. The bank overvalued my property; I paid too much for it. Alas, that logic didn't work either.

My sister works on federal housing issues and had been telling me for months that I was delusional in thinking my place was a long-term investment. You'll never make your money back, she said repeatedly. I heard her, but I wasn't ready to accept reality. I already felt like a middle-class loser compared to my parents, who made a judicious home purchase the second time around.

Finally, I resolved to let my condo go. I was emotionally ready to move on from my first home. Those final few weeks of living in Bronzeville brought heavy reflection. Would I miss the neighborhood? I rode the Green Line train frequently, absorbing all my surroundings: loose squares sold under the tracks, gawking men on corners, heavy foot traffic in and out of clothing stores, Gallery Guichard moving to the strip. Around this time, I asked a well-known Chicago affordable housing expert what he thought would happen to neighborhoods like Bronzeville—once-strong rental markets burdened by too many unsustainable condo conversions. He said the market would have to reset: A new crop of buyers would swoop in to purchase deeply discounted short sales and foreclosures, therefore stabilizing the market. That gave me some pay-it-forward comfort. My real estate agent listed my place as a short sale for $70,000. I considered this a "gift" to whoever bought the condo, and it proved to be for a single mom with twin boys. This path and deal allowed her to move into home ownership. She loved the place so much she didn't even want to change the paint. But then the bank decided not to approve the short sale. A broker valued the condo at $45,000, but the bank appraiser said $87,000, which the buyer wasn't willing to pay. This scenario reflects exactly what Cook County commissioner Bridget Gainer says: Faulty appraisers do not understand how black communities look and work. How can black neighborhoods move forward with these kinds of clueless discrepancies? What happened next was a series of fruitless attempts at negotiation with no resolution.

The bank would rather a unit go into foreclosure and remain on its loan books than go with a short sale. Eventually the bank transferred my loan to a loan servicing company, which handles mortgages and is aggressive in recouping money.

I applied for a deed in lieu of foreclosure, and it got approved after I sent the same documents multiple times and got hazed on the phone. Another appraisal came in at around $87,000. Amazing how the price went up so fast after six months (insert sarcasm!). A deed in lieu means I and the loan servicer call it quits, and both walk away. It also means my short sale "gift" to the first-time homeowner mom with twin boys didn't happen.

Meanwhile, Rod and I chose to live in Hyde Park (41 percent white, 40 percent black) because of its proximity to the lake, culture and University of Chicago. Our 3,000-square-foot top-floor apartment rental is a classic Hyde Park brick walk-up with two sunrooms.

Bronzeville and Hyde Park are a study in contrasts, even though they are only a ten-minute car ride from each other. In Hyde Park, I can walk to multiple grocery stores. Restaurants deliver. I can walk to order takeout, deposit money at a bank, listen to live music, eat at a white-linen bistro. I'm almost dizzy from the options. I love Hyde Park. Surprisingly, I veered from hood fatigue to hood withdrawal. I don't feel guilt, but the transition, I admit, makes me sound like a hayseed. I find myself returning to 47th Street for pedicures and oil changes when I could now get either mere blocks away. I still support businesses like small coffeehouses in less resourced nearby neighborhoods because they need deliberate patronage to stay in business.

But for my financial sanity and overall peace of mind, Hyde Park has been the best decision for our family. My journey led me here.

I thought to myself, *Let me give integration a whirl.*

5

SEPARATE AND STILL UNEQUAL

"Do you know what segregation is?"

"Yes—separation."

—All-black Mollison eighth-grade boys'
class discussion after reading
"Letter from a Birmingham Jail"
by Martin Luther King Jr.

MY FORAY INTO INTEGRATED EDUCATION WAS LAUNCHED OUT OF PURE CONVENIENCE.
Neither our Chatham neighborhood nor surrounding black areas
had all-day public school kindergarten, according to my parents. Only
half day.

"That was a real issue for me and your mother," my father recalled.
For dual-working parents, the Chicago public school two blocks away
was not an option.

The year was 1981. My parents heard about a new magnet-style program at a public school in the South Side Beverly neighborhood, a fledg-
ling integrated community that didn't succumb to white flight.

A yellow school bus ferried me and a load of black children—all from South Side black working- and middle-class neighborhoods—to Sutherland Elementary, a beautiful redbrick colonial-style school with double-hung, oversize bay windows. It took us about an hour to get to school each day.

"At the time, they had the 'deseg' program in the city of Chicago, and a lot of black families looked at it as an opportunity to go to diverse schools outside of their neighborhood," my mother recalled.[1] Sutherland students scored high in reading and math.

I attended Sutherland as a result of a last-ditch integration effort by Chicago Public Schools (CPS). Decades of other so-called reforms never achieved true integration, culminating in white students fleeing CPS beginning in the 1960s.

In 1980, the U.S. Justice Department filed a lawsuit against the Chicago Board of Education, alleging a dual school system that segregated students on the basis of race and ethnic origin was in violation of the equal protection clause of the Fourteenth Amendment. Back then the percentage of white students in the district was 18.6. The decree required CPS to implement a voluntary desegregation plan to create as many racially integrated schools as possible.

The consent decree is what helped allow my voluntary transfer to Sutherland.

"I loved the teachers there," said my mother, a retired special education teacher and administrator in CPS. "You had an excellent education. I couldn't really ask for too much more than what you had."

My voluntary busing experience belies what's burned in popular imagination. This wasn't 1974 Boston. No screaming white parents hurled epithets at black students as we rolled up to the school in a yellow school bus. White students didn't taunt us on the school steps. Law enforcement didn't arrive at the scene to escort us into the building. A decade earlier, white parents resisted integration in CPS, but by 1981, the percentage of whites in the district had dropped precipitously. Meanwhile the Beverly neighborhood was grappling with nascent integration, and white resident leaders promoted integration as an asset.

When they got old enough for school, my brother and sister joined me on the bus.

"All of you seemed very happy there," my mother said. "Teachers cared about you and they were very easy to talk to if there were any problems, and the administration was great."

I recognized differences, although it didn't register until college that I had participated in something weighty called "desegregated busing." Growing up, my father delivered the typical black parent lecture about being "twice as good" as white peers, but he never prepped us about our role in helping integrate a school. Our parents didn't treat us like pioneers or mini Ruby Bridges.

Normalcy ruled our school lives. White friends invited me over for sleepovers. Black and white students mimicked *Star Wars* on the playground with imaginary light sabers. Love and disdain for certain teachers transcended racial lines. We all agreed the Polish gym teacher sucked. But I observed many white students walking home for lunch. Bused black kids lived too far for that. And our moms worked. White stay-at-home moms dropped in for Friday pizza days and volunteered at PTA book fairs. On a more childlike wonderment note, my seven-year-old self observed that black kids ate wheat bread and white kids ate white bread during lunch. Imagine my surprise when a white classmate unpacked a wheat sandwich. The only racial incident I recall involved a white nemesis who snickered that she didn't know black people could afford to go to Disney World after I told her about a family vacation. I likely rolled my nine-year-old eyes at her; white and black girls alike found her as affable as a Garbage Pail Kid.

I loved Sutherland. We adored our avuncular white principal, Mr. Frantz, who occasionally stopped by our house for family barbecues. He also would pop into my classroom to scope my lunchbox. He knew my mother packed me leftover dinner since I disliked sandwiches without bacon. Once he lucked out and scored a bite of lobster.

Black and white teachers helped mold me. Ms. Traback introduced me to *I Know Why the Caged Bird Sings* in sixth grade. Ms. Becic fostered a love for language arts. Ms. Turner treated us like her children. I loved school and reflect positively on Sutherland without racial scars. Sutherland complemented my black Chatham life.

Yet in first grade, my parents transferred me out of Sutherland for Beasley, a high-performing, mostly black elementary school that required an admissions test across the street from the Robert Taylor Homes public housing development, because the school earned the reputation as one of the 1980s *it* Chicago schools. Beasley schooled a bevy of black middle-class youth from outside the neighborhood. After a month, I transferred back to Sutherland.

When people asked why I returned, I parroted my dad without fully understanding what he meant. "My father says he wants me to have an integrated education."

Today, no one talks about integration in CPS. In school reform debates, the topic isn't in vogue. Integration has been replaced by charter schools and yearly standardized testing as the nation's go-to strategies for improving education for black children. Soon I realized: Why *would* anyone talk about integration? Over the course of 50 years, the white population in CPS dropped from 50 percent in the early 1960s to 9 percent in 2014.

While city demographic changes occur in many neighborhoods, Chicago remains diverse. White people live here but don't send their children to public schools.

"In terms of dealing with overall patterns of segregation in Chicago, it was pretty much an abject failure. In terms of creating a few interracial magnet schools, it was better than nothing. But it was never seriously developed to figure out what actually could be done," Gary Orfield, a school desegregation expert and codirector of the Civil Rights Project at the University of California–Los Angeles, told me.[2]

Decades after the landmark *Brown v. Board of Education* and 35 years after Chicago's consent decree that allowed me and my siblings to attend Sutherland, the city's children still don't go to public school together. Why did Chicago fail to integrate public schools?

In short, the answer is court failure and lack of political will. Scared white families left the city and/or district. White people didn't want to give up their privilege or segregated education for blacks. On the federal level, changes in presidential administrations hurt CPS because priorities had changed. Historical and legal wrangling over public education foiled any chance of remarkable change. Now black leaders and organizations don't take up integration as a goal.

But after *Brown v. Board of Education*, which ruled separate public schools for black and white students as unconstitutional, Chicago seemed poised to change. The landmark 1954 decision strengthened Chicago black parents' resolve toward ending segregation, but the case meant little on the ground. Civil rights laws prohibiting discrimination served school districts in the South but fell victim to Chicago's powerful and well-oiled political machine. Mayor Richard J. Daley resisted desegregation up until his death in 1976.

"Most places were forced to change by some degree of civil rights enforcement, but Chicago was able to exercise enough political power to protect its singularity," Orfield explained.

In "Desegregating Chicago's Public Schools: Policy Implementation, Politics, and Protest, 1965–1985," Dionne Danns writes that the city is distinctive when compared to other major cities because no major court ruling came from Chicago. In other northern cities, federal and Supreme Court rulings were the sources of desegregation policy. Chicago policy came directly from the federal and state governments.[3]

CPS squandered the opportunity in the 1960s and 1970s when a substantial number of white students attended public schools by routinely ignoring desegregation mandates without suffering financial repercussions. Danns writes that as federal and state officials pursued desegregation, Chicago school officials "dragged their feet and continually issued voluntary plans calculated to stymie rather than promote desegregation."[4] The result over five decades has been fewer white students and increased clustering of those students in fewer and fewer schools. But with integration out of the limelight, even limited gains are beginning to disappear, and the word "resegregation" has become part of the conversation.

But not in the suburbs.

Surprisingly, from 1990 to 2010, white students in suburban Chicago attended more diverse schools. However, in Chicago, the number of highly segregated black and Latino schools jumped. The number of Chicago public schools 90 percent or more black increased from 276 to 287 while the number of racially isolated Hispanic schools increased from 26 to 84. Meanwhile, the number of integrated schools—where no one race comprises more than 50 percent of the student body—plummeted from 106 to 66.[5]

On the surface, the city's demographics don't suggest those figures. Chicago is not exclusively black and/or Latino because, unlike many other midwestern cities, Chicago has maintained a white population. The city is almost equal parts black, Latino and white. But while roughly a third of Chicago's total population is white, there aren't that many white school-age children living in the city. Here is CPS student racial data that I received from the district.

Table 5.1   Chicago Public Schools Enrollment, 2014–2015

Hispanic	180,790
Black	155,932
White	37,444
Asian	14,228
Multiracial	4,202
Native American/Alaskan	1,103
Total	396,683

Source: Author's compilation based on the *CPS Demographic Report* 2014–2015.

In 2012, there were 65,259 white children living in the city of Chicago, grades K–12.[6] Even if all of them enrolled in CPS, they'd still be far outnumbered by students who are black and brown. Many whites treat the city of Chicago as a revolving door. They bolt, presumably to the suburbs, once they have school-age families. They are replaced with single or childless whites, and the cycle resumes.

Despite the bleak numbers, experts say the city can find creative, innovative ways to curb the number of racially isolated schools in poor black and brown communities. Integrating schools isn't about getting black and white children to sit next to each other just for the sake of kumbaya harmony. Diversity is worthy, and segregation needs to be broken up because it perpetuates a system of inequity. Black children don't need their desks to be next to white children because whites are better. Integration is about the proximity of power and resources. Chicago lost potential and lost the chance to understand what the real benefits have been.

But integration could be regained.

* * *

During the month of January 1962, black parents and students staged a sit-in at Burnside Elementary in the West Chesterfield neighborhood on Chicago's South Side. As the community transitioned from white to black, the public school suffered from overcrowding. Children attended school on double shifts to accommodate overflowing classrooms. Some students started at 7:45 a.m.; others arrived at 9 a.m. Some students left early afternoon; some stayed late. Some classroom instruction took place in the teacher's lounge and the school auditorium.

Parents had a solution: They demanded that some seventh- and eighth-grade children transfer to nearby Perry Elementary. But rather than integrate that school, the Chicago Board of Education ordered the upper graders farther away to black Gillespie Elementary.

"But we didn't go, which is why we had the sit-in," recalled Tony Burroughs, one of the eighth-grade protesters in 1962. "Perry was closer and the black kids that lived closer to Perry school were not allowed to go to Perry. So our parents' stance was—if you integrate Perry, then those students that live closer to Perry would go, which would relieve the overcrowding in Burnside. We would still only have to walk three or four blocks to school, instead of 16, 17 blocks."[7]

His mother, Mary Burroughs, Burnside PTA president, led the demonstration.

"My mom wasn't really a civil rights worker, but she was very active in the community. She explained everything to us every day. Why we were having the sit-in, what would happen when we'd go every day. Why we were going, this whole thing about racism," Burroughs told me.

The Burroughs family had moved to the Burnside neighborhood in the late 1950s after neighborhoods outside of the Black Belt opened up to blacks. Tony Burroughs understood that segregation didn't uplift the race because a childhood accident had taught him society viewed him as a second-class citizen.

Ten-year-old Burroughs slid on a piece of glass while playing baseball with his brother in the alley. His parents took him to a hospital two blocks away.

"The hospital said, 'We don't serve niggers.' So we had to leave," Burroughs remembered.

The family drove to another hospital.

"We walked into the emergency room there and they wrapped gauze around my hand three times and said, 'We don't serve niggers.'"

A third hospital finally accepted him.

"I was in emergency surgery for three hours. The tetanus had crawled up my arm and the physician had to make this incision and bring the attendants to tie my arm up. My mom explained why, since I was a black person, I couldn't get service at these hospitals. So I knew what racism was about. Or at least I knew something about what it was about. So when my parents explained what was going on [at Burnside], it wasn't anything foreign to me."

Young Tony grasped the concept of racism, and the hospital incident solidified the importance of the Burnside protest. As the sit-in pressed on, the white principal removed the chairs and relocated protesters from the hallway to the basement. Officials threatened students with truancy. Police arrested mothers, including Mary Burroughs. She was fingerprinted, and *Jet* magazine captured the image.

Burnside parents filed a class-action lawsuit—in Tony Burroughs's name—against the Chicago Board of Education. They asked for a restraining order to halt the transfer of students to Gillespie and $500,000 in damages.[8]

A judge dismissed the lawsuit on the grounds that litigants had not pursued all state-level remedies against the defendant Board of Education before filing in federal court. Eventually the sit-in ended, and Tony Burroughs reluctantly transferred to Gillespie.

But the loss didn't deter Chicago parents. They had been fighting before that case and would continue to fight for integration with invigorated activists all over the city. Fed-up parents took to the streets, City Hall, the courts and school grounds in the 1960s.

In 1961, parents of 160 black children requested transfers from overcrowded black schools to nearby white schools that had open classrooms.[9] Request denied. That same year *Webb v. the Chicago Board of Education* alleged deliberate school segregation in violation of equal protection under the law. The U.S. Supreme Court found that plaintiffs didn't exhaust the state's administrative procedures before filing in federal court. In an out-of-court settlement, the Board of Education agreed to form a panel to analyze the school system "in particular regard to schools attended entirely or predominately by Negroes, define any problems that result therefrom and formulate and report to this Board as soon as may be conveniently possible a plan by which any education, psychological, and emotional problems or inequities in the school system that prevail may be best eliminated."[10] At the time, CPS was about 51 percent white.

Community groups refused to back down, and civil rights groups demonstrated. In Freedom Day boycotts, hundreds of thousands of students stayed out of school on various days during the 1963–1964 school year. Protests ratcheted up with a focus on Superintendent Benjamin Willis. Some compared Willis to Alabama's segregationist governor George Wallace, who declared "segregation now, segregation tomorrow, segregation forever" and ordered state police to prevent integrated public schools from opening.

Willis presided over the district from 1953 to 1966—through the critical period of time nationally of *Brown v. Board of Education* and the Civil Rights Act of 1964. He became one of the most controversial school figures in the nation for keeping black students in segregated, overcrowded schools, even though there were seats available in white schools.

The racist solution Willis applied to ease overcrowding was building mobile classroom units in front of black schools. Parents derided the units as "Willis Wagons."

Willis resigned in 1963 when the Illinois State Court ordered him to implement a student transfer plan to bring a small number of black students to white Bogan High School. The board refused to accept his resignation.

My parents attended Chicago Public Schools during this time. For one academic year, my mother attended elementary school on a half-day schedule in Woodlawn because of overcrowding. At the time she didn't grasp why. My father attended Burnside Elementary ahead of Tony Burroughs when whites still lived and attended school in the neighborhood. Fenger High School in Roseland was my father's neighborhood high school. Because a new neighborhood high school in his newly black South Side neighborhood wasn't built yet, he took the city bus to Fenger, where just a handful of blacks attended. Roseland was a few years off from full-fledged white flight. My dad hated Fenger. One day someone painted "nigger go home" on the school. He attended summer school so he could graduate early and escape prejudiced teachers. (Decades later, Fenger became a low-performing high school and made national news in 2009 when the beating death of Derrion Albert, a Fenger student walking home from school, was caught on camera.)

Meanwhile, the 1964 report tied to the Webb case—known as the Hauser Report—documented school segregation as a by-product of segregated housing patterns. "The intense dissatisfaction of Negroes with the prevalent pattern of *de facto* segregated public schools and with the quality of education in those schools in the City of Chicago must be understood as an expression of their rebellion against their general status in American society," the report said.[11] It noted that there were more Negro pupils than whites in classrooms and overcrowded facilities; Negro teachers with less education than white teachers; higher Negro dropout rates and lower test scores; and inferior Negro school facilities. Among the panel recommendations: changes in school boundaries to foster integration, faculty integration and free transportation for transfer programs.

True to form, the board did little with the report, and a coalition of civil rights, civic and religious groups grew tired of constant inaction. This trail of setbacks and frustrations show the deep-seated segregation permeating Chicago. It also helps us understand why the city continues to be so segregated. We'd have a much different public school system if the city had implemented recommendations in the early 1960s.

Black parents kept trying and kept losing, but they never gave up. In 1965, a coalition filed a formal complaint of discrimination with the U.S. Office of Education. It was the first major challenge to a northern school district under the newly passed Civil Rights Act of 1964 and its Title VI provision, which prohibited discrimination in programs that receive federal assistance. This covered education. Two years later, a report identified violations, and the Department of Health, Education and Welfare (HEW) sought voluntary compliance.[12] But because of blowback from Mayor Richard J. Daley and his powerful Democratic machine, the feds didn't give Chicago a plan and trusted the Board of Education to do the right thing. HEW had planned to defer $32 million in federal funds for the city with the expectation that CPS would cooperate on desegregation, but Daley threatened that the Chicago congressional delegation and Senate GOP leader Everett Dirksen, of Illinois, would end support for all federal education. HEW backed down.

In 1966, Willis retired. His successor, James Redmond, unveiled a desegregation plan, which included limited busing of blacks to white schools. This prompted white parents to picket, and voluntary busing failed. Redmond's plan also called for the creation of magnet schools. Blacks felt the plan wasn't enough. Ultimately, the federal government never pressed for formal compliance. Redmond—joined by politicians and white residents—seemed more focused on appeasing whites who were leaving the city.

In 1971, the Illinois State Superintendent of Public Instruction filed binding rules mandating that no school may deviate more than 15 percent in its racial composition from the school district as a whole. Again, this was never implemented in CPS.

Then in 1973, the governor of Illinois signed a bill that prohibited mandatory busing as a remedy for school segregation. Time and again in the 1970s, the Chicago Board of Education was told to come up with a desegregation plan, but every plan was found to be faulty.

With President Jimmy Carter in office and Richard J. Daley gone, in the late 1970s the feds finally found some money to withhold.

According to a 1979 report by the Illinois Advisory Committee to the U.S. Commission on Civil Rights documenting Chicago's failings:

> The Chicago Public School officials often mention the impossibility of desegregating a school system with too few white pupils. They continue to attach responsibility for segregated schooling to residential patterns and housing preferences, occurring supposedly independent of government action. The Office for Civil Rights, HEW, has however documented . . . a long history of actions and/or omissions by the Chicago Board of Education over the years that contributed to or caused segregation.[13]

"There was never a doubt that Chicago was violating the Constitution, but every time you'd come up to do something serious, massive political power was used to protect segregation," civil rights expert Gary Orfield explained.

In 1980, the U.S. Justice Department filed a lawsuit against the Chicago Board of Education, alleging a segregated dual school system.[14] Allegations included drawing/altering attendance boundary areas that created segregation, segregated schools within segregating public housing and failure to relieve student overcrowding that maintained segregation. CPS implemented a transfer policy that allowed white students to avoid attending schools where they'd be the minority in favor of schools where they were the majority.

Creating magnet schools was a key piece of the decree. One rule those schools had to follow was that enrollment could be no more than 35 percent white. Eventually, this decree would fade into the abyss of empty desegregation plans when it ended two decades later.

* * *

On a snowy January morning in 2015, students trickle in with their backpacks before the 8:45 a.m. bell rings at Irvin C. Mollison Elementary. En route to homeroom, they swing by the lunchroom to pick up a free breakfast. Just about every student is eligible for free/reduced lunch.

Staff and teachers call out "good morning" to students in the hallway before ushering them along to homeroom. After slurping their milk, students stand for the Pledge of Allegiance and then recite Mollison's creed—developed by staff with student input—about being black children ready to learn.

Mollison sits along a quiet stretch of Bronzeville greystones. The public school's name comes from Irvin C. Mollison, the nation's first black federal judge, appointed by President Harry Truman in 1945. The University of Chicago–trained lawyer was part of the team that represented Lorraine Hansberry's family in the racially restrictive housing case of *Hansberry v. Lee* that was decided by the Supreme Court in 1940.

Mollison Elementary is familiar with the limelight, not because of its nod to black history but because of a contentious school policy. Chicago generated national furor when in 2013 the district closed 50 schools on the South and West Sides, a move that disproportionately affected poor black students. CPS vacillated on the reasons for the mass closings—from budget woes to school utilization. The 2010 census revealed that 200,000 African Americans had left the city, but officials underestimated how resistant and angry people would be about closings and the sting they felt in already underresourced schools and communities.

The aftermath is a plethora of empty school buildings in neighborhoods already stressed with foreclosures and vacancies—visible vestiges of communities. Teachers and principals still complain that the district's promises of more resources to schools that absorbed the displaced students didn't pan out. Accusations of CPS wanting to privatize the school system prove to be far from conspiratorial, given the steady increase of free charter schools sometimes opening in the very neighborhoods where public schools closed.

One of the closed elementary schools, Overton, was less than a block away from my Bronzeville condo. Each closed school sent its students to what the district dubbed a "receiving school." Overton students could attend Mollison. On a purely personal, selfish level, the 2013 closing made me more depressed about the real estate market. Foreclosures and short sales had already rocked my block and Bronzeville as a whole.

How would a vacant school affect property values? How would the district repurpose a closed school?

School closings captured the attention of educators, parents, activists and community residents, but a more permanent problem persists. Segregation in CPS, as well as in public school districts around the country, is double: race *and* class. Black professionals don't send their children to Mollison. The school is 99.6 percent black and 91.6 percent low income. Test scores are below average. There's no PTA. Parental engagement isn't where it should be. Behavior issues bubble in some classrooms. This is what a typical black neighborhood school, a product of segregation, looks like in Chicago.

Mollison's challenges go beyond the statistics. On another January morning, an eighth-grade girl who hadn't been to school since November showed up. The school called child protective services amid rumors she lived with an older man.

For decades, Mollison students have struggled academically and come from high-poverty homes.[15] In 1991, a Mollison eighth grader approached her principal about poverty and crime anxieties in the neighborhood. Fewer than two weeks later, police found the girl's body in a nearby abandoned garage. She'd been stabbed six times.[16]

Kimberly Henderson, a black woman in her mid-40s with a pixie haircut and direct approach, is now the principal of Mollison and led the school during its rocky transition as a receiving school after Overton closed. In one year she moved the school from a Level 3—the lowest—to a Level 2. Her goal is Level 1, the highest. Mollison is no longer on probation, but it is far from being a top school. It's about making leaps in student growth, which is one of the ways CPS measures success, even if the achievement of the school's students remains below grade level.

Mollison's walls brim with appropriate school-age platitudes—"You can change the world" and "Spread your wings." African cloth, black art and college banners decorate the hallways. The school offers a Spanish-language class, and the teacher has taped vocabulary words all over the school for language reinforcement. International flags wave inside and outside the building. Bookcases are in nooks of the corridor. Every

Friday teachers and administrators don their alumni paraphernalia for "college day."

Inside classrooms, signs remind students to be respectful and watch their noise levels. Wide-eyed preschoolers hug new people who enter their classrooms. Third-grade teacher Ms. Love rings a bell on her desk when it's time for students to move to the next unit. Ms. Thomas's kindergarten/first-grade students put their hands up if a word she says rhymes. Hands down if the word doesn't. Each Mollison classroom door displays weekly attendance achievement. Ms. Longmire plays jazz as the day commences to settle students down, and a Nelson Mandela education quote is plastered prominently above a row of computers. Most classrooms are equipped with technology—iPads, computerized smartboards instead of chalkboards. Students wear uniforms of either navy or khaki. Upper-grade boys and girls learn in separate classrooms.

Mollison is applying for authorization to institute an International Baccalaureate college-prep program for its middle schoolers. The Spanish and an upper-grade math teacher are researching a grant to travel to China to learn some best education practices.

Principal Henderson looks for student growth, demands it from the teachers, shows them how to interpret test data. When she arrived at Mollison, she implemented the additional structure she says was sorely needed. Every Friday she and Assistant Principal Janelle Thompson spend all day meeting with teachers about their lesson plans. During testing season, she emphasizes action plans to move test scores up. The duo marked their third year as a team during the 2014–2015 school year. They routinely meet about reading interventions because only 25 to 30 percent of students read at grade level. In a climate of school testing, Henderson personally tells eighth graders about the importance of testing to graduate eighth grade and to help determine the high school they will attend. She tells them: "You are smart. You need to be reading."

"I really think that goes a long way in empowering the kids and making sure they understand the way we do what we do, and better yet, what the data tells us. That was a huge missing piece and I think that's [true] at most schools. Kids do not understand why we're taking the test, what the results mean; they think it's just a number. Once they start to take pride in their own work and how they're accomplishing things, I think you see more of an effort from them," Henderson told me.[17]

She takes a no-excuses approach to the difficulties facing Mollison.

"When a school's low achieving, it's the adults in the building [who are the problem]. If you don't have the right leadership, the right teachers in place who believe these kids can do it—because they can. There are some people who believe that because they're poor, they can't excel. So you have to confront that mind-set when you find it, and it is here. It's in every school," Henderson said. "I believe it's what you do between these four walls more than what happens to kids outside. Now, when kids' attendance is an issue—that's something we can't necessarily control. So I will start off by saying if a child has a serious attendance issue, that's something that's a little out of our control; that makes it difficult for us to move kids. I guess if a child has some kind of severe diagnosed mental or behavioral problems, then maybe [that presents a challenge]. When a kid's misbehaving in school, it's just generally because of something we're not doing here in school."

Henderson spent more than a decade teaching in Englewood, a low-income black South Side neighborhood. She firmly believes that what goes on in a classroom can trump what's going on at home. So what if a student didn't get homework help, guided reading or academic discipline at home? Henderson allotted time for homework at school. Doing it was more important than where it was done.

"I did not think about where my kids came from, where they were going when they left me. If Dad was at home, if he was in jail, if Mom was on drugs. None of that mattered to me. You have to believe that your instruction—while they're here for seven hours a day—has more of an impact and it does. We use excuses. And because we use excuses, when kids don't perform well, we think that's acceptable? Or to be expected? And I'm not sure I buy into that. There's very little aside from a kid not coming to school that I think we can't overcome."

When I ask her whether segregation is a problem in CPS and for her, Henderson referred to her own—and my—separate experiences at the historically black Howard University.

"I don't know about the integration part. Heck, I went to an all-black college, just like you. I don't necessarily have a problem with how the neighborhood is set up. I don't think there's necessarily anything wrong with that. I think it's wrong when we don't have the same resources. I don't have a problem with the fact that 99.9 percent of my students are black. As long as when we look across at a school that has an opposite reality, we all have the same resources," she explained.

She does see the grander picture of haves and have-nots in CPS. The district puts money toward selective-enrollment high schools, which get brand-new buildings downtown and on the North Side.

Public school funding in Illinois, as in other states, is a huge issue. Every CPS student—whether South Side or North Side—gets the same per-pupil dollar amount, and the debate about reforming property taxes to deal with affluent suburbs versus the struggling city is decades old. But some of the best public schools don't rely just on CPS allocations. PTAs, fundraisers and businesses contribute to the well-being of a school. Mollison doesn't have a PTA, which doesn't surprise Henderson. She's never taught at a low-performing poor black school that had one. But Mollison does have a Parent Advisory Council, which focuses on empowering the parents. Those parents have a presence inside the school, as by hosting a family game night.

Nonetheless, neighborhood schools in poor black neighborhoods can't compete with just a per-pupil allowance. A different set of well-resourced parents makes the difference in schools.

Researchers at the University of Chicago Consortium on Chicago School Research say schools in more advantaged areas of the city serving more economically advantaged students are much more likely to improve than schools located in areas that serve high numbers of students living in poverty because neighborhoods possessing "social capital," collective economic benefits and networks, fare better. Scholars and public educators around the country view social capital as social glue that holds schools together.

Social capital "is based on the connections and resources that families and people in the community have that they can actually use to support the schools. So if you look at the schools in the poorest areas of the city, in general, there're very few strong institutions so you don't have the strong community organizations. You don't have a lot of religious participation. You don't have churches, strong churches that can support the communities. I'm not talking about storefront churches," Elaine Allensworth, of the Consortium on Chicago School Research, told me.[18] "When you look at the very poorest neighborhoods in the city, they are really struggling to maintain strong institutions. You don't have a lot of economic opportunity. You don't have jobs for families or for kids. You also have problems with crime. That's antisocial capital. Not all communities have equal resources. If you're in a community with strong community organizations and people have the time and the connections that they can bring to bear to support the schools, it's going to be easier to have a strong school."

Principal Henderson sees another imbalance. She says: "When you zoom out, you'll also see that those poor black schools also don't have the best teachers. Also [they] don't necessarily have administrators that can deal with that reality. There's been research showing that the kids in the worst neighborhoods also have the worst teachers. I don't know that you can put one over the other and say that it's because of the community. Though poverty affects attendance in a lot of ways—that I cannot control. But again, if you've got the right teacher in the classroom, you can get around that. And I've just seen too many cases where teachers have been able to get past those inequities."

As principal, she does her best to go to bat for her teachers—who are black and white—and make them feel appreciated in tougher circumstances so they don't leave for higher-performing schools.

According to Gary Orfield, schools with concentrated poverty rarely compete with middle-class schools. "What really matters in schools are what is the quality and experience of your teachers, what is the level and delivery of the curriculum and what's the peer group like and the families of the peer group. You put kids who are very well prepared together in a competitive classroom with a teacher who knows what to do and who has a curriculum that's going to challenge those kids, and good things happen. In a high-poverty school, they face multiple problems, and one of them is there's not even basic stability. Neither the teachers nor students stay there for very long."

Schools need to be understood as rivers, not islands, Orfield explained. "People who live in poor neighborhoods basically don't stay there because they want to; they stay because they don't have other choices. And teachers who teach in them don't want to stay either. They leave as soon as they get choices. That means there is no long-term school community that really has the essentials for creating a good educational outcome."

Black middle-class parents have long worked within constructs of CPS to get their kids in better schools if they didn't go the private or Catholic route. For some of my friends, the transition to school out of their neighborhood wasn't always easy. Traveling from a less affluent black neighborhood to a more affluent white one made them feel like they lived two different lives. One friend who grew up in a rougher part of Morgan Park told me that by the time she reached eighth grade she had stopped going outside entirely and only went to the houses of school friends in Beverly. The boys she grew up with and their older brothers had become gangsters, wearing colors, twisted hats, with multiple visits to juvenile detention/group homes. "Things became increasingly sexualized, replete with all of the disrespect common in the music at the time, and all of my girlfriends started to become very sexual at an early age and had developed a penchant for stealing from the local stores. Me and my sister had lost our place, and, frankly, we didn't care. We had moved on as well."

My parents never considered sending me to our black neighborhood high school, which severely underperformed. Enrolling would have been as likely as me moving to the Soviet Union for boarding school. And I don't speak Russian. Same for my Chatham friends. Everyone I knew applied for and got accepted into public schools outside of our neighborhood boundaries, which extended well beyond Chatham into rougher sections of communities.

I tested into the seventh- and eighth-grade academic center at Morgan Park High School. Back then just two other high schools offered that accelerated, competitive junior high program. By eighth grade, my course load consisted mostly of freshman classes. Morgan Park surely wasn't the best high school in the city, but its college prep program, great counselors, respected international language program, Advanced Placement courses, sports teams and extracurricular activities made it a well-rounded experience. Hispanics from outside neighborhoods were bused in, promoting a different racial balance.

My love for school continued at Morgan Park. True to the 1990s era, boys looked like they walked off music video sets from either Boyz II Men or Jodeci. Girls rocked asymmetrical haircuts. We wore Girbauds, Champion T-shirts, carried Eddie Bauer portfolios and slung Coach bags over our shoulders. Michel'le's "Something in My Heart" and Art of Noise's "Moments in Love" were the slow-dance soundtracks at homecoming. Though our parents carefully curated our lives, we attended funerals and baby showers of peers and locker partners. A memorable school play written by a student took on teenage pregnancy, STDs, interracial dating and high schoolers having a good time dancing to Digital Underground. Mae Jemison, the first black female astronaut, had advanced through Morgan Park's widely acclaimed physics program, and our school newspaper—arguably the best student paper in the city and among the top in the state—eagerly covered her visit back. Morgan Park exhibited intraracial class diversity, and I take a lot of pride in being a CPS product. All of my peers from Morgan Park attended fine colleges and universities: Spelman, Northwestern, Penn, Princeton, Tennessee State and the University of Illinois.

Still, racial transitions in the student body and administration drew citywide attention and raised questions about how far black and white parents would go to participate in school integration.

In 1990, Morgan Park's local school council didn't renew the contract of the white principal. The vote split along racial lines—whites for, blacks against. White students walked out in support of Principal Walter Pilditch. Angry confrontations spiraled, leading to police clashes with students. The melee made the front page of the *Chicago Sun-Times*.[19] Several students, blacks included, were treated at nearby hospitals because they say police hit them with nightsticks. I don't remember much about that day except being herded into the school auditorium away from the drama and buckets of tears. At the time Morgan Park was roughly 70 percent black, 20 percent white and 10 percent Hispanic. Allegations of racism were hurled at Pilditch, himself a Morgan Park graduate, and local school council members. Some black students said Pilditch ignored racism complaints. Pilditch argued that test scores were up and that he disciplined two teachers for racial or derogatory remarks. He filed a lawsuit shortly after his firing in federal court and eventually won in 1992, in part because the court ruled those district-wide local school councils had too much power in firing principals.

Morgan Park's racial transition accelerated after Pilditch's departure and a series of black principals arrived.

In addition to its enhanced academic offerings, Morgan Park is a neighborhood high school for the integrated Beverly area, and the attendance boundaries extended to black parts of Morgan Park. In 2014, the school was 97 percent black and 87 percent low income, hardly reflective of the integrated neighborhood's demographic. Total student enrollment hovers around 1,300. In my day during the early 1990s, 2,000 students attended. Many white Beverly parents send their children to the local Catholic schools.

*   *   *

In 2009, Chicago asked for relief from desegregation efforts.

The federal court terminated the desegregation consent decree and monitoring, which required no school to be more than 35 percent white, stating that CPS demonstrated substantial good-faith compliance. "For more than 20 years the Board was dutiful in its commitment. The board filed annual reports with the Court detailing the Board's desegregation actions, integration of school-based faculty and the remediation of other practices necessary to satisfying its commitment. The United States never challenged or complained about the Board's efforts to bring about change, the efficacy of actions or the good faith with which it was operating," Judge Charles P. Kocoras wrote. His opinion said that the board "eliminated all vestiges of segregation 'to the extent practicable.'"[20]

The ruling meant that even CPS's limited and feeble efforts toward desegregation would no longer be legally mandated. Indeed, over the life of Chicago's consent decree, federal law had changed such that many believed CPS could not even use race as an admission criterion for vaunted magnet and selective-enrollment schools. District officials pretty much threw in the towel about integration, arguing it was impossible with only 8 percent white enrollment.

CPS created new socioeconomic tiers as a proxy for race:

- Median family income
- Percentage of single-parent households
- Percentage of households where English is not the first language
- Percentage of homes occupied by the homeowner
- Level of adult education attainment
- The performance of neighborhood schools in the area

It was only a matter of time before Chicago would take race out of the equation. A 2007 U.S. Supreme Court decision paved the way for the period we're in today on race and public schools. It invalidated voluntary school desegregation plans that used race as an admission criterion; the case stemmed from school districts in Seattle, Washington and Louisville, Kentucky: *Parents Involved In Community Schools v. Seattle School District, No. 1* and *Meredith v. Jefferson County School Board*.

"Class isn't race and race isn't class. They're related but they're different, and if you give preference on the basis of class alone, you're going to reward new immigrants who have high human capital but low current income," Gary Orfield told me. "Class is very poorly defined in our data systems." People recently divorced or sick may qualify as poor, but that's not the same as lifetime poverty.

Orfield's national research shows that segregation is typically by race and poverty. Black and Latino students tend to be in schools with a substantial majority of poor children while whites and Asians typically are in middle-class schools.

CPS sidesteps commenting on integration. When I've asked, officials provide hackneyed empty rhetoric and say they want good schools for all students. Steve Bogira of the *Chicago Reader* regularly writes about poverty and segregation. A top CPS official called racial integration laudable but told Bogira that the district's focus is quality for all students.

Bogira doesn't buy that philosophy. "Given what a thorny issue desegregation is, and how difficult it would be to achieve in Chicago's schools, it's understandable that education activists and officials, black and white, have resigned themselves instead to trying to make separate equal. But that's not working, either," he writes.[21] Race gaps in student achievement are most acute in black racially isolated schools.

Today CPS offers parents more high-performing high school choices for their children than it did 20 years ago. Chicago has both the best and the worst public schools in Illinois—which foments jockeying for coveted spots in the best-performing schools, especially among middle-class families. Overwrought parents of all races freak out over testing when their children are barely out of the womb. The result? White enrollment is increasing in elite public schools.

A 2014 *Chicago Sun-Times* investigation found more white students at selective-enrollment high schools on the city's North Side—some as high as 41 percent. The white population in those schools climbed after the consent decree was struck down.

The increase fulfilled predictions that minority students would be edged out of the city's top schools as a result of the judge lifting the consent decree. One parent characterized the new makeup of schools as "gated communities for children of privilege."[22]

Even though CPS is only 9 percent white, at myriad magnet, selective-enrollment, gifted and classical elementary schools, that percentage is more than double. (Conversely, white students are dramatically underrepresented in charter schools, where they make up only 1.7 percent of the overall population.) Some Chicago white parents shun outstanding schools that have a significant black population. McDade (92 percent black) and Poe (91 percent black) are public schools with selective enrollment and require testing for admission. They are among the top elementary schools in the entire state and happen to be on the South Side in black neighborhoods. These are just two examples; others exist on the high school level.[23]

White parents may decide not to vie for slots in these high-performance schools because of the distance from their homes and housing segregation patterns in the city. These outstanding schools invalidate ideas that black children are deficient and culturally incapable of high achievement. Separate but equal doesn't work, but that doesn't mean black children cannot thrive in school. Even though I emphasize that segregation doesn't work, I am not suggesting that there is something wrong with black children or black institutions. Racialized inequities are the problem.

Meanwhile, racism produces outrageous theater. Lenart is another top Illinois elementary school. In 2002, the school moved from a white South Side neighborhood to West Chatham. White parents used a code word—crime—to express their dismay about the school moving into a stable middle-class black community. Since the school moved, the white student population has decreased by more than half while the black student population continues to rise. Nevertheless, the elementary school remains a top one.

Diverse environments provide students with soft skills to succeed in an ever-evolving global society. Integration helps students of all races—including whites. Interracial contact can also reduce racial prejudice among students, and that exposure can help them later in life, in college and at work. Clearly, for some white CPS parents, diversity begins and ends when whites are the majority. Due to the city's hypersegregation, white parents equate the South Side with danger and dysfunction. In 2013, a baseball game between two selective-enrollment high schools was canceled when some North Side parents refused to let their children travel to the South Side for the game.[24] They were worried about safety. It's infuriating to witness the prejudices of people who swear they aren't prejudiced.

Kimberly Henderson, the Mollison principal, lives in Beverly and sends two of her children to high-performing elementary schools that require testing for entry. She grew up on the South Side, and her mother enrolled her in Catholic school instead of the neighborhood school.

"And I remember distinctly getting in trouble at school. The nun told them that I was bored, and the reason I was getting in trouble was because I was done with all my work and that they should test me," Henderson recalls. She tested into Poe, one of the top-performing elementary schools then and now. In seventh grade, Henderson tested into one of the academic center programs.

When Henderson had children, her view shifted from that of a CPS teacher to a parent who wanted to provide the same educational path. Her son attends one of the best high schools in the state, Lane Tech High School (44 percent Hispanic, 33 percent white, 10 percent Asian and 9 percent black). Her daughters tested into Lenart and McDade. They all test extremely high and love to read.

"It was just a foregone conclusion for me—that everybody would test to get into selective-enrollment schools."

Her fourth-grade son is the only one who attends an integrated neighborhood school—Sutherland, my alma mater, in Beverly. He has ADHD, and Henderson thinks the school can provide him with organization. Sutherland no longer has the busing program I was a part of, but it's a strong school that's naturally integrated because of the neighborhood.

All of those different schools make for hectic mornings in the Henderson house. Combing hair, cooking waffles, reminders of book bags and the day's schedule. The eldest, a senior in high school, is out the door by 5:30 a.m. to take public transportation. Henderson takes her two daughters—in third and sixth grades—to the exact same bus stop in two trips because of different pickup times. Selective-enrollment schools offer busing. Finally, she drops off her youngest son at Sutherland, just a few blocks away.

"I was still kind of bummed out because we didn't have anybody in the same school. But everybody's school, I feel, is perfect for them," Henderson told me.

She's had a jam-packed half day before she pulls into the parking lot at Mollison.

Henderson doesn't complain and is thinking ahead. She's prepping the younger three for academic centers, which are accelerated seventh- and eighth-grade programs embedded in a high school, similar to what I did for Morgan Park.

"I knew from my own experience that being in a regular grade elementary school, there was only so much we could do in terms of the rigor. Like we can never re-create what they do in the academic center," Henderson told me.

The family hasn't always lived in neighborhoods with great schools, but that never factored into how she planned to map out her children's education. When I asked her about the school choices she and her husband made, they sound a lot like what I hear from many black parents. Henderson doesn't focus on race. All of the children attend great schools that happen to be diverse or rooted in black excellence.

A recurrent argument is how schools can even begin to think about much less fix the problems of segregation if housing isn't addressed. Public schools merely reflect housing patterns. As long as segregation persists where people live, schools will by default be segregated. Indeed, housing plays a big factor because structural racism affects everything—housing, poverty, education, employment and so on. Our housing segregation patterns aren't by accident, and neither are our public schools. I take to heart Principal Henderson's no-excuses approach and her not having a problem running an all-black school. But I also see the uphill battles Mollison faces. I argue that the system purposefully leaves behind black neighborhood schools. "People basically look at the problem of segregation and say 'It is so big; there's no way we could solve it all so let's do nothing.' That's like saying cancer or heart disease is incurable. But for some people it really can be cured. So should we say if we can't really cure segregation, we don't do anything about it? That's basically the logic of Chicago and a number of big cities," Gary Orfield told me. "Imagination has completely failed in Chicago."

Chicago is a multiracial city where people aren't learning together or about each other. Despite hypersegregation, the city's diversity conceivably could open the door for interracial, interclass schools. New magnet schools across regional school boundary lines could be opened, Orfield explained.

No one solution can reverse decades of institutionalized racism. "You could take a major institution in Chicago—the Field Museum [of Natural History] or something—and create a regional magnet school together with one of the universities. How many people would want to go to that?" he asked.

Orfield suggests that nascent gentrification in some neighborhoods opens the door to support integrated neighborhoods. Changing attendance boundaries, building regional relationships for new schools or compelling the suburbs to play along by offering seats in their public schools are ideas that could work. None of these ideas is groundbreaking. Magnet schools have long promoted academic excellence while mitigating racial isolation. Connecticut, for example, has spent $2.5 billion to open new magnet schools in the Hartford region to encourage integration. Suburban districts have voluntarily offered students seats in public schools.[25] In late 2014, the state of New York education chief announced grants for a voluntary integration program to foster diversity in high-poverty school districts.[26]

A University of Minnesota Law School report in 2013 argues that magnet schools provide a number of models for enhancing education for urban students. "A survey of results for racially diverse magnets in the Twin Cities clearly suggests that students do best in stably integrated schools—schools that do not make the transition to predominantly non-white that is so common for racially diverse schools. Further, results in several other states also suggest that there are potential benefits for the region in pursuing magnet school-University partnerships."[27]

Another report by the University of Minnesota Law School—written by Myron Orfield, Gary Orfield's brother—argues for a regional integration district. It would create a variety of magnet schools and pro-integration affordable housing programs in high-opportunity neighborhoods.[28]

The imagination Gary Orfield touched on is not seen in Chicago.

To be sure, CPS has money for new schools. In 2014 the city announced a new selective-enrollment high school on the North Side near the former Cabrini-Green public housing development and right around the corner from another selective-enrollment high school. The announcement hints of pandering to white middle-class parents to not leave the city and promising that their children won't have to travel to the South Side. None of the elite testing high schools on the South Side has a significant white population.

When the controversy first raged over CPS shuttering 50 schools, I thought about the arguments in favor of closings: half-empty schools and depopulation in battered neighborhoods. Promises for better resources rang hollow. Underperforming schools closed, and students from them were transferred to equally underperforming schools a wee bit farther away. Again, this signifies no imagination. What a radical idea if CPS brought back widespread busing (currently it's for students attending selective-enrollment elementary schools) and dispersed those students to some of the top neighborhood or at least middling schools. CPS could have used the school closings to address segregation and promote integration. After all, the schools that closed were poor and racially isolated.

Sure, the circumstances were different for me and my family and our Chatham neighborhood, but I ruminate over the integrated elementary school experience of myself and my siblings—a magnet-like program and busing that worked. Educators and politicians commemorate *Brown v. Board of Education* for striking down separate but equal, but half a century later, we don't value its legacy. Instead of truly fixing school poverty and segregation in Chicago, district officials and political leaders avoid the problem and fail to provide meaningful discourse. To them, the problem is too big; that inaction implies tacit approval of separate yet unequal. And right now Chicago isn't even exploring ideas.

This photo was taken from a helicopter in 2012 looking north toward downtown. The Dan Ryan Expressway splits Chicago's South Side in two. / Photo by Bill Healy

A group of men in Englewood sit in the shade to avoid the summertime heat. Harold's Fried Chicken Shack is a popular fast-food chain. / Photo by Bill Healy

A liquor store sits on West 95th Street, just east of the Dan Ryan Expressway. / Photo by Bill Healy

Ornate greystone buildings are common in the city's Bronzeville neighborhood, like these on South Dr. Martin Luther King, Jr. Drive. / Photo by Bill Healy

Bill Ball has owned Abundance Bakery in Bronzeville for a quarter-century. The bakery is on 47th Street on a stretch also known as Tobacco Road. / Photo by Bill Healy

Me, my husband and three stepdaughters. In 2014 we moved to integrated Hyde Park on the South Side. / Photo courtesy of Natalie Y. Moore

A group of girls walk in Englewood. This building is across the street from one of fifty Chicago Public Schools that closed in 2013. / Photo by Bill Healy

Kimberly Henderson is principal at Irvin C. Mollison Elementary School in Bronzeville. / Photo by Bill Healy

My childhood Chatham home. / Photo by Bill Healy

The author and her grandparents at her eighth-grade graduation. / Photo courtesy of Natalie Y. Moore

My family in 1998 in the Beverly/Morgan Park home. / Photo © Dot Ward

Me; my grandfather, Joseph E. Moore Sr.; and brother Joey. /Photo courtesy of Natalie Y. Moore

Both sets of my grandparents with my parents on their wedding day in 1974 at Chicago City Hall. / Photo courtesy of Natalie Y. Moore

A typical block club sign in black Chicago neighborhoods. / Photo by Bill Healy

Children hold hands and form a circle in a Chicago park in 1941. This photo was taken as part of a project by the federal government to document life in the United States. / Photo by Edwin Rosskam

Dancers in the 2015 annual Bud Billiken back-to-school parade in the Bronzeville neighborhood. / Photo by Syd Falls

6

KALE IS THE NEW COLLARD

SWEET CANNED CORN AND CORNSTARCH CROWD A SHELF NEXT TO LOAVES OF
white bread and Louisiana Hot Sauce at a gas station. A window display stocks an arrangement of rainbow candy—Skittles and Starbursts. Rows of knockoff red Flamin' Hot Cheetos, Twinkies and sugary soft drinks bulge out on shelves behind the cashier. This gas station fashions itself as a convenience store or mini-mart—except customers can't walk in. The space only fits one person, the employee.

I drive past vacant lots and empty land in Englewood, a South Side neighborhood struggling with unemployment and poverty about 20 minutes south of downtown. Englewood is short on many retail amenities and services—full-service grocery stores and restaurants included. My office used to be in Englewood so I know how convenient it is to grab fast food when there's nothing else to eat in the neighborhood. I pass a Burger King and White Castle before pulling up in front of Chaz Food & Liquor, a corner store with a yellow facade and red lettering whose colorful motif reminds me of the Care Free Curl activator bottle. The store windows are dirty. Vertical metal bars guard the building on South Halsted. "Food" in the store name must be an ironic trick, as liquor and potato chips are the only items for sale. All of the store merchandise is behind either a glass door or a partition.

The gas station and the corner store are prominent grocery store options in a neighborhood where traditional grocers are scarce. Under different circumstances, this may not seem like a big deal. Why not pick up a candy bar or calorie-rich honey bun before pumping gas? In a free market society, why should a liquor store owner be responsible for selling any healthy food? Because the government says so. Both the corner store and the gas station accept food stamps and must provide nutritious options, according to federal requirements. The United States Department of Agriculture (USDA) administers the food stamp program, known as the Supplemental Nutrition Assistance Program (SNAP). There are a set of haphazardly enforced rules. This particular gas station ignores those requirements by failing to stock perishable goods. No fresh produce, no fresh meat, no dairy. It's also hard to believe that a *gas station* could meet the standard for SNAP benefits with more than half of its sales coming from eligible staple foods. Meanwhile, at Chaz Food & Liquor, bright signage boasts that the store accepts LINK, the Illinois food stamp card. The federal government prohibits the sale of liquor with food stamps. But the store makes money by selling high-fat, salty bags of potato chips (and similar junk food), all of which can be purchased with food stamps.

Gas stations and corner stores are types of fringe stores. In Chicago, more than 2,200 authorized food stamp retailers serve low-income customers. Fourteen percent include gas stations or liquor stores. Pharmacies and dollar stores comprise another 15 percent. In neighborhoods like Englewood, corner stores are what are available. They're not 7-Elevens. That's much too fancy. Most corner stores lack aesthetic appeal. Garish neon "food" and/or "liquor" lettering adorn the exteriors. Junk food trumps fresh food. Grocery items tend to be overpriced, and most fruit and vegetables are canned. Corner stores are also the poster child for peddling the infamous Flamin' Hot Cheetos—artificial red snacks that leave your fingers and tongue stained for hours. Each bag contains 26 grams of fat and a quarter of the amount of salt recommended for the entire day. In addition to the artificial coloring and flavoring, Ashley

Gearhardt, a clinical psychologist at the University of Michigan, calls this snack hyperpalatable, or highly addictive: "It's something that has been engineered so that it is fattier and saltier and more novel to the point where our body, brain and pleasure centers react to it more strongly than if we were eating, say, a handful of nuts. Going along with that, we are seeing those classic signs of addiction, the cravings and loss of control and preoccupation with it."[1]

I don't mean to be condescending by suggesting people shouldn't be able to buy candy, cookies or liters of soda pop with food stamps. It's perfectly legal. The point is that some stores are rewarded even when they violate USDA standards. Big money is involved. Across the country, SNAP provides $80 billion in food stamp benefits. Let's drill that down to a micro level. Chicago's South Side Roseland neighborhood, for example, is overrun with "fringe" grocery stores. On average, they earn $5,000 a week in food-stamp sales.

*   *   *

Everyone eats.

Food is a common denominator. Food is part of the human condition. Food nurtures fellowship.

Food access can be racist.

Most often segregation is examined and explained through the lens of housing and public education. But the mundane task of grocery shopping is an unlikely by-product of separate but unequal. "Food deserts"—large geographic areas with no or distant grocery stores, combined with an abundance of fast-food joints—contribute to health disparities in black communities. Picture grocery shopping at a gas station, liquor store or dollar store. Or trying to purchase (nonexistent) fruit and vegetables at a convenience store that loads its shelves with processed food. This is the grocery reality in many Chicago black neighborhoods, regardless of income. Black families earning $100,000 annually are not immune, proving that this issue goes beyond class and is squarely a race issue.[2] Retailers have long had an aversion to South Side neighborhoods, regardless of residents' incomes. We see racism, not classism, at work.

Despite the abundance of unhealthy food options, Englewood also leads the way in improving food choices. Tracts upon tracts of empty lots dot blocks upon blocks. Instead of considering the land as vacant deficits, urban agriculture disciples repurpose them as assets. Urban agriculture runs the gamut—from small community gardens to full-scale organic farming on acres of land—and growing food for self and neighbors in a sea of food deserts nourishes residents even as the long-term sustainability of such efforts remains dubious. Recently opened farmers' markets and the opening of new grocery stores coupled with a growing appetite for healthy food have had positive impacts. Meanwhile, a debate rages among food justice advocates about what grocery models work best in a neighborhood where junk food is the current grocery favorite. Luring big-box grocers and national chains compromises local entrepreneurship. Urban agriculture may seem like sharecropping if it is not handled delicately. Corner store owners must be coaxed into upgrading their businesses. But without a doubt, no other store created quite a stir as the upmarket Whole Foods, which announced in 2013 that it would open a store in high-poverty Englewood by 2016. That announcement ignited questions about affordability and gentrification in a low-income black neighborhood.

But again, everyone eats.

And food may be an unlikely strategy to help stabilize a place like Englewood. Attempts at transforming the food ecology are still very much works in progress. But many people are trying to change the way people shop, eat and grow food in the South Side.

To be sure, the American problems of obesity and poor health cut across race, class and geographic lines. We live in a "fast-food nation" that presents an "omnivore's dilemma." Conflicting messages abound. First Lady Michelle Obama's signature "Let's Move" program wants to solve childhood obesity within a generation through empowering schools, communities and parents to guide children to eat healthier. Juxtapose that with the Big Gulps and super-size portion messages shoved down our collective throats. School lunches appease a child's palate, while efforts to retreat from cheesy nachos and pizza have generated mixed results in school cafeterias. We also live in a foodie society that gushes over trends such as cupcakes, Sriracha sauce, bacon, gluten free and duck fat. U.S. farmers rely too much on corn and soybean subsidies, and questions persist about whether those commodities benefit the rural community and consumers. Pesticides threaten the environment. Several food thinkers, such as Mark Bittman and Michael Pollan, yearn for a national food policy to help stop preventable deaths caused by bad diets and to fix our muddled food system.[3]

In urban centers like Chicago, a broken food access system is about more than too many potato chips; it's a public health issue. In 2006, Chicago-based researcher Mari Gallagher published a report—which popularized the term "food desert"—titled "Examining the Impact of Food Deserts on Public Health in Chicago" that found that they exist almost exclusively in black areas. Simply put, in these areas, the nearest grocery store is roughly twice the distance as the nearest fast-food restaurant, which overlaps with higher rates of obesity in those neighborhoods.

"All of these findings point to one conclusion: communities that have no or distant grocery stores, or have an imbalance of healthy food options, will likely have increased premature death and chronic health conditions, holding other influences constant . . . it is clear that food deserts, especially those with an abundance of fast food options, pose serious health and wellness challenges to the residents who live within them and to the City of Chicago as a whole," Gallagher's report said.[4]

In Englewood, the death rates from stroke, diabetes-related illnesses and coronary heart disease are higher than city averages. According to Gallagher's report, people who live in majority white, Latino or diverse tracts travel the shortest distance to any type of grocery store. The report concluded that more than 20 percent, or 550,000 Chicagoans—a substantial number of them single mothers and children—live in food deserts.

Gallagher updated her findings in 2011 with a progress report. In five years, the population living in food deserts had been reduced by 166,428, with that number moving to what she dubbed a "food oasis"—a place with an uptick in healthy options. Still, 70 percent of the total food desert population is black. Gallagher concluded: "Unless conditions improve, we predict continued premature death and suffering of Chicago Food Desert residents from diabetes, hypertension, cardiovascular disease and certain kinds of cancer. We also predict continued high rates of obesity among adults and children. . . . [T]hose who suffer most will be African American adults and children."[5]

WHOLE FOODS

In a peculiar way, Whole Foods and Walmart are similar national chains, albeit on opposite ends of the economic scale. Both have an aversion to unions. Both have opened in places outside their demographic sweet spot, and fears, denunciations and head scratching have commenced.

Highbrow Whole Foods (pet name "Whole Paycheck") lures yuppies with a penchant for its organic produce and its bevy of artisan cheeses, natural health products and free-range meats. In some stores, you can push your shopping cart while sipping a craft beer or Sauvignon Blanc. Whole Foods gets pilloried for nurturing food elitism—with the sticker-shock receipt as proof. Shopping bags inscribed with "Kale Is the New Collard" further accusations of haughtiness.

Lowbrow Walmart, the world's largest retailer, oozes all the charm of a drab strip mall. The discount chain commands the market by offering competitively priced or, better yet, cheap wares. The big-box operator routinely comes under fire for not paying employees fair wages and hiring undocumented workers—and then turning them over to authorities. Walmart represents the homogenization of suburbia and rural life. Thanksgiving Day is barely a holiday for shoppers and employees; Black Friday commences before the turkey gets cold.

Whole Foods and Walmart eventually tapped out their respective core bases: affluent urban areas and rural and suburban markets. Hence, both have made new urban forays, viewed as plucky moves. Walmart originally met resistance during the 2000s in union stronghold Chicago. It took years for the Arkansas-based company to gain city approval to build a store, which resulted after Mayor Richard M. Daley overrode the city council. To shore up support, Walmart officials used the hooks of food deserts and lack of jobs in South and West Side neighborhoods.

Consequently, stores have opened in the very same places devastated by deindustrialization and unemployment. Englewood seemed to be a place where Walmart would affix its blue font and golden spark logo. Instead, Whole Foods shocked Chicagoans when it announced that it would open an 18,000-square-foot store in Englewood.

Walter Robb, co-chief executive of Whole Foods, made the announcement in Englewood at Kennedy-King College, one of the city's two-year colleges that has a lauded culinary program.

"We realize the first step is to listen to what people in Englewood actually want. We know that we can do certain things but we know without partnering with the community, it doesn't really amount to anything. This is not a helicopter-in drop, build a store. This is a situation where we start to meet people and learn and listen to what's needed here," Robb said.[6]

Michael Bashaw, Midwest regional president of Whole Foods, responded to questions about affordability in a neighborhood that has 25 percent unemployment and 42 percent of residents living below the poverty level by saying: "We think this is an opportunity to bring a store to a community that would like us to be there and we would like to be a partner with the community. Some items may be somewhat cheaper and some will be similarly priced. We do competitive pricing analysis constantly. And we know that we are more competitively priced than what some people would perceive based on identical items." Executives touted the private-in-house 365 Everyday Value line as being competitively priced.[7]

The immediate response to the announcement resulted in comments sections of news stories filled with race-baiting about residents stealing from the store, killing each other and continuing to eat unhealthy sticky buns and soda pop. *The Economist* quoted an Englewood resident saying it is easier to buy guns and drugs than food in the neighborhood—fueling the stereotype of guns and violence as all-day, everyday norms.[8]

Twitter lost it. Tweets included racist musings from whites and low-expectation reactions from blacks. "@WholeFoods is opening a store in Englewood, Chicago. . . . Whoever thought this is a good idea has gotta be on drugs." "@WholeFoods is making plans to open a store in Englewood. Chicago will have the healthiest gangbangers in the nation." "They're building a whole foods in Englewood. One of the worst pars [*sic*] of Chicago. Foolish."[9]

Shortly after the Whole Foods press conference, I read a Facebook post from a black person predicting that "niggas have been given notice" that they will be kicked out of Englewood by 2016. Gentrification jitters fluttered at the idea of Whole Foods entering the neighborhood. But it's not Pottery Barn. It's *food*. Everyone eats. A perverse type of reverse racism surfaced during the hullabaloo of the announcements: Poor black people and black people, in general, didn't *deserve* a Whole Foods; let them cling to their honey buns and Flamin' Hots.

Englewood is part of a broader strategy for Whole Foods, which has expanded its reach by committing to food deserts and under-served "inner-city" markets. In 2013, the Austin-based chain won over Detroiters, making it the first national grocer to open in the city in years. Food justice advocates partnered with the chain to ensure employment opportunities and healthy-cooking classes. Local products line the shelves, including a hibiscus tea that Marcus Garvey's Black Star Line chef created. These days the chef's great-granddaughter is mass-producing the recipe in Detroit. On grand opening day, the Detroit store sold more produce than any other store that opened in the history of Whole Foods. In New Orleans, a Whole Foods anchored a local fresh food retailer initiative to bring healthy eating and economic revitalization to a corridor with commercial challenges after Hurricane Katrina. A Whole Foods broke ground in Newark, New Jersey, an area dogged by images of urban decay, in the summer of 2015.

In fall 2014, I met Whole Foods co–chief executive Walter Robb at a press conference in the community garden of Miles Davis Academy, a public school in Englewood. Whole Foods Foundation pledged $20,000 to eight local public schools to support their gardens to help school-children learn to eat healthier. Robb, dressed casually in jeans, engaged with students who cheerfully showed off their lemon sorrel and oregano. Robb and I chatted briefly about Englewood and various food dynamics in the neighborhood.

While many black neighborhoods are overrun with crappy food, there's nothing special about eating "farm to table." Black people have done it. Even on the South Side of Chicago, my father had a hobby backyard garden in the 1980s where he grew tomatoes, greens, radishes, peppers and a dozen other vegetables. We were organic and didn't even know it. Leftovers were put in plastic bags and given to neighbors and family members. I learned that, at the end of summer, we could take green tomatoes, wrap them in newspaper and put them in a dark area of our basement to turn them red.

My pleasant exchange with Robb led to a phone interview a few months later about Whole Foods' position in the grocery ecology. Robb is keenly aware of the store's image as a purveyor of white elitism. He told me that several years earlier, he started reflecting on those critiques and wanted to know why. "Natural food or whole food—with a small 'w'—in its truest form is really just foods of different cultures and different communities. I mean, you're talking about different grains that have been eaten on the planet for forever, right? And if you look at traditional diets of different cultures, there's nothing elitist about them at all. In fact, in some ways, this whole [healthy eating] movement began with looking at simplifying things and looking back to traditional whole foods, traditional whole diets."[10]

Robb's journey in trying to change the elite paradigm of Whole Foods began with his friend USDA secretary Tom Vilsack, who took him to Detroit in 2009. There Robb learned the health disparities between the black city and the white suburbs. He says finding a way to serve broader communities became a moral issue.

Robb approached Whole Foods senior staff and his co–chief executive and asked for a bit of faith and trust in his pitch. "As I started learning about Detroit and seeing what was happening there, this seemed like a very constructive step for us to take as a company and a direction in which we could make a contribution. And the more I learned, the deeper it went, the further it went, the further it took us into elitism and racism and cultural relevancy and community relationships and how people perceive companies and all these areas we unfolded in our journey in Detroit," Robb told me.

Robb learned that black Detroiters didn't need lectures from white people on how to eat healthy. He's also had black people tell him that he shouldn't make the store a "Half Foods"; he should ensure the store is stocked with quality products because no one wants a bootleg version. When Mayor Rahm Emanuel called Robb to consider a Chicago location, Robb drove around Englewood and observed the wilderness of open urban food-less space. But he bristles at the term "food desert": "I think it's insulting to the communities to sort of suggest that they have nothing going on, when in fact there's a tremendous amount going on. It's a term that needs to go away, that needs to be replaced by something that's much more positive and constructive."

Robb explained that Whole Foods isn't embarking on a charity mission by opening stores in underserved areas. In Detroit and Englewood, the business model evolved because the real estate costs were much lower in their respective parts of town, which, in turn, makes items in the grocery aisles cheaper.

"But it is a business. Detroit is profitable and I expect Englewood will be a successful business as well. I know people are making fun of us and saying all sorts of things and I don't really care because in the end, we're putting real money down, we're creating real jobs, we're making really new suppliers. As long as it's done respectfully in a way that's culturally relevant and that's guided by the community, I think it's a positive thing," Robb explained.

That said, Whole Foods doesn't plan to be ubiquitous. Chicago, Detroit, New Orleans and Newark are just four stores in grocery-challenged areas. The company predicts 500 stores globally by 2017, and the longer-term goal is to have 1,200 in the United States. "But [opening stores in food-challenged areas is] a meaningful part of our growth because it's so purpose driven, right, intentional around taking our purpose and trying to make it real. And you know, I said in Detroit, we have brought a point of light to the city of Detroit. But I hope that we're a large enough, big enough, open enough company to recognize that Detroit is a point of light for us. Or, in other words, I hope we can learn as much as we can contribute," Robb concluded.

A little more than a year after the store opened in the Midtown neighborhood, *Slate* writer Tracie McMillian challenged whether Whole Foods could change the way poor people in Detroit eat. "At the prices I saw this fall, it's hard to see how eating a healthy diet, with lots of produce, would be an affordable option if you were to shop primarily at Whole Foods."[11] McMillian found that fresh items were 58 percent more expensive and packaged items were 4 percent more costly compared to other area stores.

But Robb is undeterred. For him, shopping is voluntary, and Whole Foods' presence is not causing anyone to give up choices. And he maintains that in some instances, there's a trade-off in buying the cheapest or the most expensive food.

"I'm under no illusion that we're the guiding light, but I definitely think it's been a positive step and a constructive step and it's part of what needs to happen here. And I see this as being a step in my own personal learning and growth as a citizen, as what I hope will be a more multicultural society that has more tolerance and is accepting and understanding of different situations. So that's what I've experienced. And my hope for Whole Foods is as we take these steps, we stretch, we bend, we learn and how that will help our company to improve is still to be seen."

Naomi Davis, the founder of Blacks in Green, a local nonprofit dedicated to environmental principles in black communities, shakes her head at Whole Foods.

"It is a Trojan horse for the gentrification of Englewood," she told me.[12] "It's been a long time coming. It's a plan that was hatched a long time ago that's coming into fruition." Davis explained that the new street lamps and street paving from years earlier are her telltale signs. "If they [the city] had invested that money into an academy for incubating neighborhood businesses, you'd have a completely different neighborhood." The city did invest in a new community college with a culinary program. "But the private side is a luxury grocery? If economic development isn't structured to increase household income, what the hell is it doing?

"Whole Foods hasn't gotten its lie straight. They say [the Englewood store] is not philanthropy. But then suddenly it's all about 'we want to make sure our food is affordable.' How do you do that within your business model? Nobody has explained," Davis continued.

Food justice advocate and Englewood resident Sonya Harper disagrees. She told me that, growing up in Englewood, her family never shopped in the neighborhood. It's not something she thought about. It was as habitual as eating dinner together. Harper says Whole Foods has made a meaningful connection in Englewood in a way no other grocer has.

Practically speaking, Whole Foods' presence is simple.

"It'll increase our options by one," Harper told me.[13]

I attended one of the early community meetings an Englewood neighborhood group held with a Whole Foods representative. Residents asked about affordability, but the prevailing sentiment was that people were happy something new was coming to their often-maligned neighborhood. Jobs. More food options.

* * *

On a narrow, one-way street, Donna Summer's "Bad Girls" blasts out of a one-story home in Englewood. It's a Saturday morning, and the song is part of a soundtrack for weekend chores. On the same street—smack in the middle of a residential block—Growing Home's Wood Street Urban Farm celebrates an open house. Baskets of collard greens, arugula, scallions, radishes, kale, beets and turnips bask under the warm autumn sun. Swarms of bees circle the bounty on this September day. Homemade apple coleslaw soaked in lemon and honey sits out on tables along with freshly made guacamole and a black bean salad. I overhear a woman tell her friend that she would never eat that kind of food before coming here.

The year-round urban farm opened in 2007 in the shadow of a viaduct on a vacant Englewood lot. Several years later, it became the city's first USDA-certified organic farm. Several warm hoop houses ensure harvests throughout the year, even in the frigid winter. Every Wednesday in the summer and fall, farmers set up a market, selling everything from purple basil to lemon cucumbers.

This is a picture of urban agriculture.

In 2005, Englewood residents designed a quality-of-life plan for their neighborhood. In the quest to uplift the community via schools, housing and economic development, urban agriculture surfaced as a twofold strategy: employment engine and method to increase the availability of fresh produce. That led the nonprofit Growing Home, Inc. to expand its agriculture-based job training program to Wood Street. The transitional employment is aimed at helping people who were formerly incarcerated, homeless and overcoming substance abuse. Trainees learn to farm in Englewood and on a farm 75 miles south of Chicago. More than 90 percent of Growing Home graduates go on to full-time permanent employment.

DeAndre Brooks already had a passion for food when he started at the Wood Street farm in 2012. He had tired of going in and out of jail on gun and drug charges. While working for a carpet-cleaning business, Brooks cooked dinners on the side and delivered fresh catfish, jerk chicken and pork chop meals to beauty salons and currency exchanges. A friend told him about Growing Home, and after he finished his training, the nonprofit hired him full-time. As a crew leader, he grows and harvests at the farm.

"It's a desert over here," Brooks said of Englewood. "If you don't try to push out the word of how food should be, you'll never know. All you know is what you see in your local market." He's slowly weaned his children off Flamin' Hots and introduced them to Swiss chard. Brooks's long-term goal is to have his own food truck with soul food without beef and pork.[14]

Opportunities beyond the Growing Home farm are important to Sonya Harper. She returned to her community to do outreach for the social enterprise up until 2015. As a black woman, sometimes her work presents conflicts. She's a convert to the urban agriculture movement and agrees with the premise, but she's irked that most people excited about urban ag in Englewood aren't from the community or people of color.

Harper is part of the grassroots Grow Greater Englewood coalition, which is trying to act as a food-system watchdog as well as drum up community interest. When one local foundation doled out grant money, Harper says no one from Englewood applied. And she doesn't just want residents toiling on the land owned by others. "My vision is that I would like to see at least half of any urban ag projects be done by any entity in the community with black people. I'm just going to say it," she told me.

Urban agriculture is in demand. The city has embarked on a long-term green and healthy neighborhood initiative over the next couple of decades that includes urban ag. But the discipline of urban ag is very skills based, so many larger nonprofits with direct experience are signing up; and many of those groups aren't black-run. Some efforts already have gone belly up, such as a couple of farmers' markets and a former city bus that loaded up with fresh produce and drove around food deserts. In 2015 the bus hit the streets again with a new business plan. Other programs rely on subsidies and grants to stay afloat. And as utopian as growing greens on vacant land sounds, how does someone earn a living wage harvesting collards?

That's the quandary for L. Anton Seals Jr., a community activist who serves on the Grow Greater Englewood coalition with Harper.

"Developing urban ag may be a Trojan horse in our community. There's a reason why we [in the United States] have large agribusinesses. [Farming] takes a long time. If you want to grow something, you're not on your time. Seeds won't grow faster because you want them to. We live in a midwestern city—November through March—you're not doing that." He also works with the Eat to Live Garden in Englewood that is supported in part by a North Side community farm. Seals says the urban ag movement focuses too much on employing rather than using the tracts of land for black self-determination, so that blacks can grow their own crops. Eat to Live hopes to foster small business incubators. "What I envision is black-owned stores offering locally sourced fruits and vegetables from Eat to Live—folks making stuff and putting in stores; soap, shea butters, pies all in one place."[15]

Seals told me that he understands that behavior has to be changed to get people to shop at urban ag and that not all growers will be black. "When it comes to advocacy, I'm still struggling with this. You want access but then big places want to come to Englewood." He paused, showing his own sense of conflict. "It's still being figured out. There hasn't been a big pool of money because the yield is so low."

Meanwhile, Chicago's last black-owned full-service grocery store closed in 2008. It was in Chatham. After 25 years, the owners wanted to move on, and their sons expressed no interest in the business. Two Arab businessmen bought Chatham Food Center.

Language around food access is tricky. On one hand, the term "food desert" is a potent visual descriptor. On the other, it paints a negative image. "To me, when you think of a desert, you think of something dry and desolate and nothing happening, and it ignores the assets that are already there. When you take that approach, it's a sexy term and people latch onto it. It doesn't boil down for a sound bite. It made it easier for people to come in and say we'll give water for your desert," Seals explained. By "people" here he means corporations.

Naomi Davis is a transplanted New Yorker who lives in Chicago and often waxes about her childhood in a middle-class black Queens, New York, neighborhood awash in small businesses. She's a big proponent of neighborhood-owned businesses and keeping cash flows and profits within a community. Local models and support for mom-and-pop grocers have been overlooked, she told me. Davis believes the big-box or corporate model is counterproductive for black communities because that model extracts wealth from neighborhoods. "Why would Michelle Obama get behind fake grocery stores to come to the neighborhood, such as Walgreens?" The Chicago-based drugstore chain— a staple in any neighborhood, including underserved ones—has committed to being an oasis in a food desert. "I don't have a particular beef with Walgreens, but enterprises like Walmart are not the solution— period or exclamation point. And yet they've been touted from the White House on down, congratulated. An apple is $1.39 at Walgreens. *One* apple. That's not a grocery store; that's a convenience store at the corporate level."

* * *

The corner is a place to talk shit, drink, socialize, chill.

In the song "The Corner," Common rapped: "We talk play lotto & buy German beers" and "It's so black packed with action that's affirmative." The Last Poets chimed in: "The corner was our Rock of Gibraltar, our Stonehenge / . . . Our testimonial to freedom, to peace and to love."

The intersection of race and food is also at the corner.

On West 69th Street in Englewood, a small corner store is near a heavily trafficked corner next to an empty, garbage-strewn lot. The store's name isn't even on the building, but plenty of pictures of products are: popcorn, meat, milk, detergent and juice. Security bars adorn the outside. The owner painted them blue, but the effect is still a prison feel. Inside, the front of the store is packed with candy, chips and artificially flavored drinks. The floor tile is cracked. When it rains, the ceiling leaks, dripping onto those cracked tiles.

A store like this can be found on any street in any food desert. Despite their unsavory reputation, corner stores are important in such neighborhoods because they are the existing economic food model. That model isn't inherently bad. The problem is that these stores perpetuate unhealthy eating. When run properly, they can fill in food gaps. Corner stores don't have to be de facto junk-food depots.

The Inner-City Muslim Action Network (IMAN) understands the corner store paradigm and the intersection of race and health. Black neighborhoods, Arab store owners. Community organizers launched Muslim Run in 2010 to appeal to the sensibilities of Arab Muslim store owners: sell less junk, stock healthy food.

"Oftentimes we think about Latinos and blacks, but what about Arabs and blacks, right? Arabs are operating in these neighborhoods 60, 70 hours a week. And also, what does it really mean to be a store that is owned by Arabs, Muslims?" Shamar Hemphill, who's black and an IMAN organizer, asked me. "Sociologists always talk about this middleman minority complex. These stores operate within that same realm if we're not pushing them to do that or anything beyond just my store's making some dollars. It's beyond a community obligation, it's a human rights violation if you have a store and you're operating it at low standards."[16]

When Muslim Run first started, IMAN interviewed Arab store owners and black residents. Racial stereotypes peppered responses from both groups. The former thought black customers were shady, and the latter thought Arab business owners treated them like shit. Many owners argued that they didn't stock fresh produce because people wouldn't buy it. After IMAN doled out grant money to stores for refrigeration and fresh apples and bananas, people actually did buy them.

At the 69th Street location, the corner store owner replaced candy in the front with produce from local urban agriculture endeavors. IMAN has adopted the store. Organizers want to help it stock organic, halal meat and ensure that there's a consistent rotation of fruit in the front in addition to injecting some aesthetic appeal. IMAN believes corner stores can be beautiful: no metal bars, no bulletproof glass. Positive interactions between black and brown people.

"There's a culture where people come in and may not immediately feel like—yo, why do you have this here? Why is this there? Why is this old? Why isn't this clean?" Hemphill said of the store. "But what we're doing is working through some of the best business strategies and practices to begin to show them—because remember, they don't have a model or they don't have a business degree to really show them. We're going to have a business liaison come in every week that's a resident from the community that will check in with about looking at the products, what's old, what's right. Remove this off the floor, set this here."

Ashraf Asmail is from Palestine and moved to the United States in 2003. He co-owns the corner store with his brother, who opened it originally. At IMAN's urging, Asmail agreed to experiment with selling fresh produce. His English is a little broken, but I ask him why he decided to participate.

"Because I thought this is a real good idea. At the end of the day, this is junk and because, for me, I know, I'm a human and I study nutrition, okay? Real food is better than something junk. The vegetable and the fruits is rich, you know? From one apple you can survive. But not from a candy or from cigarettes or whatever," Asmail explained.[17]

He says people have definitely been buying the fruit. "If I make my cost and I'm losing nothing and everything's moving fast, I got two benefits. I'm not losing nothing and they got something healthy and fresh."

On a weekday afternoon, IMAN showed up at the no-name 69th Street corner store. A group of visiting Malaysian musicians lined up in front and beat their drum to incredulous onlookers. The store has hosted community meetings and eventually will offer cooking demonstrations in back.

"What we're trying to do is show the viability of what we can use—how we can use our spaces, our corner stores. More than just stores where we purchase food. We know it's the intersection in cities like Chicago. Most people come and hang out, and what we want to do is give them a whole different type of experience, and we want to show the store owner that he can utilize the space," Hemphill explained.

Uplifting corner stores as a food access solution is logical. Durable chains Aldi and Food-4-Less have an Englewood presence, but traditional grocers eschew neighborhoods like this one. Therefore, why beg them to open? Corner stores can be bright as a sunflower and as nutritious as a honey crisp apple.

When I moved to the integrated South Side neighborhood Hyde Park, I had walkable grocery options. There is a full-service grocery store and a lovely corner store a block away with a clean interior and kind staff. The shelves are stocked. The halal store sells an array of olive oils, lentils and spices. If that seems too "exotic," consider the coffee machine, fresh meat, shiny fruit and sticks of appropriately priced butter. And yes, the store carries Flamin' Hot Cheetos and other chips, but they aren't the dominant display. My own understanding of corner stores and their neighborhood benefits expanded once I lived near some with ample variety.

That wasn't always my reality. I used to live in a food desert in Bronzeville, but because I had a car, I could drive to get the groceries I needed. If I had stayed in my neighborhood, my option would have been the junk-food corner store variety with dubious-looking meat.

I also shop at Whole Foods. The store may have changed public discourse about food like no other grocer, bringing terms like "organic," "artificial additives" and "genetically modified foods" to people's consciousness. But the chain is nectar for white yuppies. That pesky "Whole Paycheck" label is not for naught. I've vacillated between loving the store and giving it the side-eye. In the past, I've yelled at myself, an admitted impulse shopper, for spending $150 on two bags of food. And for a spell I rejected Whole Foods because I felt its premise cultivated elitism around healthy eating. Yet excellent customer service, smoked gouda spread, eggnog gelato and English cheddar cheese seduce me.

When I lived in a food desert, I had car privilege to shop elsewhere. When I moved to a food oasis, I experienced life in a healthy neighborhood.

In my years of reporting on food access issues in Chicago, I learned that building new grocery stores isn't the only answer. Food justice advocates promote more. Nutritional education must be a component in neighborhoods where fresh produce on store shelves isn't the norm to change shopping habits and behaviors. A number of farmers' markets offer cooking classes to teach people how to sauté green vegetables. Opportunities for community engagement, from cooking demonstrations to working with mothers of infants on public assistance, have emerged. These days public schools promote healthier school lunches with student cooking contests or campus gardens. Each year food stamp spending at farmers' markets increases in Illinois and the Midwest as a whole. But putting a dent in food deserts and improving health outcomes is going to require a long-term strategy. The demand for fresh food won't happen overnight.

* * *

Chicago's meatpacking district sits in the western shadow of downtown. In 1990, Oprah planted her Harpo studio flag there and changed the desolate warehouse strip into a funky turf of glittering restaurants, champagne salons on cobblestone alleys and art galleries in lofts.

One Friday night, I met up with my friend Jenny at the newish Green Street Smoked Meats. Reviews raved about the meats. We arrived at 5 p.m., when the spot opened, and already a line had formed for the cafeteria-style service. The atmosphere is shabby chic, rustic barnyard. No servers take your orders, and you eat off napkins and paper plates. An early-bird crowd consisted of families with babies in fashionable strollers. As the night progressed, groups of friends and dates gathered at the communal tables, tearing apart meat with their fingers. Jenny and I ordered salmon, a slab of ribs, fried pickles and broccoli salad. When the cashier rang everything up to $51, I thought I misheard. The food tasted good, not great. Even though I knew it was in a high-rent area and part of a "scene," I still couldn't get over how much everything cost. I'm not cheap, but something bothered me about the experience. Jenny summed it up: "It's no Lem's."

Lem's Bar-B-Q is a South Side takeout institution. Rib tip and hot link smoke billows down the entire block. A whole slab costs $25 and comes with fries. I have no idea if Lem's wants to expand. People who dine at Green Street are part of a foodie scene. Both restaurants exist in their respective enclaves with their respective clienteles, but what nags me is that food gaps in Chicago aren't limited to grocery stores. Those gaps seep into other areas as well.

For example, the South Side is short on sit-down, non-diner restaurants compared to the North Side, but there's no shortage of comfort food. Southwest Side Latino neighborhoods boast the best taquerias. Never mind all the white fried chicken joints spilling over downtown and the North Side. We have Harold's Chicken Shack, a venerable chain that masters the sublime mild sauce, all over the South Side. Food Network's *Diners, Drive-Ins and Dives* highlighted the wrong fried shrimp place in Chicago, Big & Little's. Haire's Gulf Shrimp on South Vincennes runs circles around the competition, and it always tickles me to read white Yelp reviewers who consciously note how far they drove to get, in their estimation, the best local fried shrimp. At my job, we once conducted a tummyache-inducing doughnut crawl as part of a radio experiment to pinpoint the best independent-owned shop in Chicago. The underdog winner hailed from the Roseland neighborhood on the South Side—and it cost a third less than all the doughnut du jour eateries that have popped up in the city.

Perhaps the division between North and South Side restaurants shouldn't be judged by which one has the most white-linen tablecloths, craft cocktails or number of servers. But those disparities resonate with me for myriad reasons: lack of capital for would-be entrepreneurs, co-opting of food deemed as ethnic and perceptions some have about crossing their own mental/physical boundary within the city for savory sustenance.

Orrin Williams thinks so too.

As a black urban ag vet, he and his partners want the South Side Washington Park Perry Street Farm to stand in contrast to other local programs. Located on the other side of the expressway separating Englewood and Washington Park, Perry Street celebrated its first harvest in 2014. Kale and watermelon grew on the one-acre plot. Across the street is a single-family home that serves as the farm's headquarters. It stands alone in the middle of an open field. No other houses are on the block.

The erstwhile living room walls are chalkboard on one side and dry-erase boards on the other. Scribbled on them are the phrases "South Side renaissance," "community economics" and "impact soil." As Williams and I talk, I can hear the gurgling of aquaponics. In the building, old water bottles grow basil and lettuce with the help of pet store fish.

Williams wants people to be farmers and make a livable wage by doing so. He doesn't knock the job training urban ag initiatives but told me: "We don't want to be a workforce-development program. We want people to come with skills that we can put to use."[18]

Perry Street harvested another crop in 2015, but all the rest is in the infancy stage as grants are applied for and different funding models are explored. The strategy is to build up the community via a food system.

"How long are we going to be dependent on California with its droughts? That's food insecurity." Like L. Anton Seals Jr. and Sonya Harper, Williams understands that growing and selling fresh fruits and vegetables may not be enough to create living-wage jobs. How can bagged lettuce, pies and kale chips be transformative?

But a grocery store co-op could be. Williams says Perry Street Farm is creating a small village that mirrors the way other neighborhoods place value on local small businesses, not chains. For Williams, a nearby cafe could buy its herbs and salad mix from the farm. The South Side could have its share of locally sourced cafes and restaurants that are warm and inviting—more than takeout. The goal of the Perry Street Farm creators is to use a food-based enterprise system to grow small businesses while providing fresh food.

There are a great many ideas about how to fix our segregated food system: improving corner stores, holding grocery stores accountable, promoting entrepreneurship, holding food stamp retailers more accountable and educating consumers around healthy food choices. No one way is going to cure food ills; a multipronged strategy is necessary ultimately to change the way people shop, eat, regard their health and grow food.

This is nothing lofty or esoteric. Because, after all, everyone eats.

7

WE ARE NOT CHIRAQ

For as long as there is residential segregation, there will be de facto
segregation in every area of life.

—Martin Luther King Jr.

I HATE THE NICKNAME CHIRAQ.

The slang term combines "Chicago" and "Iraq" (pronounced shy-rack), a sly, albeit ham-fisted, way of linking violence in the two locales. Some young people brandish the Chiraq moniker with the same kind of pride reserved for the Michael Jordan era of the Chicago Bulls. Rapper King Louie is credited with inventing the terms "Chiraq" and "Dril-linois." He's a drill artist, and drill music is a subgenre of pulsating hip-hop originating in the South Side (hence "Drillinois.) The trend is being capitalized on with Chiraq T-shirts that juxtapose a machine gun with the city's skyline or the word emblazoned over a state map or decorated with the red, black and green colors of the Iraqi flag. There's no solidarity with Iraqis, just a failed metaphor. The term has expanded beyond the city. Nicki Minaj made a "Chiraq" song featuring local rapper Lil Herb. Meek Mill made one too, featuring local rapper Lil Durk. Not to be out-done by non-Chicagoans headlining "Chiraq" songs, South Sider Katie Got Bandz freestyled her own version. All of the rappers used the same beat. When acclaimed filmmaker Spike Lee in 2015 decided to call his movie, centered on South Side violence, *Chi-Raq*, controversy over the name ratcheted up a notch because of the pall it casts over the city. The movie is a satire that borrows from the Greek comedy *Lysistrata*, in which women perform a sex strike to stop a war.

My disdain for the word isn't about respectability politics or blocking Lee from the moviemaking tax breaks some local politicians proposed during the filming. The name "Chiraq" is more than a pop culture moment or young black people in the city reciting a harmless badge of honor. It's actually racist. "Chiraq" plays on fear running throughout the black community. We are internalizing what we are told about black places being violent. Language impacts us. The media influences us. We fear black bodies. We fear young people of color. We become what we think we are. We think we are Al Capone 2.0 Chicago in blackface. If comparisons are going to be made between Chicago and Iraq, compare the federal spending in the Middle East with what is spent in U.S. urban neighborhoods. People who don't live or visit these neighborhoods think there are Wild West shoot-outs on every corner. War imagery denotes tanks, bombings, assault rifles and people under siege. The metaphor ignores the real predicament in segregated neighborhoods and dismisses residents as mere anonymous war casualties.

Chicago activist Mariame Kaba once told me that by constantly referring to some communities as war zones, we trap ourselves into considering only those solutions that are steeped in a punishment mind-set. The state is then the punisher. Kaba explains:

> When we adopt war metaphors to characterize how we live in our communities, we put a ceiling on our imaginations for how we might address violence and harm. After all, you can only respond to tanks with more artillery and not with a peace circle. Restorative or transformative justice requires us to build trust and to establish relationships. This is difficult to do in "war zones" where suspicion and lack of trust are the order of the day.[1]

Chicago is not the murder capital of America, much less murder capital of the Midwest—more on murder rates versus number later. Violence in

Chicago has long been misinterpreted, celebrated and racialized when in fact it's actually a symptom of inequity. Racial and economic segregation allow violence to fester in low-income black communities. The most brutal enclaves of the city are the most troubled Chicago neighborhoods—poor, characterized by excessive unemployment, blight, food deserts, underperforming schools, high rates of preventable diseases, lack of economic development. Each year thousands of adults return to just a handful of black Chicago zip codes after they get out of prison. A large pool of parolees living in those communities adds a collective burden to those underresourced locales.

To reduce violence, the aforementioned issues must be considered. Diversions sidetrack us from productive solutions or from focusing on the systemic problems of poverty and unemployment. The myth of black-on-black crime is a red herring that ignores the fact that people who commit crimes generally commit them against people they know and near where they live. The term "black-on-black crime" downplays poverty, racial inequality and "white-on-white crime." By keeping a running tally of shootings, local media help cultivate our sense of fear and despair. Terms like "war zone," "Chiraq" and "urban terrorism" seep into our consciousness. According to the running narrative, violence is the default in black neighborhoods, which exhibit few redeeming characteristics, and black people are incapable of avoiding crime.

Still, Chicago has too many murders.

And America has too many murders.

Chicago does clock in more murders than any other U.S. city and is more violent than New York and Los Angeles. Yet Chicago is smaller and much more racially segregated than both of those cities.

But Chicago is *not* the murder capital of the country or planet. Figures from the Chicago Police Department show that homicides peaked in the early 1990s and then followed a national trend of a decrease in violent crime through the rest of the decade, and the city as a whole has seen a decrease in crime. Neighborhoods downtown, white and closest to the central city, saw dramatic decreases. Pockets of the South and West Sides worsened—areas with acute poverty, unemployment and hypersegregation. According to city public health statistics, a current snapshot of Englewood reveals that unemployment is at 25 percent. Forty-two percent of the neighborhood's residents live in poverty; for children, the number is almost double that, and 29 percent of residents don't have a high school diploma.

The following chart documents just how many murders Chicago has had over a 40-year span.

Table 7.1 Chicago Murders, 1973–2013

Year	Number of Murders
1973	862
1978	787
1983	729
1988	660
1993	703
2003	601
2008	513
2013	414

Source: Chicago Police Department Annual Reports.

Statistics can be manipulated, interpreted and understood in various ways.

People conflate murder *rate* with raw murder numbers and mistakenly say that Chicago has the country's highest murder rate. That's inaccurate. A rate counts murders per 100,000 residents. In 2012, Flint, Michigan, had 62 murders per 100,000, making it the city with the highest murder rate in the United States that year. Chicago, in contrast, had a rate of 18.5 murders per 100,000. From 1985 through 2012, only six cities had the country's highest murder rate, and Chicago isn't one of them. The cities are: New Orleans, Louisiana; Washington, D.C.; Detroit, Michigan; Flint, Michigan; Richmond, Virginia; and Birmingham, Alabama.[2] (The most violent city in the world is San Pedro Sula, Honduras, which has a rate of 171.20 homicides per 100,000.)

* * *

Contrary to what outsiders believe, black lives do matter to black people. Pundits and politicians like Rudy Giuliani, Glenn Beck, Juan

Williams and Joe Scarborough enjoy upbraiding people for protesting police murders of black people instead of protesting so-called black-on-black crime. Their flawed logic asks how people can protest Trayvon Martin's death at the hands of George Zimmerman and not protest murders in Chicago. The simple answer is that protests happen in Chicago on a fairly regular basis, but the national news cameras usually aren't around to broadcast those moments. It's easier for pundits to accept black pathology as the answer. But beyond the ridiculous notion that black people can't care about various gun issues, replacing black-on-black crime with black-on-black love is a Chicago campaign dating back to the 1980s and Ed Gardner, the founder of hair care company Soft Sheen Products. Messages of black uplift and unity are as old as the Great Migration.

Dozens of community groups and activists work on reducing violence and advocating social justice on the South Side. In the Roseland neighborhood, Diane Latiker, a local black woman, is considered a hero. In 2003, she opened her home to area children as a safe haven and founded Kids Off the Block, which now has a community center and has served thousands of youth. Black Youth Project mobilizes young people around politics, hip-hop and feminism. Build Chicago works to give positive alternatives to youth exposed to drugs, gangs and violence. UCAN leads classroom-based violence interruption projects, has a peace hub for young people and addresses trauma for those exposed to violence. Black community activist Zarakyah Ben Sar Ahmadiel believes bad diets are a casualty of violence and promotes a vegan "peace diet" program to children. He teaches how nutritional neuropsychology can in part help prevent violence.

Today I see fear among black Chicagoans. I'm not saying it's never justified, but it teeters on being the primary emotion for folk. When I lived in Bronzeville, in my all-black building, one condo owner who moved in after me constantly expressed fear of our block and wanted security cameras placed all over the three-story walk-up. During a condo association board meeting, he spurned the women in the room by asking where we were from because he felt we weren't concerned about his safety. The assumption was that we knew nothing about the South Side when actually all of us were from there. I told him to go to a block club or community policing meeting if he had safety concerns. He never did. Another friend of a friend who had newly moved to Bronzeville reiterated how scared he was to live there with his children. I asked if he had gotten involved with one of the many active neighborhood improvement associations. He hadn't. A suburban friend of my ten-year-old stepdaughter spent the night at our Hyde Park home but was afraid to walk to the store with her and my husband for ice cream. She thought she was going to get shot. My stepdaughter tried to reassure her by pointing out we live two blocks away from President Obama's home and Secret Service is abundant in the neighborhood. The girl relented but ducked in and out of the store to avoid imaginary bullets. Even simple good-in-the-hood stories fall on tin ears. A young woman who planned the first-ever Englewood 5K on a Sunday morning in 2014 said people wanted to donate but not run because of the location.

Stereotypes and misconceptions influence how people interpret violence.

Every generation thinks the one behind them includes the worst children ever to grace the earth. Yet dismissing young people does nothing about the conditions of the neighborhoods they hail from. I also hear that music is worse today. No doubt there's a lot of nihilistic music on the airwaves, which does contribute to a culture of violence. But when I hear Gen X-ers point fingers at today's hip-hop mainstream music as the major culprit, I find myself amid a wave of amnesia. "Gangster rap" began in the late 1980s. N.W.A. and raunchy group 2 Live Crew's "Pop That Pussy" alarmed the country and our parents. We argued that the music didn't define us. While I do believe music is influential and drill artist Chief Keef needs an intervention, music didn't create the segregated circumstances of neighborhoods that allow gun violence to burgeon. I'm still waiting to hear how music led wayward white youth to commit mass shootings in Littleton, Colorado (Columbine High School); Newtown, Connecticut (Sandy Hook Elementary School); Charleston, South Carolina; Roseburg, Oregon; and Aurora, Colorado. Music also doesn't explain away crime over the past 50 years.

I try mightily to not wear my self-righteous truth-and-justice journalism cape. But some days these conversations test me. My father and

I were at a party and one of his retired police officer friends perched on his soapbox and talked about how crime is worse and different today. "Women didn't get killed. Children didn't get killed," he argued. I quietly sipped my vodka tonic because, well, what's the point in arguing, I thought, or debunking that lie with facts? This retired detective must know he's spewing fallacious rhetoric! The conversation moved on. Minutes later he and my father recounted hanging at a South Side lounge in the 1980s. A woman pulled a gun on a man outside of the bar. The police officer, off duty at the time, intervened. Naturally, the irony of the story was completely lost on him. When I brought up that this was a woman with a gun, he didn't understand the correlation and looked confused. As someone gently told me, I must stop jousting at windmills.

Finally, many Chicagoans refuse to believe the numbers—that homicides *are* down. Media cultivation theory says too much television can lead you to think the world is a much more violent place than what's reality. A simple example: watching marathons of the television series *Law & Order* could lead someone to think the world is a much more dangerous place than it actually is. The Chicago news cycle of constant reporting on crime makes people think our city is far more dangerous than it is.

I also believe that the Obama factor piques the curiosity of the national and international media who descend upon the city regularly to report on violence. For example, an international news outlet woke me late one night in 2013. Multiple shootings had occurred in a South Side park in a mostly Latino area after I had gone to bed. Thankfully, none of the shots was fatal. I quickly figured out why this was international news. Several hours later I did a quick phone debrief with the anchor, and the opening question referred to Chicago as the president's hometown, using the opportunity to connect the dots about segregation, violence and poverty.

In Chicago, police receive too much blame and credit for spikes and dips in crime. While community policing and strong community relationships are vital for the city, police officers don't control the circumstances in which most violence occurs. Meanwhile, police credibility continues to erode in some communities. The gun violence solutions

often touted by politicians involve deploying more police officers on the
streets or bringing in the National Guard. For them, apparently, a heavy
police state is easier than dealing with structural racism.

When unraveling the impact and implications of Chicago violence,
we fail to recognize that the media have played a role in contributing to
the narrative. We become what we think we are. Chicagoans are time
and time again fed how violent we are, and many people internalize that
cognitive belief. The perception of crime is higher than the reality. From
the mob to gangs, violence has percolated through the streets of Chicago
for the past hundred years. The city has seen it all before; there's nothing
new under the sun. We just don't remember.

* * *

The Chicago Crime Tour leaves every couple of hours on weekends, its
pickup and drop-off location steps away from Magnificent Mile shopping on Michigan Avenue and the Ritz-Carlton Hotel. Yellow crime
tape flutters on the black limo bus that takes tourists on a 90-minute
tour. The tour guide, probably an actor or aspiring comic, stands up
front to regale passengers with tales of criminals, gangsters and mob-
sters for $39.95.

The jaunt starts in Streeterville, the neighborhood of lakefront
high-rises and gleaming skyscrapers, named after Cap'n George Wel-
lington Streeter. The Civil War veteran stole lakefront land and tried to
run guns to Honduras. Then the bus curves up Lake Shore Drive and
pulls up to the former Biograph Theater. Federal agents killed Public
Enemy No. 1 John Dillinger at the mouth of the alley next to the theater. As the tour guide explains how women dipped their handkerchiefs
in Dillinger's blood, another crime bus, the Untouchable Tour, whizzes
by. These tours are a cottage industry.

We return to our seats on the bus, and our guide narrates details
about the 1929 St. Valentine's Day Massacre and later shows us the private speakeasy of Public Enemy No. 1 Al Capone, atop a tall downtown
skyscraper. Holy Name Cathedral is the final stop, the site of a 1926
bloodbath. Tales of white men and white immigrants, the birth of graft

and corruption in the Windy City. Tourists drink all this up like a stiff Prohibition-era cocktail.

The bus winds downtown and throughout parts of the North Side. There are no stops on the South Side. No mention of policy kings—the rich black men who helped build institutions on the South Side through numbers running, the precursor to the lottery. Nor is there any mention of black gang kingpins Jeff Fort of the Blackstone Rangers or Larry Hoover of the Gangster Disciples or any excursion into Latin King territory on the West Side. The hokey crime tour commemorates particular crime and mob aspects of Chicago. Riding along is like enjoying the plot of a black-and-white movie—a story of yore, a peek at an underworld. The message is that white mob activity is a slice of history, precious and memorialized.

The tour is also a reminder that Chicago has always been a violent city.

"This Is the Murder Capital," blares a *Chicago Tribune* editorial headline. "Chicago recorded 108 homicides in the first three months of this year. That sets a record. In the same three months, New York, which has twice as many inhabitants, had only 75 killings, less than two-thirds as many. . . . We live in the most murderous city in the civilized world and there is no excuse for us."[3]

Although this sounds like a grossly exaggerated condemnation of the twenty-first century, this editorial ran on April 12, 1925. Even then the *Tribune* counted deaths. That same year the newspaper ran a "hands of death" graphic calculating deaths from what the editorial board judged one of society's biggest menaces: automobile fatalities. An editorial urgently wrote: "Fighting automobile deaths is unlike fighting death from disease in this: a dozen men in a laboratory can forever end the scourge of typhoid; a labor battalion under competent direction can free a tropical province of yellow fever, but we can't delegate the job of making the streets safe." The "hands of death" also took on guns. The *Tribune* again declared Chicago the murder, crime and automobile death capital of the "white world."[4]

On July 14, 1937, the *Tribune* reminded readers about "the hands of death" in a short paragraph: "A crime clock which records the homicides and other felonies in Chicago appears on the editorial page where it will . . . be a daily feature. Also on the editorial page hereafter will appear the massacre clock which records auto deaths and injuries."[5]

Prior to Prohibition, saloon homicides usually involved poor, young single men. Between 1875 and 1920, at a time of industrialization, immigration and population explosion, Chicago's homicide rate more than quadrupled, and Chicago ranked as the most violent major urban center in the United States.[6]

Jokes about murder city haunted Chicago during the 1920s. Editorials and articles on the East Coast and overseas referred to criminal anarchy. Local newspapers also enthused about the anarchy. Powerful publishing magnate William Randolph Hearst used the *Chicago American* and *Chicago Examiner* newspapers to capitalize on the bloody stories. In an absurd art-imitates-life scenario, a circulation war broke out between the *American* and the *Tribune*. Both newspapers hired thugs to threaten newsboys and subscribers. One bootlegger hijacked *Tribune* delivery trucks. Gunmen and mercenaries actually killed rival readers. Between 1913 and 1917, 27 newspaper employees, civilians and hired guns were killed.[7]

None of this was labeled "white-on-white crime."

In *The Condemnation of Blackness: Race, Crime, and the Making of Modern Urban America*, Khalil Gibran Muhammad chronicles the idea of black criminality. He writes: "At the dawn of the twentieth century, in a rapidly industrializing, urbanizing, and demographically shifting America, blackness was refashioned through crime statistics. It became a more stable racial category in opposition to whiteness through racial criminalization. Consequently, white criminality lost its fearsomeness."[8]

White social workers operated in settlement houses to help white immigrants gain a footing in the United States, but those resources followed the segregated color line. Black social workers lacked the funds for black or colored settlement houses. "Among whites, struggling neighborhoods were considered a cause of crime and reason to intervene. Among blacks, they were considered a sign of pathology and reason for neglect," according to Muhammad.[9]

Eventually European immigrants shed their criminal identities and blended in with the majority white population. Simply put, according to Muhammad, white criminality was seen as society's problem, and black criminality was black people's problem. The same situation is happening today.

THE MEDIA STUDY

Learning bits of the history of Chicago crime coverage led me to wonder about the origins of fear and the media's role in perpetuating it.

Growing up, our household subscribed to the *Tribune*, the *Sun-Times* and the black newspaper *Defender*. I recall reading the mainstream dailies and watching television thinking that the South Side reporters described wasn't *my* South Side. The limited coverage prioritized crime.

Due to my love of writing and reading, journalism seemed like a good path to pursue. My desire to be a journalist wasn't to be an apologist only creating "positive" stories about black people but to show the breadth of our communities. The *Defender* did a much better job of capturing black life than other local news agencies. The *Sun-Times* did better than the *Trib*. My news consumption as a child was limited by the hegemony of three news channels and daily newspapers. Now more choices exist because of media demassification, which allows for greater quantities of local, regional and national news. A 24-hour news cycle, cable and the Internet enable more democracy—and sometimes confusion for consumers.

As a news media practitioner, I'm comfortable critiquing the insensitivity of the industry. The journalism adage "if it bleeds, it leads" drills to the heart of how news sensationalizes catastrophes. News outlets count murders as casually as a sleepless person counts sheep. Unfortunately, the Chicago media crime narrative is national, consistent and unfair. That coverage led me to wonder how to quantify my hunches. Is the past simply prologue, as Shakespeare's *Tempest* proclaims? I decided to explore media treatment of violence.

What has Chicago crime coverage been like over the decades? To be sure, television news is the biggest offender in regard to crime coverage in any city. But analyzing TV news is too complicated. I decided to examine the print editions of the two major dailies, the *Tribune* and *Sun-Times,* over a 40-year period.

For this to be a random study, I picked 14 days in two constructed weeks.

The weeks included these dates: January 1, first Thursday in February, second Saturday in February, third Wednesday in March, first Sunday in April, last Friday in May, first Tuesday in June, second Friday in June, July 5, third Monday in August, first Tuesday in September, fourth Monday in October, last Thursday in November, fourth Sunday in December.

The years covered are 1973, 1978, 1983, 1988, 1993, 1998, 2003, 2008 and 2013.

Scanning the local sections of the newspapers for murders, homicides and shootings, I categorized whether the story made the front page, had visuals and where the crime took place (North, South or West Side). Were race, age and gender of the victim mentioned? Was the story a brief or a sympathetic tale?

Articles included victims of shootings and injuries from violent crimes, not just murders. Some days had multiple stories on shootings or murders. Front-page coverage was rare.

For each year, I assessed a total of 28 days for both newspapers, which added up to 252 days total for me to sift through. I found that a shooting or murder made it into print in 184 articles—or 73 percent of the sample. In 1973, I located 27 stories—the most. In 1983, I found 11 articles—the fewest.

I concluded that, over the past four decades, violent crime has historically and consistently been covered in Chicago by the two mainstream dailies. In the stories I reviewed, race was never mentioned; I could tell ethnicity or race only if a picture accompanied the article. Most of the crimes covered occurred in the black parts of the city's South and West Sides.

When police officers or children were victims, the stories seemed sympathetic. However, not every child death was allotted a story. Many consisted of briefs, either a paragraph or a few sentences. Funerals or children turning their lives around also produced articles.

I also found:

- 2 stories about the "mob"
- 5 stories on police officers shooting or killing a civilian
- 8 stories of violence on a Chicago public housing property
- 15 stories on law enforcement officials shot or killed

That's 48 stories involving children as victims. Some stories from the 1970s read like true crime novels by going beyond the who, what, when, where and why formula. A March 21, 1973, *Sun-Times* front-page article described a housewife who shot and killed two robbers as they fought with her husband. She had managed to reach for a hidden pistol. Twenty-six percent of the articles focused on victims under 18 years of age. In 1993, the *Chicago Tribune* launched an award-winning, and Pulitzer finalist, yearlong series called "Killing Our Children" about violence in the region. On February 4, 1993, a story detailed one 14-year-old's dual life as a quiet girl who loved her family and one whose race toward adolescent rebellion led to her death.

The peak in murders occurred in early 1990s Chicago. Of the stories the *Tribune* ran during the sample that year, most struck a sympathetic tone or received full-blown ink. While coverage of children's murders has remained steady in terms of numbers through the decades, the identification of young people as Chicago Public School students began in 2008. On June 3, 2008, for example, the *Tribune* reported that a 16-year-old boy accidentally shot his 19-year-old friend while playing with a gun—the twenty-second CPS gun-related fatality that school year and the twenty-fifth student killed that year. This trend cropped up on the watch of Arne Duncan, chief executive of Chicago Public Schools from 2001 to 2008. If a CPS child was killed, the district made it a point to say so. I don't doubt Duncan's passion for children or how wrenching it is for a school community to lose a child. But the constant IDing became an epithet for CPS or an indictment of public education.

After all, none of these children was slain on CPS property. School shootings are not a phenomenon in Chicago.

Covering the deaths of children also raises ethical questions of who is "undeserving" to die. Every decade a "good kid" is killed, and the murder morphs into a public rallying cry. Protests, marches, speechifying all follow.

In 1984, a teen shot and killed Ben Wilson, the county's number one high school basketball player. In 1992, a sniper killed seven-year-old Dantrell Davis as he held his mother's hand walking to school in the Cabrini-Green public housing development. In 2007, Blair Holt, 16, died on a city bus as he tried to protect a classmate from a hail of bullets. In 2013, Hadiya Pendleton, 15, died from a gunshot weeks after she performed at President Barack Obama's inauguration. These high-profile deaths inspire rallies, speeches, fundraising and renewed promises from adults to protect children.

Still, youth violence had been on the decline. According to a University of Chicago researcher, 2006 saw the largest decline in youth violence in Chicago—down by almost 40 percent. Professor Dexter Voisin once told me that widely covered murders give people the impression that violence is up. "Conventional thinking has been a lot of this violence has been between gang members. But now we're finding young people, honor students, individuals who are not part of gangs who individuals don't see as deserving to die because they're good kids."[10]

Stories counting the deaths of CPS students are a precursor to the more recent reporting that resembles a baseball scoreboard. Local media are notorious for writing roundups of deaths. With the web and social media, Chicagoans—and the rest of the world—wake up on Monday mornings to a roster of deaths by the numbers.

A case in point from my sample is a January 1, 2013, brief in the *Sun-Times* that detailed multiple shootings, and on July 5, 2013, the *Sun-Times* published this lead: "Five men were killed and at least 15 other people were wounded in shootings throughout the city this holiday weekend." The story was a jumble of names, addresses, ages and neighborhoods of people injured or killed.

A convoluted September 3, 2013, article in the same newspaper attempted a summary: "Five other men and a 16-year-old boy were killed and at least 17 other people were injured in shootings across the city since Friday night." According to the last sentence in the story: "Fourteen others have been injured in shootings since Friday night. In the most recent nonfatal incident, a 36-year-old man was shot in the abdomen at 6:35 p.m. in the 11700 block of South Marshfield, police said."

News coverage isn't an exact science. Some days are slow news days. Editors differ on news judgment and which stories reporters should be dispatched on. Some caveats to my analysis: I counted only the number of stories, not the number of injuries or murders in the stories, which were sometimes multiple. Another limitation is that I didn't include Internet stories in my analysis.

It is difficult to determine the right way to cover homicides in Chicago. Journalists and scholars ponder the role of journalism and ethical responsibilities in reporting on underserved neighborhoods. The voyeuristic exercise of counting deaths is not a good method, for it tells us nothing except that bad shit sometimes happens in "bad" black neighborhoods.

Gene Demby, writing for National Public Radio's race blog *Code Switch*, summed up what we are actually talking about when we talk about violence in Chicago.

We have a default template for the way we process mass shootings. We scour through every available scrap of the perpetrators' interior lives—Facebook postings, YouTube videos, interviews with former roommates—to try to find out what drove them to kill. The sites of the massacres become kind of shorthand: Columbine, Sandy Hook, Fort Hood. We conduct protracted, unsatisfying conversations about gun rights, and about mental illness, and about how we have to make sure that they never happen again. We also have a template for the kind of carnage we saw in Chicago last weekend, in which at least 80 people were shot in 21 separate shooting incidents. At least 14 people died. The conversation and the coverage here is different, less probing. There are no attempts to illuminate the killer's psyche, no news coverage of the anniversaries of the shootings. These incidents are generally not treated as discrete events, but as part of a grim, undifferentiated parade of violence in the Chi. *It's a war zone. Welcome to Chiraq. Send in the National Guard.*[11]

Attempting to show humanity amid death, the *Sun-Times* in 2013 launched a feature in its online edition, "Homicide Watch Chicago," which pledges not to treat murders as simply run-of-the-mill stories. Reporters recount every murder in the city "so that together we might fight the tendency to view homicides as just another rising or falling number, like mortgage rates or batting averages."[12]

Those good intentions fall flat for me, even though in principle treating all murders as equal seems like a good rule to follow. It moves away from "innocent" victims and people who "deserved" to die if they were criminals. Unwittingly, however, "Homicide Watch Chicago" confirms black crime and supports prejudice. Documenting deaths raises questions for me. Why not list seat-belt deaths? Those due to hypertension, drug overdoses or suicide? How useful are profiles of the deceased? What are we trying to tell residents about murders? What about other forms of crime? Why not profile perpetrators? While there were 729 murders in 1983, there were more than 2,200 rapes.[13] In 2013, the Chicago Police Department told me officers respond to nearly 200,000 domestic calls annually. That's more than 547 calls a day. Is that more newsworthy? It's not covered, that's for sure.

In addition to journalism not being an exact science, no official handbook regulates what journalists should prioritize in their coverage. Some journalists think reporters should cover more shootings than homicides. Are homicides down because medical technology saves more lives? Do more cops make a difference? Amid this debate, newspaper layoffs, buyouts and budget cuts have left a leaner press corps. Is reporting death that much of a priority? Perhaps more reporters should be dispatched to cover Illinois state government or local county politics. Whatever the choice may be, repercussions follow.

Chicago clinical psychologist Nicole Tefera specializes in childhood trauma, an area she doesn't think gets enough attention. Violence is broader than who shot whom on what day of the week. She counsels children who have been exposed to community or interpersonal violence: physical abuse; domestic violence; witnessing the murder of a caregiver, parent or friend. Her job is to help them heal "because human beings are not designed to deal or should not deal with those experiences." Therapy allows them to better focus in school, cope with life and curb behavioral issues.

Tefera told me that media coverage can generate trauma too. She explained that so many children are affected by violence that the media couldn't even begin to address all the stories of individual people. "Sometimes people and families affected by violence look for their stories to be covered by media—whether newspapers or TV—and when it's not covered, that's equally distressing because, for them, their son or daughter or friend or sibling didn't matter. That's another piece that's not really discussed," Tefera said.[14]

She too questions the types of violence journalists choose to cover.

"When you turn on the TV, you're not hearing about the latest domestic violence incident where someone died of the injuries sustained or didn't die but suffered significantly. But you will hear about someone shot if the person died or didn't. It gives the appearance that gun violence happens more frequently than other types of violence," Tefera explained. "When I think about violence, I think about not just the violence I hear about or reported about, I'm thinking about individual cases of children in the child welfare system that aren't attended to properly or women in domestic violence shelters because they're fearful of their perpetrator or I'm thinking about young women, teenagers, involved in human trafficking. The way violence is reported is one-dimensional and it would leave you to believe 'Chiraq.'"

Tefera says it's hard to strike the right balance. She also says that gun violence coverage is politicized, with the debate focused on the right to carry weapons. She doesn't see enough correlation between poverty and an increase in interpersonal violence or substance abuse.

"If an alien is only watching the news, the alien would come away with: Wow, there's really good people trying to do good things and terrible things are happening. They wouldn't have a balanced view. An alien should walk away with: This is a large metropolitan city. Violence does occur and in these forms and [to] all kinds of people. Sometimes it's random and sometimes it's intentional."

*   *   *

Often the victims and offenders of gun violence are young men of color. I attended high school in the early 1990s and knew a few young men who died of gunshots. Experts are researching how to prevent those deaths.

The well-regarded University of Chicago Crime Lab says there is value in "focused prevention," which involves using resources to prevent youth gun violence rather than addressing the problem after the fact. Research from the crime lab suggests that one way to prevent youth gun violence is to give youth prosocial activities, such as school, so they can avoid risky behaviors like using guns. Improving health and reducing poverty are part of the equation too.

Project Safe Neighborhoods (PSN) in Chicago is an initiative of the U.S. Department of Justice implemented in 2002 to reduce gun violence. In 2009, PSN's research found that the victims and offenders of gun violence in Chicago consist of a small group of individuals who have had repeated contacts with law enforcement. More than 60 percent of homicide victims and 80 percent of homicide offenders in the PSN target areas had at least one prior arrest. The population most at risk of committing a murder and of becoming a murder victim is highly concentrated among a small population. The active PSN area population consists of about 1,500 individuals, or less than 1 percent of the area's total population.[15]

Andrew Papachristos, a Yale sociologist, documents crime trends in Chicago while bringing facts and sanity to violence discourse. In 2013, he noted that all but 10 of the city's 77 communities experienced declines in violent crime. Those neighborhoods with stubbornly high homicides were poor black ones. "Chicago is by far not the 'murder capital' or 'crime capital' of the U.S.," Papachristos writes.[16] The overall violence rate in Chicago is closer to that of Houston or Minneapolis and is half that of Detroit and St. Louis.

Papachristos also wrote an editorial in *Crain's Chicago Business* distilling his data for a nonacademic audience, debunking crime myths in the city at the same time. Again, he put statistics in context and concluded: "End-of-year totals are convenient figures for politicians and the media, but they do not tell the whole story. When thinking about crime, both time and history matter."[17]

Yet emotion gets in the way of facts. Multiple comments on the piece accused Papachristos, a reputable scholar, of lying and purposefully creating erroneous data. The word "thug" was used repeatedly to describe black males.

A media-fed crime diet will do that to you.

Yet it's hard to swallow that perception is reality.

I have empathy for families who have lost loved ones, whether they were victims or perpetrators. I am not dismissive of crime, trauma and bloodshed in our communities. I don't have all the answers on how to tell stories while being fair and exhibiting integrity.

I harp on these points because the fact-finder in me strongly believes that the city can't be fixed unless we have a true handle on the problem. Otherwise, feckless solutions arise. To wit, in 2013, Illinois Republican senator Mark Kirk proposed $500 million in federal funds to arrest 18,000 members of the Gangster Disciples street gang. Congressman Bobby Rush, a South Side Democrat, pilloried Kirk's idea as an "upper-middle-class, elitist white boy solution to a problem he knows nothing about."[18] The junior senator is stuck in the era when the streets were ruled by gangs, not by renegade crews of young black men formed by blocks or gang factions.

The two politicians later played nice, and when Rush gave Kirk a tour of Englewood, nary a resident mentioned the Gangster Disciples. Rather they harped on the lack of jobs, decades of disinvestment and how the neighborhood can't police itself out of problems.

Kirk responded to a room full of residents: "Oftentimes when people say you cannot police your way out of this, I would say thank God that Illinois and Chicago didn't believe that. We could've just let Al Capone run the whole place."[19] Residents groaned, and Kirk continued blathering about those boogeyman Gangster Disciples.

From silly solutions to collective self-righteousness, that's what Chicagoans receive. I've covered way too many discussions on youth violence with newsmakers and politicians who like to hear themselves talk. And sadly, the pendulum always swings toward policing. Panic responses— like bringing in the National Guard—end up being a part of the problem, not a solution.

"It's asinine [to bring the Guard in] because the National Guard is not a police force—it is an occupying force. Its job in an urban setting would be to restore order—at the point of a gun. There would be no mediation, no conciliation, and no investigation," Lou Ransom, executive editor of the *Chicago Defender,* wrote in 2009. "We must be careful not to overreact and embrace draconian 'solutions' simply because we now have a national and international audience. We have to address all the causes of violence, not just the violence."[20]

Monday morning hand-wringing about Chicago weekend shootings is nothing more than social media masturbation. Our city may be the face of urban violence, but what's happening in our neighborhoods can be seen in segregated cities across the country. Crime is inevitable in big cities. The commonalities in neighborhoods with the highest rates of violence are unemployment, disinvestment, mortality from preventable diseases and poverty. These neighborhoods are black, and these ghettos were constructed by design by decades of unscrupulous housing policies. Black people are put in the impossible situation of using bootstraps to lift themselves up or living in these conditions with dignity. We must remember the redlining, white flight and the white violence that greeted some of the first blacks to move into those neighborhoods.

Should the focus be gun control? Are black male mentoring programs the answer? Is lamenting bad black behavior a solution? Gun control is a political wasteland, and until the equivalent of the National

Rifle Association emerges to oppose them, getting any legislation passed will be hard. Mentoring and youth employment programs have shown positive outcomes.

Teen unemployment in Illinois is among the highest in the United States, and for low-income minorities, the rates are even higher. For example, only 8.7 percent of black teens in Chicago were employed in 2010–2011. Twenty-one percent of white teens were employed.[21]

According to a study conducted by the University of Chicago and the University of Pennsylvania, a public summer jobs program for high school students (nearly all black) from disadvantaged neighborhoods in Chicago reduced violent crime arrests by 43 percent over a 16-month period.[22] The jobs included camp counseling, community gardening and office work. Prior to the program, 20 percent of the students had been arrested and 20 percent had been crime victims. They lived in neighborhoods with an average unemployment rate of 19 percent and high violent crime rates.

Jobs must be a part of the solution—as well as job training, reduction in high school dropout rates, mental health services, better policies surrounding disparities in drug offenses/convictions and rehabilitation programs for those incarcerated and reentering society. Drugs should be decriminalized—for everyone. A reformed Chicago marijuana law allows police to ticket people in possession instead of jailing them. But two years after that law was instituted, police in 2014 were still cracking down in poor minority areas.[23]

Poor communities need serious investment, a comprehensive, compensatory effort. "This is not a novel conclusion. Black activist and civil rights groups have long called for such policies," writes Chicago opinion journalist Salim Muwakkil. "The nomenclatures have ranged from 'urban Marshall Plan' to 'comprehensive affirmative action' to 'reparations,' but they embodied the same reasoning. Descendants of enslaved Africans are victims of an exceptionally destructive historical injury that requires exceptional economic investment in public repair."[24]

Pushing for a domestic Marshall Plan—a nod to the $13 billion the United States gave various battered European countries to rebuild and restore economic infrastructure after World War II—goes back decades. Labor leader A. Philip Randolph called for one in the 1960s. In 1963, the National Urban League lobbied for one for Negro citizens.

A 1966 article in the *Boston College Law Review* proclaimed:

> Approaches other than the Marshall Plan technique have been attempted and have failed. Poverty and unemployment will not be eradicated piecemeal. Only a sustained, coordinated, and centrally directed program to enrich our national life can be effective. The stakes are high. We cannot assimilate our Negro millions racially if we fail them economically. We cannot unify the nation and make equality a fact rather than a dream if we do not unleash our total resources for this crusade. The ways of the Marshall Plan are many and diverse. Positive hiring and training by businessmen is not enough. Our steps are limited only by our ingenuity, skill, and genius as a people. Those who earnestly seek to uplift the republic will not be weighted down by methodology.[25]

What a great concept for Chicago and black America.

In 1990, the National Urban League renewed its call for an urban Marshall Plan. President John E. Jacob asked the government to shift $50 billion in Cold War spending to make the Marshall Plan happen. "At a time when we hear policy-makers talk of a new Marshall Plan and a new Economic Development Bank for Eastern Europe, we need to press for an Urban Marshall Plan and an Urban Investment Bank that invests in our own people and in our own cities," Jacob said.[26]

Segregated areas needed money flowing to them for new opportunities for employment and economic development. To rise out of the abyss of racial segregation and poverty, black neighborhoods need resources, not military intervention. Letting neighborhoods wither on the vine with more cops on the streets won't work. Violence is merely a corollary of backlogged disparities and bad policies in black neighborhoods.

Cities know how to be creative in cutting sweetheart deals for new sports stadiums or companies moving their headquarters to central business districts. Cities need to apply that same inventiveness beyond downtown areas to see a serious reduction in violence. Crime isn't an isolated occurrence. If the larger structural issues in neighborhoods, such as segregation and racial inequality, aren't addressed, any other solution will only be fleeting.

Because we are not Chiraq.

8

SEARCHING FOR HAROLD

CHICAGO HAS BOASTED SOME OF THE MOST POWERFUL MAYORS IN THE UNITED States since the mid-twentieth century.

For more than 20 years, Richard J. Daley—known as the Boss—ruled with authority, overseeing grand downtown projects and urban renewal and blocking integration at every turn while playing national Democratic Party politics. He died in office in 1976.

Eldest son Richard M. Daley served a little bit longer, also overseeing grand downtown projects and urban renewal plus a mass of pretty flower beds planted around the city. He seized control of the public schools and public housing while shepherding in splashy lakefront projects. When Daley decided not to run for another term in 2011, former Chicago congressman and Washington, D.C., bigwig Rahm Emanuel took the city's helm. His first term was marked by the controversial decision to shutter more than 50 public schools, but Emanuel has also used his influence to bring in new businesses, not just downtown but in struggling black neighborhoods.

Of course other mayors, including the first woman, have held office in between. At every turn, black Chicago voters have lent major support to these elected officials. But in the 1980s, this group of voters saw one of their own take the reins at City Hall: Harold Washington, the first black mayor of Chicago, was elected in 1983.

Washington's legacy looms over the City of Big Shoulders, stronger than the odor of the infamous stockyards, deeper than our famed deep-dish pizza. His name continues to be invoked in political campaigns. Former low-level aides jot it on their resumes when they run for office. Other politicians trot out relatives who served in the Washington administration as validation of their own bona fides. Republicans recycle archival tape of the mayor disparaging particular Democrats during any given election season.

Today no one dares to utter a cross word about the man—as if everyone was always down with Washington, as if the "Council Wars" never occurred, as if outsiders hadn't dubbed the city "Beirut by the Lake" for its notorious political brawls and as if racial politics didn't color and polarize the city during his incumbency.

Washington is almost like a religious figure to black Chicago, and his speeches seemed like church revivals. "You want Harold? You got Harold!" the bigger-than-life man often bellowed to crowds. Washington, a burly, dark brown handsome man with a thick mustache and salt-and-pepper hair, grew up in the fabled Democratic machine but flipped it on its head. At the time of his win, the city was alive with politics. People flocked to the polls. A remarkable 82 percent of registered voters cast ballots in the 1983 race, compared to 32 percent in the 2015 mayoral race.[1]

Harold Washington was the unlikely candidate whom the media initially dismissed. Chicago, a place where "ethnic" means white and whiteness has an actual identity (Irish, Serbian, Polish, Czech, etc.), elected a black man who seized the ethnic (note: not racial) narrative by saying "It's our turn." Blacks wanted a better share of political power and jobs in the Democratic machine. In the 1983 primary, two white candidates split the vote, leaving Washington the winner. White Democrats couldn't accept that fate and actually changed political parties. A white Republican contender—like a two-headed salamander in this Democratic stronghold—threw his hat in the ring, and he too lost. During the

1987 reelection campaign, white candidates jumped into the fray again. Rinse, cycle, repeat. Washington triumphed again.

During the Ronald Reagan years, urban centers experienced massive budget cuts. Amid the resulting chaos, Harold Washington was able to build a multiracial coalition, drawing support from white lakefront liberals from North Side luxury high-rises and black South Side high-rise public housing residents—a testament to his appeal across racial and class lines. Washington opened up the establishment to people who previously had been shut out and battled an obstinate group of white city council members who tried to stymie him every step of the way. The fighting looked eerily similar to President Barack Obama's experience with Congress.

Washington lived in Hyde Park, an integrated South Side bastion of intellect and political independence. A former state legislator and congressman, he loved legitimate exchanges of ideas and words. His notion of fun involved eating alone at a Chinese restaurant while wading through a stack of history or philosophy books. Washington vacillated between salty language and SAT vocabulary words when he spoke. He married once as a young college man but divorced ten years later and never had children. It's not a cliché to say he lived and breathed politics. Even friends and top aides admitted he didn't reveal much about himself.

Washington, 65, died of a heart attack at his desk in City Hall the day before Thanksgiving in 1987. His weight had ballooned to 284 pounds while in office, and stress etched lines across his face. Washington smoked, ate too many cheeseburgers and slurped a lot of soda pop.

I was in sixth grade in library class when the school announced the mayor's death over the intercom. I mourned. The city and weather were dreary. I wrote in my diary that I felt sad, as if a grandparent had died. My parents took our family to see the mayor's body lying in state at City Hall. For several hours, we waited in line with other sorrowing Chicagoans. To this day, it's common to hear some black folk whisper conspiracy theories—that his death was actually an assassination via poisoning.

Washington was an accessible, comfortable and familiar presence to black Chicago. He shook hands in soul food restaurants on Sundays after church, mingled at park events and effusively greeted people wherever he went. I have a couple of autographs from him. Even if you didn't completely understand politics, you knew Harold did right by black folk. Chicago's first black mayor is more beloved here than the country's first black president.

Alas, the era is gone. Harold can't be re-created, but his ghost haunts this city as we search for a coalition builder of his ilk. Sure, the city still elects blacks to political office. It's no accident the South Side is the political home that put Barack Obama in the White House. This city has long churned out political and economic heavyweights. In 1928, Oscar De Priest was the first northern state black congressman elected in the twentieth century. He and other black politicians gained control from white politicians in the predominantly black Second Ward, in the Black Belt, to develop the nation's most powerful black political organization. Decades later, in 1992, Illinoisans elected South Sider Carol Moseley Braun as the first black woman to serve in the U.S. Senate. Only five blacks have ever been elected to the U.S. Senate; two of them are from the South Side.

Chicago black political thought isn't monolithic, but Harold Washington crystallized an opportunity for forces to come together under his progressive umbrella. When he died, black politics in Chicago fractured and died as well, and the fissure has yet to be repaired. The battle between two black city councilmen to replace him polarized the black voting bloc as each sought to be crowned Washington's heir apparent. Lack of political unity, ego and hurt feelings allowed for a white political scion to win in the 1989 special election. Richard M. Daley ruled for the next two decades without any real competition. He neutralized the black vote while rewarding Hispanic and white loyalists. Chicago has not had an elected black mayor since Washington.

"Unfortunately, the state of black politics in Chicago is consistent with the state of black politics in the U.S.—disorganized, divided, weak and rudderless. In Chicago, it's weaker than it has been in decades and is a long-term trend we can trace back to the demise of the Harold Washington coalition in the 1980s," University of Chicago political scientist Michael Dawson told me.[2]

Black political players and thinkers of disparate stripes in Chicago agree: The bitterness in the fight to take control of City Hall post-Washington wrecked black politics. The lack of organizational capacity and leadership left wounds and scars, resulting in the lack of a tight black political agenda.

* * *

"So I told Uncle Chester: Don't worry, Harold Washington doesn't want to marry your sister," legendary columnist Mike Royko wrote after Washington won the 1983 mayor's race. It was a strange thing to write since Royko himself noted that he never mentioned the race of previous mayors. "But you can't write about Harold Washington's victory without taking note of his skin color. Yes, he is black. And that fact is going to create a deep psychological depression in many of the white, ethnic, neighborhood people who read this paper in the morning."[3]

The fear of a black mayor, of course, was rooted in racism, but those white, ethnic neighborhood people worried more about their lifeblood in the Democratic machine with jobs and clout. One of Washington's campaign ads declared that the machine didn't work anymore.

During his two-decade reign over Chicago, Mayor Richard J. Daley was regarded as the master of the machine. But the Chicago Democratic machine began in 1931 with Mayor Anton Cermak (a Bohemian immigrant who was shot and killed when a gunman aimed for President-elect Franklin D. Roosevelt). It's a political organization with ward committeemen and precinct workers. "The second integral part of the machine is the city and county government, which has been intimately tied into the machine in a relationship somewhat analogous to the one in Russia between the Communist party and the Soviet government. For many Chicagoans, the party is more important than the government itself," political scientist and machine historian Milton Rakove wrote in 1984.[4] The machine is about loyalty and job rewards. We Chicagoans refer to it as patronage.

Blacks participated in machine politics when they arrived after the Great Migration. Congressman William Dawson, of the First District, represented parts of the South Side. As a leader of the black wards, Dawson delivered mayoral votes to the machine. He also served as Democratic Second Ward committeeman.

Royko explains in his book *Boss:*

> Politically, the Negro was even more exploitable. In the South he didn't vote. In Chicago he could vote for the Democrat of his choice. The Machine's precinct captains would go right into the voting booth with him to make sure he voted properly. The major weapon was the threat. Negroes were warned that they would lose their welfare check, their public housing apartment, their menial job, if they didn't vote Democratic. Dawson ran everything on the South Side, but on the West Side, where most new arrivals from the south settled, they didn't even have black politicians exploiting them. The white officeholders and ward bosses remained after the white constituents fled.[5]

Dawson's great-nephew is revered University of Chicago political scientist Michael Dawson, cofounder of the *Du Bois Review: Social Science Research on Race* and principal investigator on many important studies on black politics, including one that created a data set on public opinion polls on the U.S. racial divide. The younger Dawson's surname taught him what the power of backlash meant. "Black nationalists, black progressives, black radicals didn't trust anyone with the name Dawson and I realize there were really good reasons for that," he told me. When Dawson returned home from college during the summer in the 1960s, his father, a lifelong member of the machine, got him a patronage job. Michael Dawson was an activist and sought to be a community organizer. He opposed the war in Vietnam, and a Second Ward committeeman told him "every antiwar protester should be put up on a wall and shot. The second thing that convinced me not to stay as an organizer in the city was hearing from my father at the time not to get too close to the head of the African American Cultural Center. He was the captain of gang intelligence, and no one knew. My father told me I'd be under surveillance. It was clear to me that the black Dawson machine was to disrupt black radicals and work with police."

Born in 1922 in the Black Belt, Harold Washington encountered the machine, which helped rear him. He knew when to enter and exit.

Washington's father ran his own law firm and served as a Democratic precinct captain on the South Side. His mother flowed in and out of his life, and Washington considered his father his hero. Harold served four years in the army in World War II and upon his return received the G.I. Bill to attend Roosevelt College in Chicago. There he met a coterie of black men who became lifelong friends—Dempsey Travis, a future real estate magnate; Gus Savage, a future congressman; and Bennett Johnson, a book publisher. Washington graduated from Northwestern University School of Law in 1952 and afterward took over his father's law practice. Like his father, Washington immersed himself in local politics and learned the workings of the machine under the tutelage of Third Ward alderman Ralph Metcalfe, the former Olympic track star. Washington also worked as assistant corporation counsel for the city.

In 1964, Metcalfe sponsored Washington for a seat in the state legislature. Several years later, the Cook County Democratic organization, led by chairman (and mayor) Richard J. Daley, decided that the independent Washington had to go. But the people in his district loved him. Washington stayed and then won a state senate seat in 1976, often bringing back money to his black district, which had many poor pockets. He supported women's rights, helped organize the legislature's first black caucus and introduced a bill that made Illinois the first state to give schools and state workers a day off for Martin Luther King's birthday.

In the Harold Washington lore, few people bring up that he ran for mayor after Daley died in 1976 and that he captured only 11 percent of the vote. Although the Democratic machine alternately feared and loathed him, Washington continued to represent his district in the state capitol.

Metcalfe had become a congressman in the First District, and when he died suddenly in 1978, Washington won his seat despite not having the backing of the Democratic organization. The machine even ran two unknown candidates with the last name Washington as an attempt to thwart him.

Then the reign of the first Daley ended with his death in office.

World War II veteran Michael Bilandic, whose ethnic roots were Croatian, followed Daley as mayor. He had been Daley's anointed mayor from their Bridgeport community, and he previously had served as alderman in the Eleventh Ward. In addition to the Irish, Italians and Poles, Croatians settled in Chicago. In the early twentieth century, their first enclave was just south of downtown.

Jane Byrne, an Irish Daley protégée, took on Bilandic in 1979 after he botched snow removal during a brutal blizzard. To recover, one of his commercials featured his blond socialite wife pleading with voters to "keep Chicago strong"; perhaps the aim was to win some women voters. The tactic didn't work, and Byrne became the city's first female mayor. Chicagoans may tolerate corruption and machine politics, but you can't play around with plowing their snow. Byrne captured much of the black vote but once in office proved disappointing when she realigned herself with machine politics. She alienated black voters by replacing black members on the Chicago Housing Authority board with white ones. She even pulled a serious PR stunt in 1981 by moving into a Cabrini-Green public housing apartment to draw attention to poverty. The move flopped. Byrne critics—some later say unfairly—nicknamed her "Calamity Jane" for unpredictable and supposedly loopy behavior.

But Byrne was vulnerable and increasingly looked like a one-term mayor.

The path to Washington's win didn't start with the man himself. A group of black activists plotted in basement meetings to find the right candidate. Unabashed black nationalist Lu Palmer spearheaded the campaign to recruit Washington to City Hall in 1980. Palmer was an outspoken radio host, and my own parents were fond of quoting him: "You send your child to college black and they come back Greek." "It's enough to make a Negro turn black!" That year Palmer founded Chicago Black United Communities, an independent political group focused on electing blacks. He also organized a conference in 1981 in which the "We shall see in '83" slogan, referring to the mayoral race, was born.

Jesse Jackson Sr. emerged as a contender, but he polled low and his personality was seen as difficult. Jackson had formed Operation Breadbasket, the economic arm of the Southern Christian Leadership Council in Chicago, in 1966. After the death of Martin Luther King in 1968, the council accused Jackson of using the organization for personal gain and suspended him. In 1971, he resigned and formed Operation PUSH. When Washington won the mayoral election in 1983, it was clear that Chicago wasn't big enough for a black mayor *and* Jesse Jackson. In 1984, Jackson formed the National Rainbow Coalition, welcoming blacks, women and gays. Jackson ran for president and used the multiracial coalition playbook in his campaign.[6]

In 1982 Washington announced his candidacy after securing commitments on voter registration and fundraising. Ed Gardner, founder of the Chicago-based black hair care company Soft Sheen Products, was among the first in line and is credited with helping register more than 250,000 voters.

Washington's base was black, but he needed a broader coalition to win. His downtown campaign office reflected a mix of people. On the South Side, black nationalists strategized for the campaign in a 47th Street storefront office. Conrad Worrill, director of the Jacob H. Carruthers Center for Inner City Studies at Northeastern Illinois University, set up shop there.

"'We got to have Farrakhan,' I told Harold," Worrill recalled during an interview, referring to Chicago-based Nation of Islam leader Louis Farrakhan. In the early 1980s, the minister set out to rebuild the Nation of Islam, which had splintered and weakened after the death of leader Elijah Muhammad in 1975. His movement was growing and tapped into black pride during the Reagan years. Worrill took Washington to Farrakhan's home after the 1983 primary. "They had a nice chat talking and bullshitting," Worrill said. Worrill handed Farrakhan a flyer and asked the minister if he could mass-produce it. Farrakhan agreed. The flyer spread like wildfire and upset some white folk. The flyer said: "We Discovered It, We Should Govern It."[7] Below were sketches of Jean Baptiste Pointe du Sable, the Haitian fur trader who was the first modern settler of Chicago, and Harold Washington. The tagline: "On April 12 Vote for HAROLD WASHINGTON."

The primary pitted Washington against two white ethnics of Irish descent: incumbent Byrne and Richard M. Daley, the Cook County state's attorney and son of the Boss. Washington's strategy to win was 80 percent black voter turnout and 80 percent of their vote. Though he didn't quite hit those numbers, he won the Democratic primary anyway with 36 percent of the vote. Byrne received 33 percent and Daley finished with 30 percent. White Democrats scrambled at the outcome, and some even switched parties. Wealthy Republican lawyer Bernie Epton emerged to challenge Washington in the general election. Epton's slogan? "Before It's Too Late," a not-so-subtle race ultimatum.

Washington won the general election with 51 percent of the vote.

The 1980s was late for Chicago to elect its first black mayor compared to some other major cities. In the 1960s and 1970s, Gary, Indiana; Cleveland, Ohio; Washington, D.C.; Atlanta, Georgia; Detroit, Michigan; and Los Angeles, California, had all elected black mayors. But the concept of black control of a central city is a "hollow prize" because of white flight and an exodus of resources.

*   *   *

"Council Wars," a play on the movie *Star Wars*, kicked off right after Washington took the oath of office.

Chicago has one of the largest city councils in the country: 50 aldermen each running little fiefdoms with meandering boundaries. Alderman Ed "Fast Eddie" Vrdolyak—a lawyer of Croatian descent with a penchant for expensive suits representing the white Southeast Side steel mill area—opposed Washington from the start. He orchestrated a split among council members; Vrdolyak had 29 white members on his side compared to 21 members for Washington. The split blocked Washington's agenda at every turn. Various budgets and measures deadlocked. Appointments to city agencies got blocked. Elected officials acted sophomoric. One time Vrdolyak fluttered his arms and sang out "pretty please" in a falsetto voice to the mayor. Washington pointed a gavel at Vrdolyak and snapped, "You're about to get a mouthful of something you don't want, mister." A couple of other aldermen jumped in and one threatened, "Sit the fuck down, or I'll knock you down."[8]

Technically, Chicago's governing structure is "strong council" and "weak mayor." In practice, that governing style has meant little. The city council had always been a rubber stamp for Boss Daley and the machine, but with the arrival of a black mayor, it suddenly "discovered" its independence. The 29 bloc looked like a bunch of white bigots determined to obstruct the mayor at every turn.

On live television in 1986, Washington and Vrdolyak sparred and scoffed at each other via minicam. The news reporter couldn't get a word in as the two politicians talked over each other.

"Ed Vrdolyak systemically is discriminating against Hispanics in the city," Washington barked.

"He just ain't got it," Vrdolyak interrupted. "You don't have the slightest clue about what being mayor in Chicago is."[9]

Washington accused the media of taking race sides. Predictably, the press recoiled at accusations of complicity in race-baiting. In a December 1983 editorial, the *Tribune* gave Washington credit for not giving in to the machine but noted: "The worst thing about him is that he keeps suggesting that racism has something to do with the frustrations of being an independent mayor. The only difference between his problems and those of anyone else is that he can blame it on the white media."[10]

But one black columnist for the *Tribune* knew better. Leanita McClain wrote about the vicious racial environment after Washington's win.

I have been unprepared for the silence with which my white colleagues greeted Washington's nomination. I've been crushed by their inability to share the excitement of one of "us" making it into power. I've built walls against whites who I once thought of as my lunch and vacation friends. . . .

An evilness still possesses this town and it continues to weigh down my heart. During my morning ritual in the bathroom mirror, my radio turned to the news-talk station that is as much a part of my routine as shaping my eyebrows, I've heard the voice of this evil. In what would become a standard "bigot-on-the-street" interview, the voice was going on about "the blacks." "The blacks" this, "the blacks" that, "the blacks, the blacks, the blacks."[11]

What McClain heard also echoed in white neighborhoods on the Southwest and Northwest Sides. After Washington's election, residents started Save-Our-Neighborhood/Save Our City, an umbrella organization to deal with race. Their solution came in the form of an insurance program for homeowners, ostensibly white ones, who feared property decline if "the blacks" moved in. All homeowners in a designated district paid a small tax, and the money went into a fund in an equity program. If the appraisal was less than the original purchase price when homeowners decided to sell, homeowners would receive a cash claim for the difference. Home values actually remained steady. Essentially, this was psychological insurance for white owners in the "bungalow belt," referring to single-family homes of that style. The mayor backed the program until black city council members balked.

Meanwhile, Washington persevered against Vrdolyak's maneuvering by using his executive power to cut the city's payroll, fix the deficit and balance the budget. He ultimately emerged triumphant in the Council Wars. Council remapping, which reflected Latino and black population gains, gave him the edge he needed in votes. The Vrdolyak 29 no longer blocked his hostage department appointments.

The feud between the mayor and the council thus ended in 1986. Washington enjoyed his triumph before seeking reelection.

When the 1987 mayoral race rolled around, the same candidates and characters endeavored to unseat Washington. All were white. First up was Jane Byrne, who was more aggressive this time as she jumped in to seek the Democratic nomination. Washington beat her with 54 percent of the vote in the Democratic primary.

That didn't deter white ethnics who still disliked Washington as chief executive. Some left the machine in name only.

Don Haider, an unknown Northwestern University professor and former Byrne budget director, entered the race as a Republican candidate and won the primary. Vrdolyak, the Cook County Democratic chairman who had long flirted with the Republican Party, declared his candidacy in the new Solidarity Party. He and Democrat Tom Hynes, the county assessor, played chicken about who would run. Hynes ran under the new Chicago First party banner. Ultimately, Hynes ran but dropped out two days before the election. Enter Vrdolyak.

In its endorsement of Washington, the *Tribune* acknowledged the fight the mayor had to present a balanced budget, put in a neighborhood repair program and distribute city services fairly. "For four years, Mr. Washington won most of his battles with Edward Vrdolyak over the size and distribution of the city's work force, its tax structure and its capital programs, and Chicago is better off because he did."[12]

Washington won again with 54 percent of the vote, a mandate. His platform always included better minority city hiring, and his workforce was more diverse than that of previous mayoral administrations.

According to political observers Melvin G. Holli and Paul Green:

> Given Chicago's changing demographics and the intensity of Washington's black support, it would have taken a miracle for anyone to deny him renomination and re-election. In effect, any opponent would have had to achieve the nearly impossible—that is, win over almost all of the city's nonblack voters. Washington had an iron grip on his core constituency, and no one could take that vote away from him. Add incumbency and a growing personal attraction to city Hispanics and liberal whites, and you have a simplified blueprint of the Washington victory coalition.[13]

The twice-elected mayor thought he'd won folks over and that eventually holdout whites would come to his side. But his tenure was ended by his November 1987 heart attack and death at the age of 65.

As Chicagoans mourned Harold Washington's sudden death, and while his body was still on the hospital bed, political power games geared up. Columnist Mike Royko rightly predicted that the wildest wheeling, dealing, trading, extorting and hustling in Chicago's memory were to come.[14]

Two days after Washington's death, Jesse Jackson Sr. cut short his trip to the Middle East to fly back to Chicago to mediate the rupture in the name of black solidarity. A series of meetings with black and Hispanic leaders yielded no agreement on who Washington's successor should be. By law, the city council had to elect an acting mayor from its ranks until a 1989 special election could be held. In the meantime, David Orr, a white North Side lakefront alderman and Washington ally, briefly served as interim mayor until an acting mayor could be chosen.

"Whatever was being deliberated or prayed over in secret did not translate into a name, it translated into a process," Jackson said after the meeting.[15]

Two names of black politicians emerged: Eugene Sawyer of the Sixth Ward, a black middle-class stronghold that included Chatham, and Tim Evans of the independent, diverse Fourth Ward, which included Hyde Park.

As political maneuvering ramped up, activists organized a public tribute for Washington that could accommodate more people than the thousands who attended the funeral. Fifteen thousand people showed up at the University of Illinois–Chicago pavilion, and in the middle of the memorial, Tim Evans strolled down the aisle. The event mutated into a rally for the alderman.

"Some of the people for Gene had started peeling off that Tim Evans was more progressive or better than Gene Sawyer. This was the greatest tragedy in black history. Both came from the regular Democratic Party. Tim Evans could speak better but everyone knew Gene had helped more black people," Conrad Worrill told me.

The special session in council chambers to elect a new mayor, held December 2, 1987, looked crazy. Outside of City Hall, thousands of demonstrators allied in favor of Evans. Inside, arguing, wheeling, dealing and politicking rumbled.

At 4 a.m., to a surprisingly large television audience, the city council chose Eugene Sawyer as acting mayor in a 29–19 vote.[16] Only six blacks on the council, including Sawyer himself, voted for him. Someone scrawled "No deals. You're a traitor to Mayor Washington's dreams" on the door of the Sixth Ward Democratic organization.[17]

Some blacks rejected Sawyer because white aldermen backed him. Two of those aldermen, Ed Burke and Richard Mell, thought they could control him. During this tumult, Democratic analyst and fourth-generation Bronzeville resident Delmarie Cobb had a morning show on the black radio station WVON. She told me: "One of the things that I said often is who do we want to run the machinery? If you keep saying Gene is a machine politician, who do we want running the machine? Someone who looks like us or who doesn't? He's on the fifth floor, he's got the seat. While we're trying to replace him, which is a crapshoot, we have someone in that seat who lives in our community who you can knock on his door or pick up the phone and cuss out and will be accountable to the black community."[18]

Sawyer's council appointment lasted for 16 months. A 1989 special election would be the real test to determine who would fill out the rest of Washington's term. Richard M. Daley, then 46, determined that now was the time to put his name on the fifth-floor door to the mayor's office.

* * *

L. Anton Seals Jr. often was dragged to community meetings and political events by his father, who worked for the Washington campaign and in City Hall. In 1989, Anton Sr. worked in the Eugene Sawyer camp and took his son, a high school freshman, to a meeting at a downtown hotel.

"Lu Palmer says if we don't get our acts together we won't see the fifth floor again until that boy is my age," the younger Seals recalled to me. Palmer squarely looked at him. "I was the boy in the room. I'll never forget that. Damn, he was right."[19]

Conversely, the local media expressed exhaustion over the racial dynamics of the election. They thought a white person could save the city from racial scars.

"A Daley election would go a long way toward healing the breach in black politics created by the death of Washington," a *Tribune* political reporter wrote in February. Daley embraced the role as racial healer.[20]

Although nice-guy Sawyer was the first alderman to endorse Washington, and his ward delivered strongly for the mayor, he lacked the Evans charisma. Sawyer was quieter and a nuts-and-bolts kind of guy.[21] He knew government and showed Washington the municipal ropes once he took office. The photogenic Evans served as Washington's floor leader.

Despite his position, he wasn't seen as one who did his homework. Lu Palmer backed Evans because Washington hadn't backed Palmer when he ran for the First District congressional seat.

The 1989 election was even nastier than the 1987 council vote that selected the interim mayor. Evans supporters labeled Sawyer an Uncle Tom and a sellout. Evans decided to let Sawyer run in the Democratic primary alone but vowed to return in the general election.

Daley bested Sawyer with 56 percent of the vote. Next he faced Evans, who ran under the Harold Washington Party. Daley also faced Vrdolyak, finally a Republican. Daley won with 55 percent of the vote. Evans won the black vote but the turnout was nothing like the turnout for Washington. The alderman also couldn't compete with Daley's margins in white ethnic Northwest and Southwest Side wards. Other politicians read the tea leaves. Alderman Luis Gutierrez, a Washington soldier, endorsed Daley and began his role as a Hispanic spokesman in the city before moving on to a seat in Congress.

The Harold Washington movement officially died with the election of Daley.

"The fracturing of the black unity that we had, we've never been able to resurrect or hold on to. Tim got his ass kicked and Daley walked in," Worrill told me.

The second Daley era began in 1989, and so did the slow dismantling of politics that allowed Harold Washington to be elected in the first place.

Daley never won or fully needed the black vote. Whites backed him. Hispanic clout grew under him, and the newly created Hispanic Democratic Organization became a player in the machine. Daley did get some black pastors to praise his name and notably sold them vacant lots for one dollar. His administration had some high-profile blacks, such as Valerie Jarrett, who held a number of positions such as deputy chief of staff. She hired Michelle Obama to work for him. Daley may have talked about being a racial healer, but he never created economic development for the postindustrial South and West Sides. Segregation remained under his watch, and he did little for black neighborhoods.

No one had the money, clout or troops to defeat him.

In the 1995 mayoral race, Daley crushed former Illinois attorney general Roland Burris, a politician who enjoyed statewide election in other posts. In 1999, Daley crushed South Side congressman Bobby Rush. Neither could raise the money necessary for a campaign despite their name recognition and popularity with blacks. Slowly, some of Daley's most outspoken city council critics joined hands with him. In 2003, he received a majority in black wards, but the victory proved hollow. His opponents were so unknown that a write-in candidate might have fared better. No candidate ever came close to dismantling Daley's monarchy. Over the years, the mayor effectively neutralized the black vote, further dismantling black political unity.

In 1995, Daley seized control of Chicago Public Schools from the state, with mixed results. Daley has never been indicted, but some of his employees were convicted of taking bribes over jobs. In 2008, Daley leased Chicago's parking meter system to a private company for more than $1 billion, which voters are still pissed about because of the new outrageous rates. In an ultimate goon move, in 2003, Daley sent bulldozers escorted by Chicago police in the middle of the night to tear up Meigs Field, a tiny lakefront airport. The covert mission solidified Daley's plans for a new park.

*   *   *

I'm loath to participate in conversations that start with "the problem with black people" or "if black people could just stick together" or "black people are like crabs in a barrel." This trope isn't new. *Black Metropolis,* the sweeping sociological study of the 1930s Black Belt, recorded Negroes uttering the same thing: "I know this much—we are divided against one another more than any race in the world." "The Negroes might be able to do something if they would stick together."[22] My argument about the lack of a black political agenda shouldn't be conflated with the idea that black people are more disorganized than other ethnic groups are.

The Evans–Sawyer rift is widely accepted as the demise of black politics in Chicago. Black Chicago voted for Harold Washington as a revolt against the machine politics that meant separate but unequal. His untimely death, and the splintering that followed, meant the end of that revolt and of black politics as it was then known.

Conrad Worrill's office on the South Side Northeastern Illinois University campus fits that of an old-school black nationalist. Reparations posters and pictures of Fidel Castro are tacked to the wall. He's run out of shelves for all of his black history books. Worrill has a stack of files on Harold Washington. He admits to being duped into the Evans camp initially but told me he realized greater forces were trying to manufacture a black split.

"I think we have lost our way. It appears the more elected officials we have in government the least influence we have," Worrill, now 74, explained. "That ought to say something to us. Our fight—I come out of the black nationalist tradition, the Africanist tradition—inside of America has always been a fight for the greatest good for the greatest number. We broke down racial segregation under the law, we opened up American society. We went into the black power phase of our movement and black consciousness. What is it we are fighting for? What do black people need at this moment of history? Other periods it was clear: we wanted to dismantle racial segregation under the law."

On the other end of the generational spectrum, Charlene Carruthers, now 30, was two years old when Harold Washington died. She's national director at the Chicago-based Black Youth Project 100, an activist group, and the South Side native says the young people she encounters don't invoke Washington's name. Although she was too young to witness or remember the 1987 political fracturing, she senses something amiss locally.

"I'm not sure there is [such] a thing as black politics. I see much more middlemen, negotiators. There's not been a single black candidate to me who has actually spoken to black community issues that are important," Carruthers told me.[23] Maybe someone's good on schools but not public safety, for example.

Carruthers explained that black politics, of course, is needed in Chicago. She rattled off the problems: unemployment, intracommunity violence, schools, lack of quality of mental health care, foreclosures, access to healthy food. "It disproportionately impacts the black community. Not just because they are poor; it's absolutely informed because they are black. Redlining didn't disappear after Harold [Washington]. The effects didn't disappear. There's continued divestment. We don't need more elected officials that are just black. We have city council. We need champions in the city."

Policy wonk Will Burns is a black alderman representing integrated Hyde Park (the former ward of Tim Evans) and some parts of black neighborhoods. "What we don't really have are tables or spaces within [the] black public sphere to connect with each other and establish consensus on a black political agenda. We don't have an equivalent of a Latino Policy Forum. We have groups that purport to represent the interest but very little coordination or collaboration," Burns told me.[24]

There's arguably too much emphasis on electoral politics when assessing black politics. Voting isn't the only form of engagement, and black Chicagoans do not vote at lower rates than the rest of the city. I must offer a caveat on the death of black politics because black folk *are* involved in civic engagement. Chicago boasts myriad grassroots organizations—some black, some multiracial—involved in issues affecting the black community. They want restorative justice, affordable housing and accountability in public housing. In 2014, young people of color in Chicago took their complaints of police brutality all the way to the United Nations.[25] They are credited with forcing Mayor Rahm Emanuel to dump police superintendent Garry McCarthy just after Thanksgiving 2015. They shut down the Michigan Avenue shopping district on Black Friday after a police dashcam video went public. The video showed a white police officer pump 16 fatal bullets into 17-year-old Laquan McDonald. The aftermath of the McDonald case has made Chicago once again one of the center-stage cities in racial politics, #blacklivesmatter. Young people have found ways to consistently disrupt the flow of the city to demand political accountability.

Today these activists are conducting peace circles at transit stops, massaging dirt for community gardens, holding police accountable at community meetings, storming police board meetings for justice in cop shootings. There's plenty to organize around for a black agenda: jobs, wages, good schools and better police relationships.

Some have even suggested this is the rebirth of black politics. But much of this activity operates outside of the electoral constructs. It's hard to imagine voter turnout in any city topping 80 percent, as it did in Chicago in 1983. Avid voters don't understand voter apathy; however, low turnout says something more about the crop of candidates than about the voters.

Former white Chicago police commander Jon Burge oversaw the torture of arrestees on the South Side in the 1970s, 1980s and early 1990s. Eventually, a federal court convicted Burge for lying about torture, but not for the torturing of black men. Richard M. Daley was the county prosecutor before he became mayor and fought claims of Burge's abuse.[26] For years, groups organized for reparations for police torture victims. Some men had already received settlements that totaled more than $100 million from the city, but that wasn't enough. In a striking win—the first of its kind in the nation—the city in 2015 agreed to a reparations package that includes $5.5 million, and the nonfinancial benefits include victims and their family members: counseling, a public memorial and a social studies unit on torture survivors for all Chicago public school eighth-graders, and free tuition to any of the junior city colleges.

* * *

Given the historic machine politics of Chicago and the tradition of long-ruling mayors, I've come to view the city as like Rome, a city-state that operates independently.

The transition from King Richard to Emperor Emanuel rattled and emboldened Chicago voters. Richard M. Daley may not have died in office like his father, but he lorded over the city for two decades, and no challenger came close to beating him.

Mayor Rahm Emanuel's brusque style and some of his policies have peeved Chicagoans. Some of the critiques are from people who are tired of an iron-fisted, noncollaborative mayoral rule. The plebeians wanted change or at least to be heard.

Rahm Emanuel returned to Chicago with some White House orchestration. Daley retired in the fall of 2010, and Emanuel left his position as Obama's chief of staff to return to Chicago and run for mayor. With the election slated for February 2011, a purposefully narrow campaign window allowed campaign-fund-rich Emanuel to prevail. Emanuel swooped in and won the black vote, mostly by default because of his Obama connection.

The black old guard tried to choose a consensus candidate the way they had done in supporting Harold Washington. Their result was pitiful. West Side congressman Danny Davis was the initial choice. He withdrew, knowing too many blacks couldn't be in the race and one of them win. Former U.S. senator Carol Moseley Braun became the black candidate. Her performance was embarrassing: She won only one precinct—not ward—in the entire city. That's one out of 2,570 precincts.

"I hate to use that word, but Harold was a consensus candidate. Harold had the ability to galvanize and mobilize the black poor, the black middle class and black elite. He had the ability to bring those folks together," J. R. Fleming, a radical activist who works on affordable and public housing issues in Chicago with the Anti-Eviction Campaign, told me.[27] The group has moved homeless people into abandoned foreclosed homes renegade style.

According to Fleming, Davis and Moseley Braun were consensus candidates among the black elite and black elected officials. This race is emblematic of the generational politics in which the old black guard doesn't engage the next generation. There's not enough passing of the baton in electoral politics. Congressmen hang on to their seats. When elected officials do get the boot, it's often because a younger black demographic has moved in the area.

In 2015, Emanuel, the city's first Jewish mayor, faced a tough reelection campaign and was forced into a runoff with Mexican American challenger Jesus "Chuy" Garcia, a Cook County commissioner. Garcia was a third choice after black Cook County Board president Toni Preck-winkle and firebrand Chicago Teachers Union president Karen Lewis, also black, didn't run. Emanuel wore sweaters in his commercials to soften his image. Some voters viewed him as a get-things-done-guy who cleaned up Daley's financial quagmire. Others saw him as a vindictive power player who closed schools and is beholden to the rich and to corporate interests. Emanuel won, and each time he ran he wouldn't have emerged the victor without the black vote—he received more than 50 percent of the vote from black wards in both elections. The state of black politics doesn't allow black voters to understand how powerful they could be. With no political unity or political ask, they don't make demands of Emanuel as they could based on numbers.

Today Chicago is in a different era. New dynamics are at play politically. Income equality across all races is growing across the nation. Service industry jobs have replaced manufacturing jobs. Poor black communities suffer from double segregation. Cities like Chicago have moved toward neoliberalism, an approach that shifts the government from the public to private sector. The term shouldn't be confused with what traditionally is considered liberal. Think liberal economics in the sense of free and open markets with no state interference. Neoliberalism in Chicago means privatization of city services, such as parking meters, expansion of charter schools, antagonism toward unions and corporations having more of an influence on city government than people. Given federal, state and local budget cuts, one could argue that neoliberalism allows cities to do more with less; it's the pragmatic course to take. But the ideology aggravates class differences within the black community and exacerbates the inability of a black mayoral candidate to step forward and address the needs of the haves and have-nots. The University of Chicago's Michael Dawson argues that poor blacks suffer under neoliberalism while elite blacks who align with it benefit. "The combination of the social, political, and labor-market isolation of America's black inner cities with the increasing political salience of class in the black community has left the black poor with far less access to social, political, and economic capital, while at the same time leaving them in a state of relative political disengagement," he writes. "America's ghettos and barrios are the domestic equivalent of countries that are marked by international neoliberal regimes as immature, ungovernable, and the site of battles between Good and Evil."[28]

What's happening in Chicago isn't unique. Nationally, Dawson says that the mainstream often dismisses black political ideals. To wit, there's a huge gap in opinion polling on how blacks and whites viewed Hurricane Katrina.

"The aftermath of Hurricane Katrina demonstrated the continuing weak condition of black politics, and while the election of Barack Obama may serve to counter somewhat the debilitating nihilism of recent decades, it has not in and of itself contributed to an increase in political capacity."[29]

*   *   *

We don't know what else Harold Washington could have accomplished had he lived. Or are we too stuck searching for that answer and using his legacy to comfort us? A nostalgia lives on. Black folk have been known to harbor a "messiah complex" in which we yearn for a leader to save us. Will there be another Harold Washington? Or at least another black mayor in Chicago?

"That's not an unreasonable focus, but I'd prefer to see black communities emphasize what they think a politician should be. What's their policy on policing, schools, economic development? It's a better long-term strategy to think about programmatic strategies and find a [compatible] candidate," Dawson told me, or "you could end up with Clarence Thomas."

According to Dawson, blacks need to rebuild black politics, including its radical wing. Skin color doesn't equate to pushing a policy agenda, which is sorely lacking. The War on Drugs, economic development and police brutality are among the issues that the right candidate could run on.

Coalition politics helped elect Obama. Chicago's first deliberate coalition came together under Harold Washington.

Black voters viewed Jesse Jackson Jr. as the anointed one. The former South Side congressman, who served from 1995 to 2012, flirted with the idea of running for mayor. He always spoke in clear racial economic terms, including championing a third airport in the region to spur economic development and jobs for blacks. He distanced himself from his father, notably when the latter was caught on a hot microphone talking about cutting off Obama's balls. But Junior's mayoral hopes were dashed permanently by his prison time for spending $750,000 in campaign cash on luxury goods. There's no doubt that Jackson could have built a coalition in a mayoral bid.

"Coalition politics work best when you're strong. The black base has to be organized first. You have to have a base to enter coalition. If you can't bring voters, what can you do for me?" Dawson told me.

According to Worrill: "We haven't found the resolve as a political entity in the city to figure out what the black political agenda is. Therein is the problem. The Latinos/Hispanics seem to be more unified in their resolve around contracts services employment, etc., in their own communities even though they have differences."

Harold Washington's integrated coalition changed white and black politics in Chicago. To win today, candidates have to have the optics of a multiracial coalition even if their policies belie the actual ideology. Richard M. Daley boasted a multiracial cadre of supporters. Obama spoke directly to black voters while assuring whites he understood them. Yet the peril of coalition building is that black candidates have to go out of their way to appear to be the candidate "for everyone."

Voters of all races expect that black elected officials will represent a wider set of interests than blacks alone, but if they do so, who's looking out for black interests?

African American interests are wide, and there's no one way to be black, but it seems black politicians can't look *too* black. Today nonblack candidates often represent black politics—not because these candidates include an unapologetic black agenda but because they appeal to individual interests of people who are black.

9

SWEET HOME CHICAGO

I AM AN UPPITY NEGRESS.

I used to wear a black T-shirt with that phrase emblazoned on it in white bubble letters. I consider myself uppity not in the sense of being bougie or stuck-up. I'm uppity by speaking up as a black woman. I don't let race or gender hinder or box me in.

Historically, whites have used the word "uppity" or phrase "uppity nigger" to describe blacks who didn't "stay in their place." Those black women and men who didn't capitulate to white authority sometimes faced violence.

I thought about that shirt and the concept of being uppity after the death of suburban Chicago native Sandra Bland. She spoke up for herself and challenged a Texas state trooper who pulled her over after a minor traffic violation in July 2015. A dashcam video showed that the trooper threatened to Taser her. He dragged Bland out of her car when she asked why she had to put out her cigarette. He slammed her on the ground. Then Bland, 28, sat in jail in an orange jumpsuit for three days, and authorities say she committed suicide. All for not using her turn signal after the trooper tailed her and she sought to move out his way.

I covered Bland's funeral at her home church, DuPage African Methodist Episcopal, in a western Chicago suburb. Family and friends wore all white. They talked about how the Black Lives Matter movement inspired Bland so much that she returned to her college alma mater in Texas for a new job. Joyfulness filled the sanctuary as they remembered her young life. Bland's family disputes that Sandy, as she's known, hanged herself in a jail cell. U.S. senator Dick Durbin spoke about the need for her death to be investigated. On his trip to Chicago for the funeral, he observed that plenty of people change lanes without using their signal and still keep their lives.

Outside Bland's funeral, strangers held signs reading "#sayhername." In cases of police- and state-sponsored violence, the stories of black women have largely been rendered invisible because society isn't used to standing up for black women; black men dominate the narrative around violence. Bland's story is a notable exception. Her death is a tragedy, no matter if she committed suicide. An overly aggressive law enforcement official didn't like that she asked him questions. He bullied her and must have viewed Bland as an uppity negress who didn't submit to his authority. Watching the video of their exchange made my stomach hurt.

I also remembered my own run-in with Chicago police at age 19 while I was home from college on Christmas break.

It was 1995, and a group of black childhood friends and I decided to go ice skating downtown. Three of us stood inside the warming center to rent skates when a police officer singled us out and ordered us to leave. Why? I asked. He didn't say. I was embarrassed to be pulled out of line and felt I had the right to know why, especially when I hadn't done anything wrong.

After we went outside near the rink, a sea of white police officers descended. One officer threw a friend on the ground. I screamed, "What's going on?" and then another officer placed me in handcuffs. Then I yelled, "Get this white bitch off me!" The officers threw three of us into a police van. The other two friends wisely remained quiet. I knew I'd gone too far as we were hauled off to jail, but I had no idea why the situation had escalated.

Turns out one friend had exchanged words with an employee, who felt threatened and called the police. As the police instructed her to leave, she told them she still had friends on the premises. That's why the officer interrupted our ice skate rental.

Once at the police station, officers made fun of us for being college girls. In return, we retorted that out of all the criminals in the city, they handcuffed three teenagers. They brought us in for resisting arrest. We were searched, they took off most of our clothes, our mug shots were taken, then we were put in separate cells with bologna sandwiches. I kept quiet and went to sleep. By now humility had set in.

Our disappointed and worried parents came to get us. My mother was in tears. That night my parents gave me and my siblings the don't-talk-back-to-police talk. I should've known better. In high school, I drove a 1984 brown Pontiac Bonneville. I remember instances of police officers pulling me over only to check my ID. Without first seeing me, I think they assumed I was a guy because my car was seen as a "gang car." During those episodes, I kept quiet and patient.

Still, my parents didn't blame me completely for the ice skating debacle. I know I shouldn't have cursed at the female officer, but rage had boiled in my silly 19-year-old veins. Three months later, I returned to Chicago for my court date. The police report said I screamed "bitch" repeatedly at the top of my lungs—which was untrue; I only said it once—and officers feared for their safety. I am five feet tall and probably weighed 90 pounds. I had no weapon on me. The case got thrown out.

My story could easily have turned out worse.

I was no martyr during my police run-in, but I recognize how quickly things can turn for people without power faced with people in power. I have no doubt that race played a role in our arrest. Why was backup called? Why were we handcuffed? Why weren't we treated like teenagers? I asked questions and never got an answer outside of the silver bracelets slapped on my wrists.

Having a police story is almost like a rite of passage for black people.

*   *   *

From New Orleans to Ferguson to Baltimore, we are having another national conversation around race, institutional racism, police brutality and a rigged criminal justice system.

I see the deliberateness of segregation. I remain steadfast in my belief that segregation is crippling because it's the common denominator in innumerable challenges in black communities, from housing to jobs to food access to education to violence. Communities should be uplifted without conceding to whiteness as superior, and investment should never cease in black communities. But unofficial "separate but equal" isn't working out too well for us. Banks, businesses and housing and education policies participate in and perpetuate segregation.

Exploring contemporary segregation in Chicago and its insidious effects has challenged me. Throughout my reporting, some people have questioned whether my antisegregation stance is anti-black and pro-white. No, it is not. That said, the term "black segregation" sounds as if black people are to blame for the conditions that have thrust them into onerous circumstances. Often black space is talked about solely from a deficit angle. We don't use the term "segregation" to describe white homogenous areas. Martin Luther King Jr. once said that segregation is the Negro's burden and America's shame.

The phrase "white segregation" should be applied frequently. White segregation is furthered, both historically and currently, with housing, banking and school policies. In *Racism Without Racists: Color-Blind Racism and the Persistence of Racial Inequality in the United States*, sociologist Eduardo Bonilla-Silva describes the high level of white social and residential segregation. Nothing irks a white person more than to be called racist because often that conjures up card-carrying membership in the Ku Klux Klan or unflinching use of the word "nigger." That narrow definition of racism gives the illusion that whites are somehow color-blind. Bonilla-Silva refers to white segregation as a white habitus, "a racialized, uninterrupted socialization process that *conditions* and *creates* whites' racial taste, perceptions, feelings, and emotions and their views on racial matters."[1] The consequences of "white habitus" promote a sense of white belonging and solidarity while projecting negative views toward nonwhites. White segregation turns blacks from the white orbit, reinforcing stereotypes, prejudice and the idea that discrimination is abstract. Segregation is one of the spokes in white supremacy, and it should be dismantled.

Still, black communities are beautiful and complicated places. Chatham produced me. Bronzeville's struggles don't cancel out a strong legacy. Englewood is full of neighbors who care about their community.

Even the First Lady basks in that exquisiteness.

In a 2015 commencement speech at King College Prep High School on Chicago's South Side, Michelle Obama instructed graduates to seize the narrative about their communities:

> Too often, we hear a skewed story about our communities: a narrative that says that a stable, hardworking family in a neighborhood like Woodlawn or Chatham or Bronzeville is somehow remarkable, that a young person who graduates from high school and goes to college is a beat-the-odds kind of hero. I can't tell you how many times people have met my mother and asked her, "How did you ever manage to raise kids like Michelle and Craig in a place like South Shore?" And my mom looks at these folks like they're crazy, and she says, "Michelle and Craig are nothing special. There are millions of Craigs and Michelles out there, and I did the same thing that all those other parents did—I loved them, I believed in them, and I didn't take any nonsense from them."

This is the story of the South Side I lived. Black life in Chicago is a place of loveliness and contradictions and negotiation. And not just for black males; I'm speaking for a particular portion of South Side black girls as well. Knowing how to talk to police. Knowing how to interact with a cross section of socioeconomic black people. Knowing how to switch between myriad black and white worlds.

Growing up, we had our garage broken into and heard police sirens. I learned how to ski and play the piano, dance to the percolator and the waltz, be a debutante and a Girl Scout, fix my face in the fancy department stores and on the subway.

I learned how to be down and uppity.

* * *

Chicago's slogan is that we are a city of neighborhoods.

The mentality is both provincial and identity-driven. Our neighborhoods connect and divide us.

Can black neighborhoods achieve equity? How can the city be desegregated? Chicago's not a snow globe waiting to be shaken up to disperse people all over. One of the perplexities of Chicago is that diversity and segregation can go together easily within the same landscape.

As I contemplate these questions, I think about a neighborhood that's organically changing despite its filthy racial history.

Black kids grew up intuitively knowing not to roam Bridgeport. If they crossed the invisible "no blacks allowed" sign at the border, someone might hiss "nigger" at them. The White Sox baseball park offered the only safe space for blacks to wander, because whites knew that black spectators would return to their own neighborhoods after the ninth inning. Besides sorry race relations, the white South Side neighborhood is noted for its historic political heft; Bridgeport produced five Chicago mayors—including two with the last name Daley.

This traditional Irish enclave, mothership to the Democratic political machine, has a long history of animosity toward blacks. A commission that investigated Chicago's 1919 race riot concluded that it was not only impossible for Negroes to live there but dangerous. In the 1950s, whites routinely used violence to keep blacks from moving in. Even decades after the tumultuous transition toward open housing in Chicago that shifted racial patterns, Bridgeport remained mostly white, its parishes and ethnic clubs intact. Working-class whiteness endured in the small frame homes and bungalows while Latinos comprised a small and growing demographic on one side of the neighborhood. Mayor Richard

M. Daley stunned the city in 1993 when he moved out of Bridgeport to a nascent neighborhood on the outskirts of downtown, perhaps understanding that a mayor who purported to be the mayor for all had to physically leave his roots behind.

The mayor's move notwithstanding, racial incidents in Bridgeport continued.

In 1997, a posse of white teenagers beat a black boy into a coma. In 2005, a Confederate flag was draped over a wooden porch across the alley where my sister's black friend lived. When I asked why he lived there after I dropped him off one night, he responded pragmatically: cheap rent. In 2012, a black comedian and his wife settled with a white couple over a housing discrimination lawsuit after the white couple backed out of a verbal agreement to sell them their house.

An expressway separates Bridgeport from Bronzeville. In 2006, the city shut it down for major repairs. The road work allowed me to get reacquainted with the neighborhood since one of the alternative routes ran straight through Bridgeport.

As I sped along, I spotted new bars, art galleries and signs in Chinese and Spanish. The acclaimed Chinese American artists the Zhou brothers opened an 87,000-square-foot art center in 2004 that hosts studio space, exhibits and parties. Two rising black male artists used studio space there, and when I visited them, they gave me a knowing look that said, "Yeah, two black Chicago dudes in Bridgeport. How did this happen?" I stumbled upon Pancho Pistolas, a Mexican restaurant with tasty margaritas and al fresco seating. Inside, the place served a surprisingly diverse crowd that included black patrons.

When Brandi, my Chatham childhood friend with whom I had my "L" train race moment, moved back to Chicago, I suggested we meet at Pancho Pistolas for lunch. "Bridgeport?" she asked incredulously. "Yes, trust me," I replied. "It's weird, but Bridgeport is changing."

I experienced some cognitive dissonance hanging out in Bridgeport; it's hard not to think of the neighborhood's legacy. I've never been chased out, yelled at or felt uncomfortable. I also only go to places that express openness.

Today more than half of Bridgeport is composed of Asian and

Hispanic households. The other half is white. The neighborhood isn't a model of racial utopia by any means. Blacks visit and leave. An influx of artists, spacious new townhomes and Michelin Bib Gourmand—a coveted dining list—restaurants have not gentrified Bridgeport. A blue-collar aesthetic exists amid the neighborhood's reinvention. Old-school watering holes dot some of the streets along with old athletic clubs and diners with blue-plate specials.

One of my favorite bars in the entire city is Bridgeport's very own Maria's Packaged Goods & Community Bar. It's a classic slashie—half liquor store, half neighborhood tavern. Maria Marszewski, a Korean woman who married a Polish cop, worked the front liquor store. She began operating the bar in 1986, and white women in the neighborhood would scream racial shit at her all the time. But inside her tavern, Maria wouldn't tolerate overt racism, and that's how she created a diverse environment.

In 2010, she handed over the bar to her sons Ed and Mike, and the brothers retooled it.

Wood tables and wood paneling give a log cabin look. Beer-bottle chandeliers hang from the copper ceiling. Maria's is cozy and takes its music seriously, but the bar doesn't take itself too seriously. It has the casualness and familiarity of a dive but without the grit. People of different races and ages park at the bar, including neighborhood folk. During the Christmas holidays, I brought my visiting sister. We heard Wu-Tang Clan and a dog barking "Jingle Bells" during the same DJ set while a bartender wore an ugly Christmas sweater.

The community bar portion takes its name from people who bring in a drink recipe and get it on the menu. Craft beers and cocktails are emphasized at reasonable prices. Old Style, a Chicago classic beer, is on the menu, as is "a random shitty beer" for two bucks. I've gotten used to listening to Biggie or A Tribe Called Quest or classic soul at Maria's. The cognitive dissonance is slowly fading. I look at Bridgeport mostly through a positive lens: A neighborhood can change. Diversity begets positivity.

Over the years, I've gotten to know co-owner Ed Marszewski, who's committed to neighborhood change. I hung out with him one afternoon sipping ginger ale as he smoked a cigarette at an indoor wood picnic table in another Bridgeport property he owns. The experimental gallery hosted a temporary park exhibit in which the artist crowdsourced plants. Hence the picnic table in the middle of a loft space.

Ed told me about his days as a teenager when his mother, a restaurant operator, first opened in Bridgeport. "People would say 'get the fuck out of here you fucking chink or gook.' I'd say 'get the fuck out of my neighborhood you fucking wop or whatever.'"[2] Growing up in the suburbs of Chicago, he learned how to fight in first or second grade and could beat the crap out of fifth graders.

"I've always been aware I'm a mutant kid," Ed says of having a Korean mother and a Polish father. "My whole life I'm growing up with racism. You realize in Chicago everyone hates everyone on the next block. It's tribalism. You get used to it. I was a union carpenter for a while. These old guys would say racist jokes. Throw the same jokes back at their face and nine times out of ten they couldn't take it."

Ed once thought Bridgeport would be the location of the racial apocalypse. "Working at Maria's, the Mexican kids would say 'hey, Bruce Lee,' which is the height of absurdity. Every ethnic group hated each other equally, but they hated blacks more than anyone else."

Bridgeport grew on him over the years. "Once people got to know you, people would stop calling [you] gook. You started to see diversity around 2005," Ed told me.

When Ed and Mike took over Maria's, they wanted to make the bar warm and relaxed. They stocked the shelves with stuff they liked to drink, cleaned it up and put good cocktails on the menu. They took out the television, emphasized music more and used the bar for community meetings on how to improve the neighborhood.

"Beer lovers and foodies don't care who you are. That is what freaked me out: the rise of the cocktail, the notion of 'cool,'" Ed told me. Maria's didn't market itself. As the demographics of the neighborhood changed and outsiders felt safer or welcome, its popularity spread.

Again, Bridgeport is hardly a racial utopia. Blacks still don't live there. Racial animus from white old-timers is real if not overt. Yet if Bridgeport can slowly change, maybe other neighborhoods can. Bridgeport seemed to evolve naturally. But usually when it comes to desegregation, deliberate action must be taken. In the Chicago region, suburban Oak Park is seen as a beacon of diversity. In the late 1960s, the suburb passed an open housing ordinance on the heels of the federal Fair Housing Act. Real estate agents were banned from blockbusting and panic-peddling, tactics used to spur nervous white homeowners who saw black migration on the horizon into fleeing. Oak Park started a housing center and community relations committee that welcomed black newcomers and monitored housing practices. The result wasn't perfect, but it was an intentional effort to have an integrated community.

That type of intentionality doesn't exist throughout the region.

Since the 1970s, Chicago's changing neighborhood story has been one of a dwindling middle class and growing income inequality. There's the Chicago Google headquarters effect in the West Loop with trendy restaurants and expensive condos, near the overpriced barbecue joint where my friend Jenny and I ate. Yet rampant and stubborn unemployment in pockets of the West and South Sides creates a dichotomy of two cities. Today the median income and housing value in once-stable communities are being squeezed.

Gentrification often is the buzzword when figuring out who are winners and losers in cities. Researchers at the University of Illinois at Chicago conducted a gentrification index in 2014 and mapped out socioeconomic trends in all of the city's neighborhoods. Scoring neighborhoods based on the index, Chicago's 77 neighborhoods were grouped into nine categories ranging from "stable upper/middle class," meaning index scores remained high since the 1970s, to "severe declines," meaning those scores dropped significantly. Only nine neighborhoods fit that "gentrifying" classification, almost all of them in downtown Chicago or just north of it, areas that have been historically white. Fourteen neighborhoods in "severe decline" were black and segregated. And black middle-class neighborhoods experienced declines in median incomes and home values. Neighborhoods exhibiting no change or stability were either white or integrated neighborhoods like mine, Hyde Park.[3]

Bridgeport is not gentrifying. According to the study, it's an "improving" neighborhood.

* * *

Journalists are often not solution oriented. In this book, I've tried not only to plainly lay out the problems of segregation but offer remedies from various people entrenched in neighborhood work. Segregation can seem so intractable, so cemented among Chicagoans, particularly those who have lived here for generations. But as education civil rights scholar Gary Orfield says in Chapter 5, on the failure of school integration, a lack of creativity continues to stifle Chicago and the greater metropolitan area.

Housing is at the heart of segregation in Chicago and America, and until policy addresses that exclusionary isolation, ghettoization will continue.

I'd love cities to establish real commissions—not window dressing, not stacked with so-called experts because it is politically expedient to include them—that contemplate segregation and subsequently offer solutions. Decades after the Kerner Commission's report, our country is still "two societies." The burning rage we watched erupt in Ferguson and Baltimore can be directly linked to residential segregation that the U.S. government created to contain ghettos. Today a growing chorus is challenging the old mentality.

Keeping in the spirit of finding solutions, I asked several activists, scholars and artists who either live in Chicago or study the city to weigh in on what the city can do to lessen or even end segregation.[4] These ideas are applicable to other urban places in America.

Mary Pattillo, professor of sociology and African American studies at Northwestern University and author of *Black Picket Fences: Privilege and Peril Among the Black Middle Class*, pushed back against the idea of integration a bit. She told me that the question about ending segregation suggests that segregation itself is the problem. She argues segregation is a problem only because it allows for the unequal distribution of resources. She says it's true that segregation allows state governments and private investors to invest in white neighborhoods and not invest in black neighborhoods and often leads to bad outcomes for black people and black families.

Pattillo is not arguing for a separate-but-equal doctrine, but "given how hard it is to undo segregation using the mechanisms we've used already, we could imagine a different direction, which is we have predominantly black neighborhoods that are underresourced, that are underinvested, disinvested systematically. We could imagine increasing resources, improving opportunities, flushing those neighborhoods with resources and they would improve. The children who live there would have better outcomes; the families who live there would have happier lives, the housing stock would be more expensive—all of the things would happen that we would imagine and that might make those neighborhoods more attractive for nonwhites to move into, and that would decrease segregation. I think the question of 'How do we end segregation?' first has to begin with the question 'Is ending segregation first the right approach, or is improving predominantly black neighborhoods as predominantly black neighborhoods—should that be our first goal, and might that result in more racial integration because it would make those neighborhoods more appealing for nonblacks to move into?'"

Achy Obejas is a novelist and poet who bought a condo in the black North Kenwood/Bronzeville area before the housing boom and bust. "I really thought we were moving toward a greater diversity of people and a greater sort of economic bounty," she told me. "It really seemed like there was this possibility because there was a lot of construction going on and most of the people moving in were middle class. It wasn't initially this big wave of white folks or anything like that; it was economically diverse. Nobody talks about that. Everybody always talks about segregation strictly in terms of race, but economics has a lot to do with that. A lot of people made a quick buck and then came the bust. People lost their jobs and, in some weird way, the neighborhood has kind of frozen in a tougher situation. We don't see the furniture and evictions the way we did a few years back anymore. But if you drive around, you'll see that we have way too many housing units in this area. I live across the street and I can count five, six empty units just from my window. It also means that we're at risk for squatters, for particular kinds of property crime. And it keeps small businesses from coming here; it keeps other kinds of businesses from coming here. The economic development that could actually anchor this neighborhood and make it attractive to all kinds of people and that would therefore diversify the neighborhood and thus organically end segregation, rather than through some forced plan, doesn't happen."

Even though I've repeated that Chicago is almost equally black, white and Latino, I've spent a great deal of time in this book describing black neighborhoods and exploring the black-white divide. But I don't mean to minimize the Latino influence that runs through the city. Primarily and historically, the Latino immigration flow to Chicago has been from Mexico. Robert Sampson is professor of social sciences at Harvard University and former University of Chicago professor/scientific director of a long-term study of Chicago that evolved into the book *Great American City: Chicago and the Enduring Neighborhood Effect*. Sampson told me that some of the cities and regions of the country that have seen the greatest declines in, or at least lower levels of, segregation, especially economic segregation, are areas that are more diverse. "We should start thinking about affordable housing, keeping crime down, improving public schools, increasing diversity and immigration of the population as major forces in society and in cities that predict the extent to which integrated communities thrive. It used to be historically, at least racially integrated communities in Chicago were relatively few and far between. They had strong institutions, like, for example, in Hyde Park you have the University of Chicago, but most neighborhoods don't. That's why I would really look to these broader social forces and I would argue that policies really need to stay in tune to the extent which they can support these general factors and if that's possible." Sampson is fairly optimistic about racial segregation but a little less optimistic about the economic segregation part. "Englewood is a very troubled area. It's poor; it's distant from the center of the city, from the lake. It also has a housing stock that has really declined tremendously. It really doesn't have a lot of the features that, at least in a typical market, create a lot of demand. The city should think outside the box and invest and allow unusual, maybe even radical, housing plans to grow in communities like that. If I were the mayor, I would offer some houses—maybe not ones that are completely run down—but perhaps give them up for free to either institutions or individuals that commit to the neighborhood."

I've longed admired Lisa Yun Lee's philanthropic and social justice work throughout Chicago. Currently, she's director of the School of Art and Art history at the University of Illinois at Chicago. Before that she ran the university's Jane Addams Hull-House Museum. "When we talk about Chicago being segregated, what we're actually talking about is a kind of apartheid that exists in the city where the segregation is not the root cause but it's a symptom of white supremacy," Lee told me. "It's a symptom of the lack of resources that are being doled out to certain segments of society. You have to look at ending segregation in Chicago in an intersectional way, and you'd have to really address issues of white supremacy. You have to be really honest about thinking about who wins and who loses by a city being segregated. I'm a cultural activist by day, and that's what really drives me. I really do believe that if you look at our city and where culture lives, we should really invest in those pockets. Things that seem trivial or to be the extras in life—dancing, house music, the kind of food you're eating—are actually at the core of what it means to be a human being in the city. If we were to really focus on the cultural life of the city and how to bring people to experience a vast array of different cultural experiences in the city, I feel like that would actually end segregation a lot faster because it's also a way people understand one another. When they start to appreciate what one another has to offer, that's where new forms start to develop so there's not just a fetishization of one notion of authenticity on what it means to be Latino or African American." Culture takes place all over Chicago, the city where house music was born. Lee is imagining culture in all sorts of spaces, not just large museums and cultural institutions. "Chicago should really take the lead: be the city of Ida B. Wells-Barnett and Jane Addams and say let's be a model for the rest of the world and not be afraid to say when we talk about desegregating the city, we're talking about creating a more equitable Chicago for everyone," Lee told me.

Emile Cambry Jr., founder of Blue 1647, a technology and entrepreneurship center in Englewood, echoes Lee. He advocates something called Sister Neighborhoods, where different communities partner with other neighborhoods. "How do we have those communities interact with those communities and make sure that it's okay to talk with those communities or make sure we have that interchange and that kind of communication? That will break down a lot of barriers. Or find ideas like that to encourage participation around things we all celebrate and enjoy, food and festivals for example. You have a lot of people who don't feel welcome in certain communities because you're either not wealthy enough, you're going to get in trouble, or some people are going to say, why are those people over here?" Cambry told me.

Artists in Chicago are responding to segregation with cultural intentionality. The Chicago Home Theater Festival, for example, brings strangers to people's living rooms, kitchens and backyards in neighborhoods all over the city during the month of May. Several artists perform, and attendees give donations. It's a hyperlocal response to hypersegregation. My husband and I attended one in the black Greater Grand Crossing neighborhood in 2014. I've never seen so many white people there. The following year, we hosted a play, dancers and performance art in our home. We hardly knew anyone in attendance. Afterward a DJ kept the party going as people munched on buttermilk pies, homemade ice cream, spinach or navy beans. It was a magnificent experience.

Of course, eradicating segregation would take years, even generations, and it's not as easy to see the first step in how to dismantle segregation. But Steve Bogira, race/segregation reporter for the weekly *Chicago Reader*, says there is an easy first step. "One of the first things we should do in Chicago is crack down on people who are discriminating against people who want to move into what are usually white neighborhoods on the North Side. This includes other areas too, where African Americans and sometimes Latinos have tried to move and they don't get calls back when they apply for an apartment," Bogira told me. In the fair housing world, testing consists of sending out people in pairs with everything equal except race—the kind my aunt and uncle did when they lived in Beverly. The Lawyers' Committee for Better Housing tests throughout neighborhoods in Chicago and finds that discrimination frequently occurs. "It's happening," Bogira said, "but we're not stopping landlords from doing it. We need to crack down on that kind of overt discrimination. There also needs to be more affordable housing for people throughout the city. This is also complicated by zoning practices, which make it easy for a community to say we just don't build properties that are affordable in our area." Chicago developers are required to put affordable apartments in all new developments of ten or more units that seek zoning changes. Developers flout that rule by making a payment to the city instead.

Experts like Janet Smith, associate professor of urban planning at University of Illinois at Chicago and codirector of the Nathalie P. Voorhees Center for Neighborhood and Community Improvement, says zoning is a regional tool that can put a dent in segregation. Many suburbs use "home rule" and exclusionary zoning to keep out affordable housing or apartments. "One of the things that's been a big push in the Chicago area and around the country is to eliminate exclusionary zoning and make zoning more inclusionary—making sure a certain amount of units are going to be set aside for affordable housing. We know there's a strong need for affordable housing and for people who are nonwhite. . . . If all of these municipalities just started to attack this problem from those regulatory perspectives, then you start to see this idea of furthering the fair housing movement opening the doors up," Smith explained.

Since the 1960s, there's been policy and advocacy from people who believe that integration is the end gain that we should be pursuing by any means possible, Smith told me. "They blame racial segregation—and I do too—on the reason the conditions are poor and undesirable, but they forget that there are other strategies that also might lead to integration: improve the housing, the schools, access to transportation, all the things that make a good neighborhood. A good neighborhood means that people want to live there. We want to make sure people really do have a choice to live where they want to live. And in regards to segregation, there's been a bit of a pushback on this in the last decade or so—partly because of this movement that wants to push people out but also because people have integration fatigue. At this rate, we're not going to reach a fully integrated society for dozens of decades in terms of the data projecting out, so why are we trying so hard and making such little progress? Maybe we need to understand, let people choose where they want to live, make the community better and not worry so much about segregation. What we do need to worry about though is when segregation is something that prevents people from having choices, prevents people from having quality neighborhoods to live in and leads to discrimination and uneven access to resources."

The 1968 Fair Housing Act hasn't filled its goals and obligation to prevent discrimination. But there's been a recent shift on the federal level with two key 2015 actions. In a move that surprised many in the fair housing community, the U.S. Supreme Court ruled that the Fair Housing Act is violated if minorities are segregated into low-income areas even if the policy is unintentional. A couple of weeks after that ruling, the Obama administration announced new rules on what's known as affirmatively furthering fair housing. Any municipality or public housing authority that receives money from the U.S. Department of Housing and Urban Development must come up with a plan for diversifying housing. To help, HUD will give the authorities reams of demographic data so communities can examine segregation and make better decisions going forward.

These were two big wins for affordable housing and integration, and neither is a radical step. Institutional racism and segregated housing patterns are often "unintentional," so the Supreme Court ruling doesn't gut the Fair Housing Act. And putting communities on notice that they actually have to think about segregation before spending their money may be just the clarion call needed. This rule will especially benefit places outside of central big cities.

Douglas Massey, professor of sociology and public affairs at Princeton University and coauthor of *American Apartheid: Segregation and the Making of the Underclass*, told me that in addition to enforcing the Fair Housing Act, residential mobility programs need to be in place. The original residential mobility program was in Chicago, known as the Gautreaux program. He says it was quite successful in opening up opportunity for low-income residents in the city of Chicago and areas throughout the entire metropolitan area and ended up improving a lot of people's lives. "It's not about black people wanting to live with white people. It's about the willingness of African Americans to deal with white people in order to get access to all the benefits and resources of American society. Inevitably, benefits and resources are unevenly distributed around the metropolitan area. To access them, you have to move. And historically in the United States, poor groups have come in, for example, and they settle in lousy neighborhoods as they move up the economic ladder and seek to move up the residential ladder. African Americans have never been given those first few steps up the ladder because the residential mobility has been so constrained. You have to bring race and segregation back into the debate in a very direct and straightforward way and not mince words. You find very few politicians are willing to do this."

And segregation has a price tag, says Marisa Novara, planning director at the Metropolitan Planning Council, a nonpartisan nonprofit that works on regional Chicago growth issues. "We have traditionally looked at the costs of concentrated poverty for people who live in poverty, and that's incredibly important. When we leave it at that, we leave out a lot of people who may feel like that's unfortunate but it's not my problem. Until we understand the real cost of living so separately from one another, we won't fully embrace what we need to do to change that," Novara explained to me. "We know a lot about concentrations by income and how that affects us as a city, and we know a lot about what that does to countries. We know that countries that are more economically concentrated perform worse in many economic measures. But we have not really drilled down yet as a city, as a region."

One of the reasons we get stuck on segregation is because it's addressed only as a hearts-and-minds issue instead of something a little more pedestrian and operational. "Why do people choose to live where they live?" Bridget Gainer, a Cook County board commissioner, asked me rhetorically. Often it's a matter of lifestyle—schools and restaurants, family and faith institutions. "The question becomes, how do we take neighborhoods that have a lot to offer and make them more attractive to residents of all stripes? Because you could argue that segregation around income is just as damning as segregation around race. Should there be a marketing plan for neighborhoods that would make it interesting for people of all races but also all income levels, or at least a wider band of income level, to live in this neighborhood? Much of what's going to drive the health and vitality of a city is going to be more mobile, younger workers who don't want to buy a house, they want to rent. Our neighborhoods are not just going to be populated with people who work in the city center and want to buy a house, have a mortgage with two kids. You used to only have to appeal to that narrow band; now you have to appeal to a greater. Do you have food trucks, do you have pop-up retail, do you have natural amenities that drive people to be around somewhere, do you have running tracks, do you have gyms? As crazy and mundane as it sounds, people are going to make decisions that fit with their life, so now we just have to get ahead of that curve to determine what is it that makes someone willing to move to a community that they don't know and don't live in. When rethinking a neighborhood, we should really go around the world. Open it up to the architects and planners and artists and people from around the world to say 'What would you do if you had an open slate here?' That's going to get people get interested, rather than saying 'How do we get a Target?'"

* * *

Segregation is a regional and a hyperlocal issue. But it's more than policy. I choose to see the humanity in the people behind the policies. Change *is* possible.

Promoting integration can be problematic because it can come off as if black people are a problem that need white fixing. My entire life is a jumble of contradictions within black self-expression. I grew up in Jack and Jill and the black cultural nationalist theater scene on the South Side. I attended Howard University, a space that allowed me to grow and articulate my brand of blackness. I've been a member of black professional organizations. I married a black man. I'm okay being called a hypocrite. I wouldn't give up any of those black spaces in the name of lambasting segregation. Desegregation isn't about black people giving up their institutions.

Self-selection and self-identification are not the same as state-sponsored segregation in either Chicago or America.

NOTES

INTRODUCTION

1. Steve Bogira, "The Most Important Issue No One's Talking about in the Mayoral Race," *Chicago Reader,* February 4, 2015, http://www.chicagoreader .com/chicago/still-separate-unequal-and-ignored/Content?oid=16347785.
2. Nate Silver, "The Most Diverse Cities Are Often the Most Segregated," Five ThirtyEight.com, May 1, 2015, http://fivethirtyeight.com/features/the-most -diverse-cities-are-often-the-most-segregated/.
3. John R. Logan and Brian J. Stults, "The Persistence of Segregation in the Metropolis: New Findings from the 2010 Census," March 24, 2011.
4. Douglas Massey, interview by author, February 16, 2015. Unless otherwise indicated, subsequent quotes are from this interview.
5. Quoted in Debra Cassens Weiss, "Ginsburg: Ferguson Turmoil Illustrates 'Real Racial Problem' in America," *ABA Journal,* August 25, 2014. http:// www.abajournal.com/news/article/ginsburg_ferguson_turmoil_illustrates _real_racial_problem_in_america.
6. Report of the National Advisory Commission on Civil Disorders, 1968 http://www.eisenhowerfoundation.org/docs/kerner.pdf.
7. Douglas S. Massey and Nancy A. Denton, *American Apartheid: Segregation and the Making of the Underclass* (Cambridge, MA: Harvard University Press, 1993), 198.
8. Nikole Hannah-Jones, "Living Apart: How the Government Betrayed a Landmark Civil Rights Law," *ProPublica,* October 29, 2012, http://www .propublica.org/article/living-apart-how-the-government-betrayed-a-land mark-civil-rights-law.
9. Robert Sampson, interview by author, February 26, 2015.

CHAPTER 1: A LEGACY THREATENED

1. Mary Pattillo-McCoy, *Black Picket Fences: Privilege and Peril Among the Black Middle Class* (Chicago: University of Chicago Press, 1999), 3.
2. Julia B. Isaacs, "Economic Mobility of Black and White Families," Brookings Institution, November 2007, http://www.brookings.edu/research/papers /2007/11/blackwhite-isaacs.

3. Mary Pattillo, interview by author, January 15, 2015. Unless otherwise indicated, subsequent quotes are from this interview.

4. Joseph Moore Jr. and Yvonne G. Moore, interview by author, January 5, 2015. Subsequent quotes are from this interview.

5. *Local Community Fact Book of Chicago,* multiple years, available at Harold Washington Library Center, Chicago.

6. Gregory D. Squires, "Demobilization of the Individualistic Bias: Housing Market Discrimination as a Contributor to Labor Market and Economic Inequality," *American Academy of Political and Social Science* 609, no. 1 (January 2007): 200–14.

7. David Rusk, "The 'Segregation Tax': The Cost of Racial Segregation to Black Homeowners," Center on Urban & Metropolitan Study, Brookings Institution, 2001, 3, http://www.brookings.edu/research/reports/2001/10/metropolitanpolicy-rusk.

8. Ibid., 5.

9. Dorothy Brown, interview by author, December 9, 2014. Unless otherwise indicated, subsequent quotes are from this interview.

10. Philip Ashton, "'Stuck' Neighborhoods: The Transformation of Neighborhood Housing Markets & the Challenges of Market Recovery," University of Illinois–Chicago City Design Center, December 2009.

11. Squires, "Demobilization of the Individualistic Bias."

12. Dorothy Brown, "Lessons from Barack and Michelle Obama's Tax Return." This article was presented on January 17, 2014, at a symposium in Malibu, California, sponsored by Pepperdine University School of Law and Tax Analysts. It is available online at *Tax Notes,* Emory Legal Studies Research Paper No. 14-283, March 10, 2014, http://papers.ssrn.com/sol3/papers.cfm?abstract_id=2414103.

13. Robert J. Sampson, *Great American City: Chicago and the Enduring Neighborhood Effect* (Chicago: University of Chicago Press, 2012), 395.

14. Ibid., 397–398.

15. Keith Tate, interview by author, January 14, 2015. Subsequent quotes are from this interview.

16. Bridget Gainer, interview by author, January 19, 2015. Subsequent quotes are from this interview.

17. "Aldermanic Briefing: Chicago Community Area Fact Sheets," Chicago Rehab Network, October 15, 2013.

CHAPTER 2: JIM CROW IN CHICAGO

1. Yvonne G. Moore, interview by author, January 5, 2015. Subsequent quotes are from this interview.

2. Isabel Wilkerson, *The Warmth of Other Suns: The Epic Story of America's Great Migration* (New York: Vintage Books, 2010), 10–11.

3. Chicago Commission on Race Relations, *The Negro in Chicago: A Study of Race Relations and a Race Riot* (Chicago: University of Chicago Press, 1922).

4. Kale Williams, "The Dual Housing Market in the Chicago Metropolitan Area," Housing: Chicago Style—A consultation sponsored by the Illinois Advisory Committee to the United States Commission on Civil Rights, October

1982, 38–47, https://www.law.umaryland.edu/marshall/usccr/documents/cr 12h8117.pdf.

5. David Bernstein, "The Neglected Case of Buchanan v. Warley," SCOTUS blog, February 10, 2010, http://www.scotusblog.com/2010/02/the-neglected -case-of-buchanan-v-warley/.

6. Douglas S. Massey and Nancy A. Denton, *American Apartheid: Segregation and the Making of the Underclass* (Cambridge, MA: Harvard University Press, 1993), 51.

7. Richard Wright, quoted in Maren Stange, *Bronzeville: Black Chicago in Pictures 1941–1943* (New York: New Press, 2003), xxxi–xxxii.

8. St. Clair Drake and Horace R. Cayton, *Black Metropolis: A Study of Negro Life in a Northern City* (Chicago: University of Chicago Press, 1993 edition), 206.

9. Massey and Denton, *American Apartheid*, 2.

10. Carole E. Gregory, "A Closer Look at Hansberry," *New York Amsterdam News*, April 14, 1954.

11. "Jim Crow in Chicago," *Pulse* magazine, republished in the *Chicago Defender* along with Cayton's response, November 11, 1939.

12. "Supreme Court Hears Hansberry Jim Crow Case," *Chicago Defender*, November 2, 1940.

13. Enoc-P. Waters Jr., "Hansberry Decree Opens 500 New Homes to Race," *Chicago Defender*, November 23, 1940.

14. Carl Hansberry, "Realtor Tells His Role in Covenant Case," *Chicago Defender*, November 23, 1940.

15. "Restrictive Covenants," Federation of Neighborhood Associations Chicago, 1944. Subsequent quotes are from this pamphlet.

16. FBI Freedom of Information Act Files, Memo from J. E. Hoover to Att'y Gen. re: EBD, June 3, 1943.

17. Booklet of speeches, Conference for the Elimination of Restrictive Covenants, Chicago Council Against Racial and Religious Discrimination, May 1946. Subsequent quotes are from this booklet.

18. Quoted in Thomas H. Wright, executive director, Commission on Human Relations, "Documentary Report of the Anti-Racial Demonstrations and Violence Against the Home and Persons of Mr. and Mrs. Roscoe Johnson, 7153 St. Lawrence Ave.," July 25, 1949.

19. Arnold Hirsch, *Making the Second Ghetto: Race & Housing in Chicago 1940– 1960* (Chicago: University of Chicago Press, 1998 edition), 59.

20. Wright, "Documentary Report of the Anti-Racial Demonstrations and Violence Against the Home and Persons of Mr. and Mrs. Roscoe Johnson."

21. Chicago Commission on Human Relations City of Chicago, "Selling and Buying Real Estate in a Racially Changing Neighborhood: A Survey," June 14, 1962.

22. Dominic A. Pacyga, *Chicago: A Biography* (Chicago: University of Chicago Press, 2009), 308.

23. Quoted in Mike Royko, *Boss: Richard J. Daley of Chicago* (New York: E. P. Dutton & Co., 1971), 130 and 154.

24. Brian J. L. Berry, *The Opening Housing Question: Race and Housing in Chicago, 1966–1976* (Cambridge, MA: Ballinger Publishing, 1979), 499.

25. Natalie Moore, "In Chicago's Beverly Neighborhood, Integration Is No Accident," WBEZ, March 26, 2014, http://www.wbez.org/series/curious-city/chicagos-beverly-neighborhood-integration-no-accident-109922.

26. Carol Oppenheim, "Salt and Pepper: Integration Recipe in Beverly Hills," *Chicago Tribune,* June 27, 1967.

27. Moore, "In Chicago's Beverly Neighborhood, Integration Is No Accident."

28. Natalie Moore, "Why Are We Still Collecting Taxes to Prevent White Flight in Chicago?," WBEZ, June 11, 2014, http://www.wbez.org/news/why-are-we-still-collecting-taxes-prevent-white-flight-chicago-110325.

29. Family letters handed down to cousin Afi-Odelia Scruggs and given to the author August 29, 2014.

30. Martha Pratt, interview by author, September 28, 2014. Subsequent quotes are from this interview.

31. Joseph E. Moore Jr., interview by author, January 5, 2015.

CHAPTER 3: A DREAM DEFERRED

1. "Opening of the Robert Taylor Homes," archival tape, courtesy of Chicago History Museum and WGN-TV, http://www.encyclopedia.chicagohistory.org/pages/410107.html.

2. Thomas Buck, "Big CHA Project Opens Today," *Chicago Daily Tribune,* March 5, 1962.

3. Quoted in Natalie Moore, "Mixed Results on Mixed-Income Chicago Public Housing," WBEZ, October 5, 2009, http://www.wbez.org/story/news/local/mixed-results-mixed-income-chicago-public-housing.

4. Lobeta Holt, CHA voucher holder, interview by author, February 3, 2014.

5. D. Bradford Hunt, *Blueprint for Disaster: The Unraveling of Chicago Public Housing* (Chicago: University of Chicago Press, 2009), 83.

6. Natalie Y. Moore, "Taylor: the Man," *Chicago Reporter,* September 26, 2007.

7. Lawrence J. Vale, *Purging the Poorest: Public Housing and the Design Politics of Twice-Cleared Communities* (Chicago: University of Chicago Press, 2013), 232.

8. Chicago Housing Authority annual reports, 1963, 1972, 1983–1984, 1991–1992, available from the Chicago Public Library.

9. Hunt, *Blueprint for Disaster,* 8.

10. *HUD's Takeover of the Chicago Housing Authority: Hearing before the Subcommittee on Human Resources and Intergovernmental Relations of the Committee on Government Reform and Oversight,* House of Representatives, 104th Congress, September 5, 1995.

11. Ethan Michaeli, interview, "Chicago Newsroom," CAN-TV, September 27, 2012.

12. Mick Dumke, "The Shot that Brought the Projects Down," *Chicago Reader,* October 12, 2012.

13. "Plan for Transformation," Chicago Housing Authority, 2000, available at the Chicago Public Library.

14. Kimbriell Kelly, "Rising Values," *Chicago Reporter,* September 27, 2007.

15. Natalie Y. Moore, "The Good Ol' Days," *Chicago Reporter,* September 26, 2007.

16. Natalie Moore, "CHA Hires Contractor to Find Residents," WBEZ, June 30, 2010, http://www.chicagomag.com/Chicago-Magazine/April-2014/chicago-neighborhoods/.

17. Alaine Jefferson, CHA voucher holder, interview by author, March 14, 2014.

18. Lawrence J. Vale, *Purging the Poorest: Public Housing and the Design Politics of Twice-Cleared Communities* (Chicago: University of Chicago Press, 2013), 306.

19. Chicago Housing Authority, in response to a Freedom of Information Act Request.

20. Kimberley McAfee, interview by author, March 14, 2014.

21. Patricia A. Wright, "Community Resistance to CHA Transformation," in *Where Are Poor People Supposed to Live? Transforming Public Housing Communities,* ed. Larry Bennett, Janet L. Smith and Patricia A. Wright (New York: Routledge, 2015).

22. Natalie Moore, "Drug Trade Fragments in Chicago Neighborhoods," WBEZ, June 9, 2010, http://www.wbez.org/story/news/local/drug-trade-fragments-chicago-neighborhoods.

23. Susan J. Popkin et al., "Public Housing Transformation and Crime: Making the Case for Responsible Relocation," Urban Institute, April 2012.

24. Keith Tate, Chatham resident, interview by author, February 22, 2014.

25. Quoted in Natalie Moore, "Report: CHA Plan Has Improved Residents' Lives," WBEZ, March 11, 2013, http://www.chicagopublicradio.org/news/report-cha-plan-has-improved-residents%E2%80%99-lives-106036.

26. Robert J. Chaskin and Mark L. Joseph, "Building 'Community' in Mixed-Income Developments: Assumptions, Approaches, and Early Experiences," *Urban Affairs Review,* July 28, 2009.

27. Alaine Jefferson, CHA voucher holder, interview by author, March 14, 2014.

28. Natalie Moore, "Social Tension Rises at Chicago Housing Authority Mixed-Income Development," WBEZ, June 5, 2009, http://www.wbez.org/story/news/local/social-tension-rises-chicago-housing-authority-mixed-income-development.

29. Dorothy Gautreaux, et al. vs. Department of Housing and Urban Development, 1966.

CHAPTER 4: NOTES FROM A BLACK GENTRIFIER

1. Olivia Mahoney and the Chicago Historical Society, *Images of America Douglas/Grand Boulevard: A Chicago Neighborhood* (Chicago: Arcadia for the Chicago Historical Society, 2001).

2. Bernard C. Turner, *A View of Bronzeville* (Chicago: Highlights of Chicago Press, 2002), 43.

3. Leana Flowers, interview by author, September 16, 2013. Subsequent quotes are from this interview.

4. Bill Ball, interview by author, June 7, 2013. Subsequent quotes are from this interview.

5. Chicago Fact Book Consortium, 1990, and Woodstock Institute, available at the Chicago Public Library.

6. Cliff Rome, interview by author, September 27, 2013.

7. Dhyia Thompson, "Economic Revita-What?" *Bronzeville Metropolis*, September 1, 2007.

8. Matthew B. Anderson and Carolina Sternberg, "'Non-White' Gentrification in Chicago's Bronzeville and Pilsen: Racial Economy and the Intraurban Contingency of Urban Redevelopment," *Urban Affairs Review* (December 2012): 1–33.

9. "The Socioeconomic Change of Chicago's Community Areas (1970–2010)," Nathalie P. Voorhees Center for Neighborhood and Community Improvement at the University of Illinois at Chicago, October 2014.

10. Jackelyn Hwang and Robert J. Sampson, "Divergent Pathways of Gentrification: Racial Inequality and the Social Order of Renewal in Chicago Neighborhoods," *American Sociological Review* 79 (2014): 726–751.

11. Natalie Moore, "South Siders Spend Billions Each Year Outside of Their Neighborhoods," WBEZ, September 1, 2009, http://www.wbez.org/story/south-siders-spend-billions-each-year-outside-their-neighborhoods.

12. Kelly Virella, "Black And White, Seeing Red All Over," *Chicago Reporter*, August, 31, 2009.

13. Emily Badger, "Retail Redlining: One of the Most Pervasive Forms of Racism Left in America," *Atlantic Cities*, April 17, 2013, http://www.citylab.com/work/2013/04/retail-redlining-one-most-pervasive-forms-racism-left-america/5311/.

14. St. Clair Drake and Horace R. Cayton, *Black Metropolis: A Study of Negro Life in a Northern City* (Chicago: University of Chicago Press, 1993 edition), 438.

15. Michelle R. Boyd, *Jim Crow Nostalgia: Reconstructing Race in Bronzeville* (Minneapolis: University of Minnesota Press, 2008), xv.

16. Quoted in Jeff Huebner, "Whose Blues Will They Choose?" *Chicago Reader*, November 30, 2000.

17. See three-part series, "Power Politics Privilege: A LAKEFRONT OUTLOOK Examination of the Harold Washington Cultural Center," *Hyde Park Herald*, December 13, 20, and 27, https://hpherald.com/backups1/lo1.html.

18. Teresa Wiltz, "Bar Fight: Chicago Says Last Call, but the Palm Tavern's Owner Is Good for Another Round," *Washington Post*, May 29, 2001.

19. Sabrina L. Miller, "Bronzeville Club-Site Buyer Linked to Tillman," *Chicago Tribune*, November 13, 2002.

20. Sabrina L. Miller, "New Name in Controversy," *Chicago Tribune*, April 16, 2002.

21. See "Power Politics Privilege" series, *Hyde Park Herald;* Thomas A. Corfman, "Foreclosure Suit Hits Tillman Pet Project," *Chicago Real Estate Daily*, October 7, 2009.

22. Derek S. Hyra, *The New Urban Renewal: The Economic Transformation of Harlem and Bronzeville* (Chicago: University of Chicago Press, 2008), 79.

23. "Black Pride and Bronzeville," *Chicago Tribune*, June 3, 1996.

24. Raynard Hall, "Inner-City Struggle," *Chicago Tribune*, June 16, 1996.

25. Alf Siewers, "Restoring Bronzeville's Luster—Boosters Hope Landmark Area Can Be Reborn," *Chicago Sun-Times*, August 30, 1992.

26. Lee Bey, "Saving Bronzeville," *Chicago Sun-Times*, April 8, 1996.

27. Quoted in Patrick T. Reardon, "Bronzeville Searches for Lost Luster," *Chicago Tribune,* June 8, 1994.
28. Richard M. Daley, "Daley Replies to Editorial on Bronzeville," *Chicago Sun-Times,* July 9, 1996.
29. Randy Price, interview by author, Fall 2013. Subsequent quotes are from this interview.

CHAPTER 5: SEPARATE AND STILL UNEQUAL

1. Joseph Moore Jr. and Yvonne G. Moore, interview by author, January 5, 2015. Subsequent quotes are from this interview.
2. Gary Orfield, interview by author, November 24, 2014. Subsequent quotes are from this interview unless otherwise indicated.
3. Dionne Danns, *Desegregating Chicago's Public Schools: Policy Implementation, Politics, and Protest, 1965–1985* (New York: Palgrave Macmillan, 2014), 9.
4. Ibid., 4.
5. Linda Lutton and Becky Vevea, "Greater Segregation for Region's Black, Latino Students," WBEZ, June 27, 2012, http://www.wbez.org/series/race -out-loud/greater-segregation-regions-black-latino-students-100452.
6. Natalie Moore, "Why So Few White Kids Land in CPS—and Why It Matters," WBEZ, November 12, 2014, http://www.wbez.org/series/curious-city /why-so-few-white-kids-land-cps-%E2%80%94-and-why-it-matters-1110 94.
7. Tony Burroughs, interview by author, October 2, 2014.
8. *Burroughs v. Board of Education of the City of Chicago,* U.S. District Court, Northern District of Illinois Eastern Division, 1962.
9. University of Illinois at Chicago school desegregation timeline, http://www .uic.edu/depts/lib/specialcoll/services/rjd/CULExhibit/Urban%20League %20Exhibit/Timeline.htm.
10. *Webb v. Board of Education of City of Chicago,* U.S. District Court, Northern District of Illinois Eastern Division, 1963.
11. "Integration of the Public Schools—Chicago, Report to the Board of Education," March 31, 1964.
12. Gary Orfield, *Must We Bus: Segregated Schools and National Policy* (Washington, D.C.: Brookings Institution, 1978), 238.
13. "Desegregation Chicago Public Schools: The Deadline Game. Briefing Memo on Chicago School Desegregation," Illinois State Advisory Committee to the U.S. Commission on Civil Rights, October 1979.
14. *United States of America v. Board of Education of the City of Chicago,* U.S. District Court, Northern District of Illinois Eastern Division, 1980.
15. Karen Thomas, "School Policies Blamed for Retention Rate Woes," *Chicago Tribune,* May 28, 1990; Tracy Dell'Angela, "While Some Enjoy Taste of Autonomy, Others Struggle with Probation," *Chicago Tribune,* March 26, 2007.
16. Matt Murray, "Killer Ends the Hopes of Girl, 13," *Chicago Tribune,* November 7, 1991.
17. Kimberly Henderson, interview by author, January 20, 2015. Subsequent quotes are from this interview.

18. Elaine Allensworth, interview by author, September 23, 2014. Subsequent quotes are from this interview.
19. Frank Burgos and Philip Franchine, "Principal's Ouster Protested—Students, Police Clash in Morgan Pk Walkout," *Chicago Sun-Times*, March 2, 1990.
20. Memorandum opinion in 2009 to *United States of America v. Board of Education of the City of Chicago, 1980*.
21. Steve Bogira, "Trying to Make Separate Equal," *Chicago Reader*, June 13, 2013, http://www.chicagoreader.com/chicago/segregated-schools-desegreg ation-city-suburbs-history-solutions/Content?oid=9992386.
22. Tim Novak, "Whites Getting More Spots at Top Chicago Public High Schools," *Chicago Sun-Times*, April 28, 2014, http://chicago.suntimes.com /chicago-politics/7/71/166698/whites-getting-more-spots-at-top-chicago -public-high-schools.
23. Chicago Public Schools demographic reports, http://cps.edu/SchoolData /Pages/SchoolData.aspx.
24. Mike Clark, "Worried Parents Force Cancellation of Payton-Brooks Baseball Game," *Chicago Sun-Times*, April 27, 2013, http://suntimeshighschool sports.com/2014/08/26/worried-parents-force-cancellation-of-payton-bro oks-game/.
25. Jacqueline Rabe Thomas, "School Choice: Future of New Magnet Schools Uncertain," *Connecticut Post*, January 6, 2015, http://ctmirror.org/2015/01/06 /school-choice-future-of-new-magnet-schools-uncertain/.
26. Tiffany Lankes, "Integration Grants Could Help Buffalo Draw Suburban Students," *Buffalo News*, December 30, 2014, http://www.buffalonews .com/city-region/buffalo-public-schools/integration-grants-could-help-buf falo-draw-suburban-students-20141230.
27. Institute on Metropolitan Opportunity at the University of Minnesota Law School, "Integrated Magnet Schools: Outcomes and Best Practices," December 2013. Myron Orfield runs the institute and is the brother of Gary Orfield.
28. Institute on Race and Poverty at the University of Minnesota Law School, "A Comprehensive Strategy to Integrate Twin Cities Schools and Neighborhoods," July 2009.

CHAPTER 6: KALE IS THE NEW COLLARD

1. Quoted in Monica Eng, "Flamin' Hot Cheetos Inspire Fanatic Loyalty among Kids," *Chicago Tribune*, October 11, 2012, http://articles.chicagotribune .com/2012-10-11/news/chi-20yearold-snack-with-high-levels-of-salt-and -fat-inspires-fanatic-loyalty-among-kids-20121011_1_ashley-gearhardt -snacks-addiction.
2. Mari Gallagher, "Examining the Impact of Food Deserts on Public Health in Chicago," Mari Gallagher Research & Consulting Group, 2006, www .marigallagher.com/site_media/dynamic/project_files/Chicago_Food_Des ert_Report.pdf.
3. Mark Bittman, Michael Pollan, Ricardo Salvador and Olivier De Schutter, "How a National Food Policy Could Save Millions of American Lives," *Washington Post*, November 17, 2014, https://www.washingtonpost.com/opinions

/how-a-national-food-policy-could-save-millions-of-american-lives/2014/11/07/89c55e16-637f-11e4-836c-83bc4f26eb67_story.html.

4. Gallagher, "Examining the Impact of Food Deserts on Public Health in Chicago."

5. Mari Gallagher, "The Chicago Food Desert Progress Report," Mari Gallagher Research & Consulting Group, June 2011, 7, www.marigallagher.com/site_media/dynamic/project_files/FoodDesert2011.pdf.

6. Natalie Moore, "High-End Grocer Coming to South Side Food Desert," WBEZ, September 4, 2013, http://www.wbez.org/high-end-grocer-coming-south-side-food-desert-108600.

7. Ibid.

8. "Whole Hoods," *The Economist*, September 4, 2013, http://www.economist.com/blrobbogs/schumpeter/2013/09/food-stores.

9. John Ketchum, "Whole Foods Will Open in Depressed Chicago Neighborhood," *Marketplace*, September 4, 2013, http://www.marketplace.org/topics/wealth-poverty/numbers/whole-foods-will-open-depressed-chicago-neighborhood.

10. Walter Robb, interview by author, November 17, 2014. Subsequent quotes are from this interview.

11. Tracie McMillian, "Can Whole Foods Change the Way Poor People Eat?" *Slate*, November 19, 2014, http://www.slate.com/articles/life/food/2014/11/whole_foods_detroit_can_a_grocery_store_really_fight_elitism_racism_and.html.

12. Naomi Davis, interview by author, November 7, 2014. Subsequent quotes are from this interview.

13. Sonya Harper, interview by author, October 20, 2014. Subsequent quotes are from this interview.

14. DeAndre Brooks, interview by author, October 1, 2014.

15. L. Anton Seals Jr., interview by author, November 10, 2014. Subsequent quotes are from this interview.

16. Shamar Hemphill, interview by author, September 18, 2014. Subsequent quotes are from this interview.

17. Ashraf Asmail, interview by author, September 18, 2014.

18. Orrin Williams, interview by author, December 12, 2014. Subsequent quotes are from this interview.

CHAPTER 7: WE ARE NOT CHIRAQ

1. Quoted in Natalie Y. Moore, "The 'Chiraq' War Mentality in Chicago Prevents Solutions," *The Root*, January 6, 2014, http://www.theroot.com/articles/culture/2014/01/chiraq_war_in_chicago_prevents_solutions.html.

2. Drew Deliver, "Despite Recent Shootings, Chicago Nowhere Near U.S. 'Murder Capital,'" Pew Research Center, July 14 2014, http://www.pewresearch.org/fact-tank/2014/07/14/despite-recent-shootings-chicago-nowhere-near-u-s-murder-capital/.

3. "This Is the Murder Capital," *Chicago Tribune*, April 12, 1925.

4. "The Hands of Death," *Chicago Tribune*, March 14, 1925.

5. "The Hands of Death," *Chicago Tribune*, July 14, 1937.

6. Jeffrey S. Adler, *First in Violence, Deepest in Dirt: Homicide in Chicago* (Cambridge, MA: Harvard University Press, 2006), 2.

7. Michael Lesy, *Murder City: The Bloody History of Chicago in the Twenties* (New York: W. W. Norton, 2007), 304–305.

8. Khalil Gibran Muhammad, *The Condemnation of Blackness: Race, Crime, and the Making of Modern Urban America* (Cambridge, MA: Harvard University Press, 2010), 5.

9. Ibid., 76.

10. Quoted in Natalie Moore, "Deconstructing Chicago Youth Violence," WBEZ, January 6, 2010, http://www.wbez.org/story/news/local/deconstructing-chicago-youth-violence.

11. Gene Demby, "What We Talk about When We Talk about Violence in Chicago," NPR, July 12, 2014. Emphasis in the original. http://www.npr.org/blogs/codeswitch/2014/07/12/330784587/what-we-talk-about-when-we-talk-about-violence-in-chicago.

12. "Homicide Watch Chicago," http://homicides.suntimes.com/about/.

13. Chicago Police Department, "Statistical Summary 1983."

14. Nicole Tefera, interview by author, November 8, 2014. Subsequent quotes are from this interview.

15. Tracey Meares, Andrew V. Papachristos and Jeffrey Fagan, "Homicide and Gun Violence in Chicago: Evaluation and Summary of the Project Safe Neighborhoods Program," January 2009.

16. Andrew V. Papachristos, "48 Years of Crime in Chicago: A Descriptive Analysis of Serious Crime Trends from 1965-2013," IPS Working Paper 13-023, December 9, 2013, http://ftpcontent3.worldnow.com/wfld/pdf/yale-sutdy-murder-in-chicago-andrew-papachristos.pdf.

17. Andrew Papachristos, "Chicago the Murder Capital of the U.S.? Let's Get Real," *Crain's Chicago Business*, July 29, 2014, http://www.chicagobusiness.com/article/20140728/OPINION/140719782/chicago-the-murder-capital-of-the-u-s-lets-get-real.

18. Lynn Sweet, "Rep. Bobby Rush Blasts Sen. Mark Kirk Gang Mass Arrest Plan: 'Headline Grabbing,'" *Chicago Sun-Times*, May 30, 2013, http://blogs.suntimes.com/sweet/2013/05/rep_bobby_rush_blasts_sen_mark.html.

19. Natalie Moore, "Sen. Kirk Meets Residents on Tour of Englewood to Understand Violence," WBEZ, August 29, 2013, http://www.wbez.org/sen-kirk-meets-residents-tour-englewood-understand-violence-108569.

20. Lou Ransom, "National Panic Not a Solution to City's Youth Violence Issue," *Chicago Defender*, October 7–13, 2009.

21. Center for Labor Market Studies at Northeastern University, "The Depression in the Teen Labor Market in Illinois in Recent Years," January 2012.

22. Sarah Heller, "Summer Jobs Reduce Violence Among Disadvantaged Youth," *Science Magazine* 346 (December 2014): 1219–1223.

23. Mick Dumke, "Chicago Decriminalized Marijuana Possession—but Not for Everyone," *Chicago Reader*, April 7, 2014, http://www.chicagoreader.com/chicago/police-bust-blacks-pot-possession-after-decriminalization/Content?oid=13004240.

24. Salim Muwakkil, "The Lessons of Black History and Gun Violence," *Chicago Tribune*, February 19, 2013, http://articles.chicagotribune.com/2013-02

-19/opinion/ct-oped-0219-history-20130219_1_black-history-month-gun
-violence-violence-plague.

25. Sterling Tucker, "The Role of Civil Rights Organizations: A 'Marshall Plan' Approach," *Boston College Law Review* 7 (April 1966): 623.

26. Quoted in Sam Fulwood, "'Marshall Plan' Urged for Nation's Cities, Poor: Social programs: The Urban League would finance the plan with $50 billion taken from defense spending," *Los Angeles Times*, January 10, 1990.

CHAPTER 8: SEARCHING FOR HAROLD

1. Natalie Moore, "Black Vote Proves Key in Chicago Mayoral Race," WBEZ, April 8, 2015, http://www.wbez.org/news/politics/black-vote-proves-key-ch icago-mayoral-race-111844.

2. Michael Dawson, interview by author, March 23, 2015. Subsequent quotes are from this interview.

3. Mike Royko, "Race and Fear," *Chicago Sun-Times*, February 24, 1983.

4. Milton Rakove, "Observations and Reflections on the Current and Future Directions of the Chicago Democratic Machine," in *The Making of the Mayor: Chicago 1983*, ed. Melvin G. Holli and Paul M. Green (Grand Rapids, MI: William B. Eerdmans Publishing Company, 1984), 128.

5. Mike Royko, *Boss: Richard J. Daley of Chicago* (New York: E. P. Dutton & Co., 1971), 134.

6. Gary Rivlin, *Fire on the Prairie: Harold Washington, Chicago Politics and the Roots of the Obama Presidency* (Philadelphia: Temple University Press, 2013), 53.

7. Conrad Worrill, interview by author, March 12, 2015. Subsequent quotes are from this interview.

8. Rivlin, *Fire on the Prairie,* 172.

9. "Harold Washington v. Eddie Vyrdolak- Live on TV," YouTube video, https://www.youtube.com/watch?v=g-ocUQuMt44.

10. "The Mayor's Real Enemies," *Chicago Tribune*, December 22, 1983.

11. Reprinted in Clarence Page, ed., *A Foot in Each World: Essays and Articles by Leanita McClain* (Evanston, IL: Northwestern University Press, 1986), 33.

12. "Harold Washington for Mayor," *Chicago Tribune,* April 7, 1987.

13. Melvin G. Holli and Paul M. Green, *Bashing Chicago Traditions: Harold Washington's Last Campaign* (Grand Rapids, MI: William B. Eerdmans Publishing Company, 1989), 115.

14. Mike Royko, "In Midst of Grief, the Dealing Begins," *Chicago Tribune*, November 27, 1987.

15. R. Bruce Dold and Mitchell, "Jackson Fails to Resolve Rift," *Chicago Tribune*, November 28, 1987.

16. John Kass and John Camper, "Council Elects Sawyer Mayor," *Chicago Tribune,* December 2, 1987.

17. John Camper, "Mayor Makes Pitch for Unity, *Chicago Tribune*, December 3, 1987.

18. Delmarie Cobb, interview by author, March 26, 2015.

19. L. Anton Seals Jr., interview by author, March 24, 2015.

20. R. Bruce Dold, "Winner Must Know When to Hold 'em, Fold 'em," *Chicago Tribune*, February 12, 1989.

21. Monroe Anderson, "The Sawyer Saga: A Journalist, Who Just Happened to Be the Mayor's Press Secretary, Speaks," in *Restoration 1989: Chicago Elects a New Daley*, ed. Paul M. Green and Melvin G. Holli (Chicago: Lyceum Books, 1991), 95.

22. St. Clair Drake and Horace R. Cayton, *Black Metropolis: A Study of Negro Life in a Northern City* (Chicago: University of Chicago Press, 1993 edition), 723.

23. Charlene Carruthers, interview by author, March 17, 2015. Subsequent quotes are from this interview.

24. Will Burns, interview by author, March 19, 2015.

25. A. Pully, "Chicago Activists 'Charge Genocide' at United Nations," *Ebony*, November 17, 2014, http://www.ebony.com/news-views/chicago-activists-charge-genocide-at-united-nations-043#axzz3T31s3c00.

26. Steve Mills, "Burge Reparations Deal a Product of Long Negotiations," *Chicago Tribune,* May 6, 2015.

27. J. R. Fleming, interview by author, March 18, 2015.

28. Michael Dawson, *Not In Our Lifetimes: The Future of Black Politics* (Chicago: University of Chicago Press, 2011), 131.

29. Ibid., 162.

CHAPTER 9: SWEET HOME CHICAGO

1. Eduardo Bonilla-Silva, *Racism Without Racists: Color-Blind Racism and the Persistence of Racial Inequality in the United States* (Lanham, MD: Rowan & Littlefield, 2006), 104.

2. Ed Marszewski, interview by author, March 11, 2015. Subsequent quotes are from this interview.

3. "The Socioeconomic Change of Chicago's Community Areas (1970–2010)," Voorhees Center for Neighborhood and Community Improvement, University of Illinois–Chicago, 2014.

4. Interviews conducted between January and March 2015.

BIBLIOGRAPHY

Adler, Jeffrey S. *First in Violence, Deepest in Dirt: Homicide in Chicago 1895–1920.* Cambridge: Harvard University Press, 2006.

Algren, Nelson. *Chicago: City on the Make.* Chicago: University of Chicago Press, 2011, 60th anniversary edition.

Black, Timuel D. Jr. *Bridges of Memory: Chicago's Second Generation of Black Migration.* Evanston, IL: Northwestern University Press, 2007.

———. *Bridges of Memory: Chicago's First Wave of Black Migration.* Evanston, IL: Northwestern University Press, 2003.

Bonilla-Silva, Eduardo. *Racism Without Racists: Color-Blind Racism and the Persistence of Racial Inequality in the United States.* Lanham, MD: Rowman & Littlefield, 2006.

Boyd, Michelle R. *Jim Crow Nostalgia: Reconstructing Race in Bronzeville.* Minneapolis: University of Minnesota Press, 2008.

Bryk, Anthony S., and Penny Bender Sebring, Elaine Allensworth, Stuart Luppescu and John Q. Easton. *Organizing Schools for Improvement: Lessons from Chicago.* Chicago: University of Chicago Press, 2010.

Chatelain, Marcia. *South Side Girls: Growing Up in the Great Migration.* Durham, NC: Duke University Press, 2015.

Danns, Dionne. *Desegregating Chicago's Public Schools: Policy Implementation, Politics, and Protest, 1965–1985.* New York: Palgrave Macmillan, 2014.

———. "Racial Ideology and the Sanctity of the Neighborhood School in Chicago." *Urban Review* 40 (2008): 64–75.

Dawson, Michael C. *Not In Our Lifetimes: The Future of Black Politics.* Chicago: University of Chicago Press, 2011.

Drake, St. Clair and Cayton, Horace. *Black Metropolis: A Study of Negro Life in a Northern City.* Chicago: University of Chicago Press, 1993 edition.

Hansberry, Lorraine. *A Raisin in the Sun.* New York: Vintage Books, 1987 edition.

Hirsch, Arnold R. *Making the Second Ghetto: Race & Housing in Chicago 1940–1960.* Chicago: University of Chicago Press, 1998 edition.

Holli, Melvin G. and Paul M. Green, eds. *Bashing Chicago Traditions: Harold Washington's Last Campaign.* Grand Rapids, MI: William B. Eerdmans Publishing Company, 1991.

———, eds. *The Making of the Mayor of Chicago 1983*. Grand Rapids, MI: William B. Eerdmans Publishing Company, 1984.

———. *Restoration 1989: Chicago Elects a New Daley*. Grand Rapids, MI: William B. Eerdmans Publishing Company, 1989.

Hopkinson, Natalie. *Go-Go Live: The Musical Life and Death of a Chocolate City*. Durham, NC: Duke University Press, 2012.

Hunt, D. Bradford. *Blueprint for Disaster: The Unraveling of Chicago Public Housing*. Chicago: University of Chicago Press, 2009.

Hyra, Derek S. *The New Urban Renewal: The Economic Transformation of Harlem and Bronzeville*. Chicago: University of Chicago Press, 2008.

Jacobs, Jane. *The Death and Life of Great American Cities*. New York: Vintage Books, 1992 edition.

Kotlowitz, Alex. *There Are No Children Here: The Story of Two Boys Growing Up in the Other America*. New York: Anchor Books, 1991.

Lemann, Nicholas. *The Promised Land: The Great Black Migration and How It Changed America*. New York: Vintage Books, 1991.

Lesy, Michael. *Murder City: The Bloody History of Chicago in the Twenties*. New York: W. W. Norton, 2007.

Long, Herman H. and Charles S. Johnson. *People vs. Property: Race Restrictive Covenants in Housing*. Nashville: Fisk University Press, 1947.

Massey, Douglas S. and Nancy A. Denton. *American Apartheid: Segregation and the Making of the Underclass*. Cambridge, MA: Harvard University Press, 1993.

Moore, Natalie Y. and Williams, Lance. *The Almighty Black P Stone Nation: The Rise, Fall and Resurgence of an American Gang*. Chicago: Lawrence Hill Books, 2011.

Muhammad, Khalil Gibran. *The Condemnation of Blackness: Race, Crime, and the Making of Modern Urban America*. Cambridge: Harvard University Press, 2010.

Obama, Barack. *Dreams from My Father*. New York: Three Rivers Press, 2004 edition.

Orfield, Gary. *Must We Bus: Segregated Schools and National Policy*. Washington, D.C.: Brookings Institution, 1978.

Pacyga, Dominic A. *Chicago: A Biography*. Chicago: University of Chicago Press, 2009.

Pattillo, Mary. *Black on the Block: The Politics of Race and Class in the City*. Chicago: University of Chicago Press, 2007.

Pattillo-McCoy, Mary. *Black Picket Fences: Privilege and Peril Among the Black Middle Class*. Chicago: University of Chicago Press, 1999.

Petty, Audrey. *High Rise Stories: Voices from Chicago Public Housing*. San Francisco: Voice of Witness, 2013.

Polikoff, Alexander. *Waiting for Gautreaux: A Story of Segregation, Housing, and the Black Ghetto*. Evanston, IL: Northwestern University Press, 2006.

Popkin, Sue. "CHA Residents and the Plan for Transformation." Urban Institute, January 2013.

Reed, Christopher Robert. *Black Chicago's First Century: Volume 1, 1833–1900*. Columbia: University of Missouri Press, 2005.

Rivlin, Gary. *Fire on the Prairie: Harold Washington, Chicago Politics and the Roots of the Obama Presidency*. Philadelphia: Temple University Press, 2013.

Royko, Mike. *Boss: Richard J. Daley of Chicago.* New York: E. P. Dutton & Co., 1971.

Sampson, Robert J. *Great American City: Chicago and the Enduring Neighborhood Effect.* Chicago: University of Chicago Press, 2012.

Stange, Maren. *Bronezville: Black Chicago in Pictures 1941–1943.* New York: New Press, 2003.

Sugrue, Thomas J. *The Origins of the Urban Crisis: Race and Inequality in Postwar Detroit.* Princeton, NJ: Princeton University Press, 1996.

Vale, Lawrence J. *Purging the Poorest: Public Housing and the Design Politics of Twice-Cleared Communities.* Chicago: University of Chicago Press, 2013.

Venkatesh, Sudhir Alladi. *Off the Books: The Underground Economy of the Urban Poor.* Cambridge: Harvard University Press, 2006.

———. *American Project: The Rise and Fall of a Modern Ghetto.* Cambridge: Harvard University Press, 2002.

Wilkerson, Isabel. *The Warmth of Other Suns: The Epic Story of America's Great Migration.* New York: Vintage Books, 2010.

Wilson, William Julius. *The Truly Disadvantaged: The Inner City, the Underclass, and Public Policy.* Chicago: University of Chicago Press, 1987.

——— and Richard P. Taub. *There Goes the Neighborhood: Racial, Ethnic, and Class Tensions in Four Chicago Neighborhoods and Their Meaning for America.* New York: Vintage Books, 2006.

INDEX